AWAKENING THE INNER EYE

Intuition in Education

NEL NODDINGS
PAUL J. SHORE
Stanford University

D0061151

Teachers College, Columbia University
New York and London

Published by Teachers College Press, 1234 Amsterdam Avenue, New York, N.Y. 10027

Grateful acknowledgment is made for permission to reprint previously published material:

Excerpts from "what if a much of a which of a wind." Copyright 1944 by e. e. cummings; renewed 1972 by Nancy T. Andrews. Reprinted from "what if a much of a which of a wind" in COMPLETE POEMS 1913-1962 by e. e. cummings. By permission of Harcourt Brace Jovanovich, Inc., and Granada Press Publishing Ltd.

Lines from "Little Gidding" in FOUR QUARTETS, copyright 1943 by T. S. Eliot; renewed 1971 by Esme Valerie Eliot. Reprinted by permission of Harcourt Brace Jovanovich, Inc., and Faber and Faber Ltd.

Passages in chapter 4, adapted from Nel Noddings, *Caring: A Feminine Approach to Ethics and Moral Education* (Berkeley and Los Angeles: University of California Press, 1984). With permission of the University of California Press.

Library of Congress Cataloging in Publication Data

Noddings, Nel.
  Awakening the inner eye.

  Bibliography: p.
  Includes index.
  1. Intuition (Psychology) 2. Educational psychology.
I. Shore, Paul J., 1956-   . II. Title.
BF311.N63 1984   153.4'4   83-18057

ISBN 0-8077-2899-3

Manufactured in the United States of America

89 88 87   1 2 3 4 5 6

To my mother, Nellie Rieth Walter.—*N.N.*

To Gracie McGinnis, who has always recognized
the importance of intuition in education.—*P.J.S.*

*Le coeur a ses raisons, que la raison
ne connait point; on le sait en mille
choses.*

The heart has its reasons, of which
reason knows nothing; we know this in a
thousand ways.—*Pascal*

CONTENTS

ACKNOWLEDGMENTS

WE WOULD LIKE TO THANK Julius Moravcsik, whose interest in intuition provided the initial stimulus, and the many students in the Stanford University School of Education whose comments and questions over a period of years contributed so much to this book's development.

Thomas M. Rotell, former director of Teachers College Press, deserves our thanks for his enthusiasm and steady encouragement. We thank our editors Kerry Kern and Karen Osborne and also the anonymous reviewer whose comments were unusually helpful. Craig B. Vittetoe and Lisa Bloch contributed useful editorial suggestions, and Ruth Bergman helped out substantially with typing. Special thanks go to Jane Wassam for typing, organizing, and maintaining the efficiency of the project.

INTRODUCTION

INTUITION HAS BEEN a topic of fascination for centuries. Everyone uses the word. Some use it both seriously and appreciatively; others use it seriously but with deprecation; and still others "just use" it without attempting to say exactly what they mean by it. In the last category, we find many otherwise careful thinkers who seize upon *intuitive* as an attractive synonym for *informal, nonrigorous, visual, holistic, unfinished,* and a host of other terms. Used in this cavalier fashion, the concept has long furnished buzz words for educators, but it has not yielded the treasure of useful recommendations that we are perennially led to expect.

Among serious and appreciative users of the terms *intuition* and *intuitive,* we find Platonists who posit intuition as the capacity of mind that connects us to a realm of ideal forms, mystics who use intuition as a means of effecting being-to-being contact, and both theorists and practitioners of various persuasions who promote programs designed to increase their clients' intuitive capacities. Neither of the first two categories should be ignored, and many persons operating in the third area are doing interesting, even seminal, work. We have put aside work in the third category until very late in the book. At that point, we will take a critical and appreciative look at a variety of positions on intuition; these are positions that could not be entirely assimilated to the conceptual framework we have established. In the case of Platonists and mystics, we shall argue early on that these positions make investigation and understanding of intuition very difficult because they posit intuition as a faculty that connects us with realms unreachable by other means. Hence, in these very interesting approaches, we find that we cannot get at intuition through the ordinary experiences of life. Our approach, we believe, is clearly designed for and applicable in the commonsense world.

We begin with a conceptual history of intuition, tracing its development from the ancient seers, and we look at intuition in religion, art, psychology, education, and philosophy. Building on the strengths and weaknesses identified in our historical account, we next engage in a search for definition of the concept. In this effort, we analyze the relationship of intuition to such terms as *receptivity, consciousness, immediacy, representation,* and *will.* Then, in chapter 4, we establish a framework built on the notion of "intuitive mode"; in this discussion, intuitive thinking is differentiated from analytic thinking. The intuitive mode is characterized by engagement of the will, involvement of the senses, receptivity, a quest for understanding or meaning, and a facilitative tension between subjective certainty and objective uncertainty.

In the following chapters, the conceptual machinery constructed earlier is put to work. We discuss the establishment, maintenance, and enhancement of intuitive modes, and how these efforts are related to both cognitive and affective education. In "Intuitive Arrangements and Presentations of Subject Matter," we describe concrete applications of intuition for curriculum makers and teachers: the structural lesson, inductive methods, creation of representations, multiple embodiments, new levels of the concrete created from former levels of abstraction, nested symbolic structures, and many others. This part of the book culminates in a chapter called "Intuition, Love, and Education." Here we acknowledge that intuition is active in the domain of interpersonal relations, and we are particularly interested in the teacher-student relation and how teaching may enhance both moral and intellectual sensitivity in students.

As authors we hope that some of the exhilaration and excitement that we experienced in researching and writing is caught by the reader. Intuition is at once a stimulating and extremely challenging subject. In exploring it we were compelled to grapple with difficult philosophical problems, stubborn linguistic ambiguities, and the awareness that many people (including a sizable group of educators) view the entire notion of intuition with great skepticism. Those readers not particularly interested in the historical or philosophical aspects of intuition might find it useful to skip over or browse lightly through the first three chapters. What follows, starting with "Intuitive Modes," is entirely readable without the preliminary philosophical argumentation. In the earlier chapters, our attention is focused on the fascinating question: What is intuition? In the later ones, we explore the question more familiar to educators: How can it be enhanced?

The result of our struggles and experiences is not intended to be the definitive word on the subject. Instead, we hope this book will be the beginning of a serious dialogue on the meaning, importance, and uses of intuition, a dialogue involving not only scholars and scientists, but teachers, artists, and others who encounter intuitive processes in their daily lives. Such a conversation is, we believe, essential if intuition is to take its place among other valuable educational concepts.

AWAKENING THE INNER EYE

Intuition in Education

Chapter 1

INTUITION: HISTORICAL AND TOPICAL DEVELOPMENT OF THE CONCEPT

> Indeed, it is difficult to say how far an absolute moral courage
> in acknowledging intuitions may not be of the very nature of
> genius: and whether it might not be described as a sort of
> interior sanctity which dares to see and confess to itself that it
> sees, though its vision should place it in a minority of one.
>
> Coventry Patmore,
"Seers, Thinkers, and Talkers"

FEW WORDS USED BY philosophers and educators have oc-
casioned as much confusion as the term *intuition*. Yet few terms embrace so many promising concepts. Derived from the Latin verb *in-
tueri*, meaning "to look upon," the word *intuition* has gradually
changed in meaning as successive generations of philosophers, educators, and laypersons have used it to describe a variety of processes and experiences. Although intuition was once thought of
primarily as a concern of philosophers and theologians, in recent
years psychologists and educators have become more interested in
the meaning and importance of intuitive thinking. Jerome Bruner,
one of the most prominent modern psychologists to grapple with the
problem of intuition, considers intuition of particular import to
educators.[1] In *The Process of Education* he raises two questions basic
to educators' investigations into intuition: What is intuition, and
how can teachers foster it? Unfortunately, Bruner confesses that it is
not clear to him just what intuitive thinking is.[2] Thus, educators
looking for a workable definition of intuition in *The Process of Educa-*

tion, although they will find many suggestions on how to foster intuitive thinking, will search in vain for a clear statement of what intuition actually is.

An examination of other writings on intuition can prove equally confusing to the educator seeking a definition or model of intuition on which to build. From the time of Kant until the present, many writers have used the term to mean some sort of spontaneous understanding or perception, but there has been little agreement about the actual properties of intuition. Aestheticians such as Benedetto Croce have linked intuition with artistic expression,[3] while Gestalt psychologists, notably Max Wertheimer, have emphasized the problem solving aspects of intuition,[4] and philosophers, among them Henri Bergson, have conceived still a different meaning for intuition, that of a disinterested consciousness that identifies itself with the object of intuition.[5] At the same time, mystics, both Eastern and Western, have used the word to mean a religious revelation or enlightenment, an experience removed from problem solving or even creativity.[6] Finally, the general public has used intuition to mean a correct hunch, or perhaps a clairvoyant or other psychic experience, and has even given a special label to women's insightful experiences, "feminine intuition."[7] The situation is further enriched (or confused) by the wide variety of styles in which writers have discussed intuitive experience. These range from philosophical essays to psychological analyses to poetry, fiction, and popular, nonscientific literature. The foci, too, of these writings have ranged over many fields: artistic, spiritual, educational, and ethical.

Faced with a bewildering array of meanings and connotations for the word *intuition,* some educators have, unfortunately, chosen to ignore intuition completely or treat it contemptuously as a catchall for any process not easily described as logical or linear. Some writers have gone even further, denouncing intuition as merely imprecise thinking. Typical of these are Siegfried and Therese Engelmann, who write:

> The feeling of intuition is actually nothing more than the by-product of a very sloppy learning situation. It can be induced merely by presenting a concept in such a way that the learner must spend an unnecessary amount of time trying to learn it. The intuitive feeling can be eliminated by improving the presentation, thereby reducing the amount of time required to learn the concept.[8]

By thus ignoring intuition and regarding it as an unimportant part of learning, educators avoid a process that has been credited with producing some of the most important advances in the sciences and one that has contributed immeasurably to the arts and humanities. Ignoring the potential benefits of intuition also cuts off educators from one the most exciting and least explored areas of learning in children and adults.

Both the interest of distinguished contemporary educators such as Bruner and the continuing lack of clarity about the meaning of intuition call for a thoughtful, thorough investigation of this important concept. The following chapters are an attempt to initiate such an investigation. First will come a brief historical review of major philosophers', educators', and writers' views on intuition and an attempt to compare and contrast their differing views of the term. The evolution of the concept of intuition and the various attempts to define the term will be examined. While this discussion is not an exclusively historical or philosophical account, it will attempt to provide information on the role of intuition in the histories of both education and philosophy. We believe such a survey is warranted since, until now, no serious conceptual history of intuition has been made accessible to educators. While obviously not exhaustive, this review may add to our understanding of intuition and encourage others to develop the subject further.

ANCIENT VIEWS OF INTUITION

Both prehistoric and ancient literate societies sought and validated knowledge in many different ways. Evidence from the external, physical world vied in importance and value with the internal impressions and insights experienced by each individual or by the whole community. There was no clear-cut division in the minds of ancient people between the external stimulus and the internal impression, for frequently the internal impression validated or rejected the external stimulus or vice versa.

When visions or insights were experienced, the integration and interpretation of intuitions or insights were considered functions of the greatest importance. One institution common to many cultures that performed this interpretive function was the seer or oracle. The seer or oracle was always a prominent member of the community, held in particular awe and reverence by all. These seers or oracles made predictions about the future of the community or provided insights into the past or present. They also helped interpret and examine the intuitive experiences of others as sources of knowledge.

These intuitive insights or experiences were regarded as messages from the gods or evidence of the exceptional powers of the seer or oracle.

The psychological state of seers or oracles might be calm and "rational," as were the Aztec, Babylonian, and Egyptian diviners; filled with moral indignation, as were the Hebrew prophets; or clearly frenzied, as was the oracle of Delphi, who predicted future events while in a trance. In some cultures seers and oracles banded together into powerful hereditary priesthoods, such as the priests of ancient Israel, while in others the seer was a solitary figure living on the edge of society and venturing into it only to give a message or answer an urgent question. In other cultures, including Native American, intuition was a personal experience in which many members of the community might participate at special times. What all types of seers and oracles shared was a claim to knowledge not normally accessible through "rational" means. This is not to say that the seer's knowledge was considered in any way abnormal or "irrational." On the contrary, it was often regarded as the most valuable kind of knowledge.[9] Many contemporary cultures have retained a serious view of intuitive procedures. We shall now take a quick look at two major non-Western societies' approaches to the use of intuition.

The Chinese have always taken what must be considered a serious view of intuition, attaching great significance to the patterns of yarrow sticks or the cracks appearing on heated bones (scapulimancy) or heated shells (plastromancy). What makes their view serious is the importance they have placed on the interpretation of these objects, an interpretation requiring the sort of nonrational associations and spontaneous insights that have typified other serious descriptions of intuition. The pattern of cracks on a tortoise shell heated over a fire, for example, must be interpreted according to a set of patterns established and written down, yet the interpreter must take the often scanty and vague information and render it into a comprehensible and useful message. Westerners have typically had little contact with the above-mentioned forms of divining, or with geomancy, the art of interpreting landforms, but the I Ching (Book of Changes),[10] based on the casting of yarrow sticks, has gained considerable popularity in the West among those who believe that an understanding of the interplay between human insight and physical reality can be gained by performing this ritual.

While a thorough examination of Hindu concepts of intuition is not possible in this brief survey, several points are worth noting.

First, for the Hindu, intuitive insights are achieved through meditation and disciplined control of the mind. Second, intuition usually illuminates large or universal cosmic issues, rather than addressing concrete problems. Finally, the intuitive experience is always linked closely with spirituality and aesthetics.

Until the twentieth century, traditional Eastern notions of intuition had little direct influence on Western philosophical and educational investigations of the topic. However, beginning in the late 1800s and continuing to the present day, there has been a growing interest in Eastern mysticism among Western intellectuals. Writers such as Alan Watts have used Eastern metaphors to describe intuitive and spiritual experiences, and the teachings of Eastern spiritual leaders have been examined seriously by Western philosophers.[11] During the last few decades, popular culture in the United States and Western Europe has also reflected influences of Hindu mysticism, Taoism, and other Asian religious and philosophical systems. The most important contribution of this infusion of new ideas for the story of intuition is the legitimation of intuitive experience in the minds of laypersons and educators. While some of the bastardized adaptations of Eastern religions appear to be of little value to the serious student of intuition, the original writings of Hinduism, Sufism, and other Eastern religions deserve further investigation. In view of Arthur Schopenhauer's contribution to thinking on intuition, Buddhist philosophy and its important influence on his thought are also areas which should be examined by the student of intuition.

The classical Greeks and Romans considered both rational and intuitive knowledge to be valid. In fact, intuitive knowledge was considered special and frequently superseded rational conclusions. For example, the Athenian general Nicias, at the siege of Syracuse, against his rational judgment, made his army postpone a retreat because of his intuitive interpretation of a lunar eclipse.[12] Unfortunately for Nicias, his interpretation of the eclipse resulted in a decisive defeat for the Athenians. Other ancient leaders often fared better, calling upon a wide range of techniques of interpreting portents and omens. From across the millennia come the exotic names of these techniques used by seers and oracles to extend the knowledge of the time: chresmology, the art of oracular pronouncement; oneiroscopy, interpretation of dreams; and the reports of the prophet (*mantis*) or priest (*hierus*) were all known to the Greeks. Among the Romans one found haruspicy, the art of interpreting the future by inspecting entrails of a sacrificed bird or beast, and augury, the interpretation of natural events as they related to matters of state. This divination from the natural world was of special interest to the Romans, and Cicero himself wrote a treatise on the subject.

For the Greeks and Romans, as well as their Middle Eastern neighbors, nonrational sources of knowledge were valued not only for their possible aid in solving real-life problems, but also for the contact they provided with the spiritual, nonmaterial world. Thus the connection between oracular practices, the intuitive insights of seers, and spirituality remained strong throughout antiquity. As time passed, intuition's connection with the discredited spiritual realm, along with its inconsistent results, led to its devaluation in some scientific circles. As we shall see, intuition's vulnerability in this area was to persist into our own time.

As Greek philosophy developed, notions of knowledge or fundamental truth obtained from intuitive sources were retained and incorporated into philosophical beliefs. The Pythagoreans, who flourished in the sixth and fifth centuries B.C., combined knowledge of astronomy and mathematics with a firm belief that numbers themselves, existing in an intuitively apprehended realm, could yield profound knowledge about the universe that was unavailable elsewhere. Local oracles, usually associated with a particular deity, made weird, often incomprehensible, predictions while in trances. No less a man than Socrates believed in a good spirit ($\alpha\gamma\alpha\theta\sigma\varsigma$ $\delta\alpha\iota\mu\omega\nu$) that guided his actions at critical moments, even causing him to disregard his friends' pleas and carry out his own judicial suicide.[13]

Kings and slaves alike believed in this possibility of obtaining knowledge from a vision, an insight, or a dream. The Greeks' outstanding achievements in science, philosophy, and the arts, fields which we still believe require intuitive insights, compel us to take their views on intuition seriously and not dismiss them as merely the superstitions of an "ignorant people."

After Pythagorus, Plato (427?–347 B.C.) was the most influential philosopher to devote significant effort to the question of intuition. Plato's Republic is filled with ideas derived not from concrete experience, but from his intuitions concerning ultimate reality, a fact often overlooked by commentators on this philosopher. In fact, the entire philosophical school of idealism that flows from Plato may be said to be based on the notion that intuition is a reliable source of knowledge. Centuries later, the German philosopher Immanuel Kant drew upon Platonic notions of intuition and truth to help formulate his own theory of intuition.[14] Today, some individuals still espouse a form of idealism in which perfect archetypes are revealed through intuitive insights. This point of view, still alive in contemporary education, is not one we shall adopt, since it tends to establish dogmatic positions in both ethics and epistemology.

Plato and his disciples valued reason (λογος), and the society envisioned in Plato's *Republic* is one that functions in a largely rational way. Yet the basis of many of Plato's views is an incorporeal idealism that derives from his own intuitions about the nature of humankind and society. Plato did not elaborate on the process which led him to his insights, but his disciple Aristotle isolated and discussed the intuitive process in detail.

Aristotle (384–322 B.C.) wrote of the knowledge that exists without proof, which he called intuitive reason (νους). Aristotle realized that unless some knowledge was known without proof, reasoning would involve an endless regress of proofs. Therefore, to begin deductive reasoning, an intuitively known truth or an inductive-empirical one is needed. Such intuitively known truths rank above even the universals of science and are, Aristotle believed, indispensable for scientific inquiry. In the *Posterior Analytics* he wrote:

> Now of the mind's techniques by which we come to know the truth, some are always true, while others, such as opinion and calculation, may err. Scientific knowledge and intuition are, however, always true. Furthermore, no other kind of thought except intuition is more accurate than scientific knowledge.[15] (author's translation)

The claim that Aristotle made for intuitive knowledge (including Euclidean axioms) is rarely made today, for intuition is no longer universally regarded as an infallible source of truth. Indeed, a mark of progress in conceptualizing intuition is the move away from viewing intuition as an unfailing source of truth toward perceiving it as a way of knowing, a way of seeing the objects of knowledge. This distinction between knowledge and truth is a crucial one and will be emphasized repeatedly in this book. When intuition is viewed as a source of knowledge or guidance, the restrictions placed on it by the exaggerated claims of various philosophical or religious systems are removed, and intuition can join other human experiences and processes as a tool for education.

The differences between Aristotle's conception of intuition and those of other ancient philosophers are also worth emphasizing. Although Aristotle had what might be called faith in the value of intuitive reason, his approach to the concept is not really religious or spiritual, as were the later interpretations of his work by medieval scholastics. Also, Aristotle's discussion of intuition centered on inquiry rather than human conduct, thus distinguishing him from the ethical intuitionists and Cynics. Aristotelian intuition is related to sense perception and memory, but goes further than either.

Aristotle calls this "a critical power that is called perception (αισθησις)."[16] It is a leap of understanding, a grasping of a larger concept unreachable by other intellectual means, yet still fundamentally an intellectual process. This notion of an intuitive leap is an important link between Aristotle and modern theorists of intuition and is something we shall discuss in our chapters on education. The notion of intuition as telescoped rationality, however, also provided the seeds of the "nonserious" view of intuition that impeded the development of the concept in modern times.

After the birth of Christ, a welter of sects and philosophical schools arose as individuals attempted to cope with the convulsive political situation and the increasing social chaos. Among the various schools of philosophy concerned with the nonrational flourishing during the days of the late Roman Empire, perhaps the most important was the Neoplatonist school, which, perhaps owing to the quality of its intellectual leadership, survived several centuries into the Christian era. The Neoplatonists' most famous proponent was the Egyptian-born Roman, Plotinus (ca. A.D. 204–ca. 270), who was one of the most important thinkers of the late classical period. Plotinus, who has been called the greatest of the Greek mystics, maintained that true knowledge is obtained through a special kind of seeing. He wrote:

> To see and to have seen is no longer reason. It is greater than reason, before reason, and above reason, as is also the desire [to see] . . . . Therefore what is seen is indeed difficult to convey: for how can a man describe as other than himself that which, when he perceived it, seemed not other, but indeed one with himself?[17] (author's translation)

Plotinus firmly believed that in a mystic experience, the observer has the sensation of union with the object that he or she is contacting. The idea of uniting or identifying with the perceived object reappears later in the writings of Bergson and will be examined and elaborated at greater length in a later section. As we shall see, however, the view of intuition that we shall take in later chapters disagrees with that of Bergson on several major points.

Another facet of philosophical interest in intuition during the classical period, known as "intuitionism," concerned itself with morality and ethics. Intuitionism, the belief that knowledge of the morally good is directly apprehended by intuition, was apparently originated in the West by the Cynics, a Greek philosophical school active beginning in the fourth century B.C. and continuing in influence for several centuries. The Cynics' ethical system emphasized virtue, which they closely identified with will power. Each man, they contended, has an instinctive sense of what is right and therefore ought not to be confined by laws or conventions of society. It should be noted that Cynism was a simple and humanistic philosophy, not to be confused with the modern meaning of cynicism.[18] The Cynics had a great faith in the individual, and although perversion of their doctrines occasionally led to moral license, there was also great potential in this ethical intuitionism for the growth of democratic institutions. Although many aspects of intuitionist movements have been discredited, the notion that ethical values spring from something other than cold reason persists and will be discussed in greater detail later.

Without erecting an elaborate dogmatic framework for intuitionism, the Cynics left open the possibility for the development of ethical values through subjective, individually reflective experiences. While their notions seem akin to Platonic idealism, the Cynics never insisted on an alternative, incorporeal universe that would provide the material of intuition. Instead they emphasized the innate potential of each person to recognize and do good in the real world. Further, Cynism is not tied to any specific theology, but instead complements quite easily twentieth century individualism and liberalism. This philosophy has been, perhaps unjustly, overlooked by modern ethicists and educators, although it was the first and perhaps the best of many systems linking intuition to ethics. As we shall see in the next chapter, intuitionism has persisted to our own time, although it no longer occupies the respected position in philosophy it once held. The general public, however, continues to hold a strong belief that individuals can distinguish between right and wrong without recourse to elaborate systems of logic and reasoning. Furthermore, courts of law hold individuals responsible for their conduct even without extensive knowledge of the law. Thus the notion of intuitive knowledge of right and wrong propounded by the Cynics can be said to be still flourishing in many quarters.

Like Cynism, Epicureanism put great emphasis on concrete, individual experience. Epicurus is sometimes regarded as an enemy of intuition, but this is not correct. A Greek of the fourth century B.C. who was one of the foremost philosophers of his day, Epicurus rejected Platonic idealism, yet maintained that humans were equipped with more than merely the five physical senses. Norman DeWitt notes:

> In addition to the five senses this equipment [which all people have] included innate ideas, such as that of justice, and these ideas, because they existed in advance of experience, were called anticipations.[19]

These "anticipations," very like "intuitions," give us knowledge with which to evaluate life experiences. Working together with reactions of pleasure or pain and physical impressions, "anticipations" enable human beings to deal justly with the surrounding universe. This limited form of nondogmatic intuitionism enjoyed wide popularity among the educated classes of the Mediterranean world for several hundred years until the decline of pagan Rome in the third and fourth centuries after Christ.

The influence of the seer or soothsayer on the educated classes of the Roman Empire appears to have gradually gone into a decline during the latter part of the classical period. There were many reasons for this decrease in influence, but the two most important causes were the rise of philosophical skepticism and the growing power of Christianity. During the Hellenistic period and especially later, during the Roman Principate, the educated classes had become less enamored of intuitive approaches to knowledge as they embraced Stoicism, Skepticism, empiricism, or other doctrines that put less emphasis on the supernatural and the divine. At the same time, however, the lower classes retained their interests in seers, astrology, and ecstatic religions, although the onslaught of Christianity virtually eliminated the seer from Western culture.[20]

THE MIDDLE AGES

The seer persisted as an important figure in other cultures after Christianity had stamped out most opposing forms of mysticism in the West. In societies as diverse as North American Indian and Anglo-Saxon, experiences that we would call intuitive continued to be regarded as valid sources of knowledge. Seers flourished in African and Asian cultures, while among the Sufis of India, a body of literature developed describing nonrational paths to knowledge that all could take.[21] Today there are still many societies employing those who can "see" more clearly than others and who can help predict the future or clarify the past or present. Space does not permit a detailed discussion of these other manifestations of intuition, but it is worth noting that intuition has been important in virutally every other world culture, while its influence in the West has remained relatively small.

In Europe, Christianity's claim to ultimate truth kept the seer from regaining his or her former position of importance and influence during the Middle Ages. Later, the rise of Renaissance science and rational empiricism alienated most (but not all) intellectuals and educators from the notion of a seer's insights as sources of knowledge. Yet in the twentieth century there has been an increased interest in the knowledge bases of other cultures and in the role of the seer as a source of knowledge. Simultaneously, more educators are showing a willingness to explore new ways of helping students gain knowledge. Among the many avenues now seen worthy of investigation is the *intuitive mode*, which has its conceptual beginnings in the activities of the ancient seer who could see or divine what was invisible to others. The intuitive mode will be central to our own development of the concept and will provide a focus for our later discussion of contemporary writings on intuition.

Although the seer largely faded from importance in the West after the establishment of Christianity, interest in the intuitive approach to knowledge did not languish totally in disrepute from the ancient period until our own day. Even after Christianity had suppressed the pagan seer, medieval theologians continued to be interested in intuition and, in fact, were the first to use the word *intuitio*. They used the term *intuition* to describe an ineffable mystical experience of identification with God. Both Augustine in an earlier period and the medieval Aquinas, among others, wrote of a spiritual revelation that is nonrational and therefore could be considered an intuitive experience. The complicating factor in medieval Christian theology's conception of intuition is that divine revelation is not only nonrational, but is often seemingly contrary to the Aristotelian concept of intuition as the mental act that makes knowledge possible. Revelation, in contrast to intuition, is not given to all. Further, basic Christian concepts such as the Trinity and the dual temporalism of the Kingdom of God can be articles of faith, but do not clearly derive from the interplay of reason and insight that constituted Aristotle's idea of intuition. Subsequently, medieval theologians were more likely to consider intuition a product of contemplation rather than a distinct way of knowing the real world.[22] As a result, medieval concepts of intuition contributed relatively little to the growth of the philosophical or psychological concept in later centuries, although they did keep the notion of intuition alive. In the long run Christianity, which began with a flurry of miracles and supernatural phenomena, did not retain fully its intuitive aspects as it became increasingly institutionalized and involved in the material world. Only occasional mystics such as Meister Eckhart and William of Ockham kept alive the notion of a personal intuitive experience, while religious legalism and the gradual rebirth of science reduced the importance of intuition.[23]

Of the medieval philosophers, the English theologian, William of Ockham, was the one most concerned with the intuitive faculty. Ockham, living in the fourteenth century, perceived correctly that scientific knowledge in his day was very limited. Yet he was convinced that many statements that could not be proven scientifically or logically were nevertheless true. To explain this riddle, Ockham proposed a system of types of cognition. The first, immediate contact with objects he called intuitive cognition; the ability to picture that which is not perceived by the senses he called abstractive cognition. In our own analysis, intuition will range over both the perceptual and cognitive domains. Like several later philosophers, Ockham allowed for the intuition of nonexisting objects, such as numbers, abstract concepts, and so forth. When intuitive cognition of nonexisting objects occurs, he said, it is through the agency of God. Here we part company with Ockham, for this view implies acceptance of a Platonic realm of ideal objects to which we have access through the intuition given to us by God. Ockham's conception of intuitive cognition is important historically because further ideas of intuition as direct contact with objects recur in the writing of subsequent philosophers and culminate in the work of Immanuel Kant.

The religious aspects of Ockham's theory of intuition are also of central importance. Man carries out God's will when he intuits, and no intuition of nonexisting objects is possible without God. The tendency to attribute any intuitive experience to an agency outside of the individual continued in philosophy for many centuries and is still present in both dogmatic intuitionism and in many popular attitudes about intuition.

FROM THE RENAISSANCE TO THE EIGHTEENTH CENTURY

During the Renaissance much attention was focused on great changes in the artistic, political, and religious worlds that were under way, and no new philosophical theories on the difficult notion of intuition appeared. However, some users in the mystical tradition continued to ply their trade with considerable success. One of the most famous prognosticators of this period was Nostradamus (1503–1566), who was active at the French court of Henry II. The cryptic verses of Nostradamus, supposedly written in a mystic trance, have generated persistent controversy ever since the 1500s, when courtiers seemed to find prophecies that came true among his quatrains. Whether any of the verses clearly predicts great cataclysms, wars, or other events is still debated, but the great interest in the writings of Nostradamus during the Renaissance shows the persistence of belief in a seer, even during an age of increased attention to science and at a royal court noted for its brilliance and sophistication.

In the seventeenth century, however, serious thinkers began to return to questions concerning nonrational sources of knowledge. This was because they recognized that to begin talking about knowledge, proofs and linear reasoning were not enough. Something else was needed to begin the process of reasoning and drawing conclusions. The notions of immediately apprehended knowledge and of innate ideas appeared. René Descartes (1596–1650), wishing to accommodate the burgeoning rationality of his own age to his personal experience of knowledge, said that "rational intuition" was the only way to gain certain knowledge. He wrote:

Intuitive knowledge is an illumination of the soul, whereby it beholds in the light of God those things which it pleases Him to reveal to us by a direct impression of divine clearness in our understanding, which in this is not considered as an agent, but only as receiving the rays of divinity.[24]

Descartes' conception of intuition is thus startlingly like that of the medieval scholastics and seems out of harmony with the rigorous mathematical system that he developed.

For Benedict Spinoza (1632–1677), intuition was a category in a tripartite division of all knowledge, the others being apprehension and rational thought.[25] In the case of both Descartes and Spinoza, the label "intuition" was assigned to the process or experience that lay somehow beyond the grasp of systematic rational analysis, and yet was very real. Even in an age of increasing skepticism, the ancient notion of knowledge gained through "seeing," that is, of knowledge that is sure and clear, was not discarded. Instead, it became associated with standard knowledge and was divorced from mysticism.

The rise of Newtonian physics in the late seventeenth and early eighteenth centuries and the attendant rationalist notion that the universe was a precise, predictable machine undoubtedly did much to discourage serious thinking about mystical intuition among many educated people. However, many others retained a belief in the non-rational and even the irrational as evidenced by this era's preoccupation with witchcraft. At the same time, a new rationalist argument was being presented against intuition. If the cosmos and all its workings could be described without need of the supernatural, the argument ran, why rely on anything but logic to solve problems in the universe?[26] The influence of religion on philosophical thought was waning, and David Hume was struggling to define human morality without a Supreme Being. Hume sought to explain what proper human conduct was through a largely nonspiritual argument, and he avoided mention of an intuitive faculty to help interpret experience or direct human activity. However, he substituted what we shall call "intuitive feeling" for the "intuitive knowledge" used by his predecessors. Hume also posed prickly questions about how we perceive and understand things around us. In response to Hume's most famous question, "How can we know anything about the external world?" rose a torrent of debate, but one man's response had crucial significance for the student of intuition.

Immanuel Kant, who lived from 1724 to 1804, was the philosopher who did the most to shape and clarify the meaning and importance of intuition. To Kant, grappling with issues of epistemology in a world moving steadily from spiritual, revelational concepts of knowledge to a more rational, Newtonian view, intuition was not *a priori* insight into a world of ideal forms. Instead, Kant defined intuition as a nonrational recognition and awareness of individual entities. In assuming such a limited position, Kant was turning back to an earlier meaning of *intuition* or *intuitus* (*Anschauung*), which was simply "to look upon." Kant's view of intuition was that the process was linked to sensual perception (*Sinnlichkeit*), which is a necessary part of the whole mental process as Kant conceived of it. He was, however, explicit on the close relationship of sensibility and understanding:

> Without sensibility, no object would be given to us, without understanding [*Verstand*] no object would be thought. Thoughts without content are empty, intuitions without concepts are blind.[27]

Kant went on to define two forms of pure sensible intuition as space (*Raum*) and time (*Zeit*). He intentionally excluded subjective, affective influences on intuition and espoused no concept of "filtering" sensible impressions through emotions, illness, or other important internal conditions. Although he lived in an era which rivaled our own in its preoccupation with sensuality, Kant seemed aloof to or unaware of the impact of biological or other physical factors on human intuition. For this he may justifiably be criticized, for one of the distinctive qualities of intuition may be its personal, subjective, and, therefore, mutable quality.

Kant's position on intuition and the process by which we gain knowledge of an object can also be criticized for another reason. His assertion that intuition yields truth was seriously challenged during the century after his death. Since Kant's arguments for intuition were based on a world view whose only geometry was Euclidean, with the development of non-Euclidean geometry in the nineteenth century, critics of Kant claimed that his arguments for intuition lost their validity. For example, in non-Euclidean geometry, the sum of the angles of a triangle does not equal 180 degrees, as it does in the Euclidean system. Thus the "truth" regarding the properties of triangles, which Kant had argued could be gained through intuition, was shown not to be universally true. Kant's critics used such evidence to attempt to discredit the entire Kantian notion of intuition. Yet this attack on Kant's claim for intuition as a source of propositional knowledge does not damage the spirit of his argument for intuition as a source of object knowledge. In the world that Kant knew, his intuitive conclusions about geometry were valid. For the objects that Kant encountered, intuition remained a useful source of knowledge. From this last idea about intuition (i.e., as an immediate source of knowledge about objects) comes much of the later constructive writing on intuition. We shall return to a defense of this basic Kantian notion in the next chapter.

Another movement triggered by the reactions against rationalism was Romanticism, which preached the natural virtues of the individual and rejected mechanistic models of the universe and the tyranny of reason. In the place of mechanistic models was proposed the "natural" human being who always lived in touch with his or her emotions and, presumably, intuitions. Jean Jacques Rousseau (1712–1778), in his educational treatise *Emile*, advocated a kind of pedagogical intuitionism based on the idea that our true feelings are smothered in us while we are young by the rigorous instruction that children receive. If left alone to develop their own feelings, Rousseau suggested, boys and girls will come in contact with the important values that spring from their own natures. The idea of the child as basically good is still with us and is exemplified by the life and works of A. S. Neill, whose book *Summerhill* described an environment where children were encouraged to act on their own intuitions.[28]

Along with the Romantic movement came a rising sense of nationalism and, in some quarters, a religious revival, reflecting reaction against what seemed to be the sterile rationality of the eighteenth century. Many felt that the unaided intellect would lapse into atheism and fatalism and devalue the passions that hold family and state together.[29] This movement, or group of movements, attracted some intellectuals, but also many laypeople with less formal education as well as some nonconforming Protestant writers. The net effects of these movements were complex, but one indisputable result was to cause the nonrational to be viewed with suspicion by both the followers of more conventional Christian movements in both Catholic and Protestant churches and the growing band of scientists and others who rejected personalized religious experience as "superstitious." With the steady advance of scientific knowledge and the rapid growth of technology throughout the 1800s, the rationalistic views of the previous century gained strength. Related to this trend was the Victorian era's profound ambivalence toward the affective side of human psychology. Although sentimental art and floridly romantic music and literature were extremely popular, in other domains such as the social sciences the nonrational and emotional aspects of human character were to a large degree downplayed. The interest of minimally reputable religious movements in nonlinear, nonrational ways of knowing only increased the reluctance of many psychologists to deal with the issue of intuition. In this respect the nineteenth century was not unlike our own era, when many nonserious writers mention intuition and, as a result, the concept is avoided by some educators and psychologists.

In a more oblique fashion, intuition suffered another blow with the final demise of alchemy, which had been practiced since the early Middle Ages. Although the well-known aim of this pseudoscience was the conversion of base metals into gold, there was also a strong mystical and intuitive component to the practice and teaching of alchemy. An example of this wedding of mysticism and primitive science is found in the career of Theophrastus Bombastus von Hohenheim, known as Paracelsus (1493–1541). A contemporary of Nostradamus, Paracelsus was a German physician and alchemist, who combined significant contributions to science with a strong commitment to the ancient incantations and nonrational traditions of alchemy. He was, however, one of the last great intellects to work in this shadowy area between science and superstition. By the 1700s scientists were growing ashamed of their previous interest in meditative states and other nonrational methods of obtaining information. This change in attitude had mixed consequences; although, on the positive side, barbaric medical practices such as bleeding and cupping and false notions about chemistry were gradually discarded, the belief in the integration of mankind into the universe was also somewhat dimmed. Furthermore, the range of acceptable procedures for obtaining information about concrete objects was narrowed to exclude nonempirical approaches, a characteristic of medicine that persists today.

We should note here that characteristic of many of the views discussed so far is the notion of intuition as linked to a holistic vision of human life and to the idea of mind and body operating in harmony. In the last several decades this connection has once again appeared, as the notions of intuitive problem solving and "being in touch" with one's body have often been held by those rebelling against a strictly empirical approach to health and medicine. Whether this trend will, however, become a permanent part of modern thought on hygiene is not yet certain.

Before we examine this issue, we must first return to a question of great concern to writers of the last century who dealt with intuition. Is it possible to develop a serious view of intuition that will acknowledge its part in standard knowledge, reveal its role in deeply important matters, and yet avoid mysticism?

THE NINETEENTH CENTURY

As we trace the progress of our concept, we note a dialectical movement about the true course of the concept of intuition as a way of knowing. Some modern thinkers reveal "forward-looking" notions of intuition directed at objects in the empirical world, others seem to revert to medieval conceptions, and still others try to make new sense of the medieval notions. In the last category, we find Friedrich Schleiermacher, the Prussian theologian who lived from 1768 to 1834. Schleiermacher recognized four types of wisdom: self-intuition, intuition of the world, aesthetic intuition, and philosophical speculations. Surprisingly, religion was placed in the "intuition of the world" category, which, predictably enough, is also where scientifically obtained knowledge is grouped. According to Richard B. Brandt, Schleiermacher wrote:

> This principle [the intuition of the world] is concerned not only with scientific knowledge, but is the foundation of all intuition and is insofar really the principle of religion, where all knowledge is posited as an intuition of God or in God.[30]

Schleiermacher's attempt to link religion and science, reminiscent of Philo, has been criticized repeatedly since it first appeared. However, his synthesis of disparate concepts under the title of intuition is important, for it represents one of the last times a major Western philosopher tried to create an all-encompassing theory of intuition and human knowledge. Even if the attempt must be considered a failure, the notion of the unity of scientific knowledge and mystical revelation is an idea that could appeal to many today who are seeking an interdisciplinary definition of intuition in the writings of Eastern mystics and others. Also, Schleiermacher's analogy of the religious experience to sense perception has appealed to those trying to make spirituality more comprehensible. In chapter 8 we will see many contemporary writers grappling with similar issues. Few will be more successful than Schleiermacher, although his results were far from totally satisfactory.

Schleiermacher's approach to human wisdom reflects the lingering tendency, which can be traced back at least as far as Aristotle, to compartmentalize vague or interrelated concepts of human understanding. While the motives behind such organization (e.g., to clarify how the mind works) are laudable, the results are frequently puzzling. Why, for example, is aesthetic intuition separated from other forms of intuition, and to what degree does Schleiermacher mean "aesthetic" as Kant did? The answers to these questions are not clear, nor is it obvious what Schleiermacher meant by an intuition "in God." Schleiermacher's efforts may best be viewed today as a somewhat interesting but not particularly useful cul-de-sac in the history of intuition. We do find, however, an intriguing indicator of things to come in Schleiermacher's emphasis on intuition itself over the thing-intuited. In his theology, God is very nearly subordinated to human intuition of God. This represents an edging toward the intuition of cognitive entities, and such a move will be important in our own scheme.

In his own lifetime Schleiermacher faced serious opposition to his views. Theologians denounced him as an atheist because he made God seem dependent upon human perception. The general public did not understand his frequently complicated and obscure arguments, and subsequent philosophers recognized that Schleiermacher made little headway in resolving the epistemological issues he addressed. Yet he remains an important link in the story of the concept of intuition, for his work illustrates the strong desire of both intellectuals and ordinary people to link perception, religious experience, and intuition.

The German philosophical schools were not the only ones concerning themselves with intuition at this time. In Italy a rather unexpected revival of Scholasticism in the early nineteenth century found philosophers debating the nature of human intuition. On one side was Vincenzo Gioberti (1801–1852), who held that knowledge was basically intuitive and that in intuition the subject apprehended the object immediately, with no operations performed by subject or object.[31] Gioberti claimed that the object itself presented to the mind was the idea, and that this idea was what intuition encountered. Gioberti's theory of intuition was not as fully developed as those of Schleiermacher or Kant, but it anticipated some current notions of intuition that view learning as a spontaneous event without any formalized operations. This is the precursor of what we will later call a "nonserious" view of intuition, a view that reduces intuition to a rapid and unconscious form of analytic thinking.

Opposing Gioberti was the Jesuit Serafino Sordi (1793–1865), who assumed the position of the medieval scholastics in asserting that human ideas are in reality ideas existing only in the divine mind. For Sordi, intuition was indeed an act, performed by either the subject or the object. He also maintained that intuition implies an image in the intuiter's mind, even if the idea has its origin in God and not human understanding. In this, Sordi drew directly on medieval interpretations of Aristotle. Although Sordi founded no significant philosophical school and has not been greatly influential during this century, his beliefs are worth mentioning, for they illustrate the persistence of Aristotelian and Thomist influences on theories of intuition over the centuries.

The nineteenth century saw in the West a fragmentation of broad philosophical movements into a wide variety of competing viewpoints. Some, such as the Utilitarians represented by Jeremy Bentham and John Stuart Mill, paid little attention to the idea of intuition, while others, including Romantics and pre-Raphaelites, harkened back to the Middle Ages and earlier, and valued a nonrational way to illumination. The mainstream of German philosophical thought, led by Arthur Schopenhauer, Schleiermacher, Georg Friedrich Hegel, and others, emphasized intuition but did not explore its role in education. That exploration must be deferred for a while so that we may look briefly at the contributions of the German school.

With the entrance of the nineteenth-century German philosophers, a crucially important development in the history of intuition must now be considered. The German philosopher Arthur Schopenhauer (1788–1860) believed that while the scientific (*wissen-*

schaftlich) intellect works only from appearances, the immediate or intuitive knowledge of reality is created by representations within the human mind, and this intuitive capacity is directed through the Will. If we are willing to embark on an existence of altruism, ascetic self-sacrifice, and a discipline of art, Schopenhauer suggests, the human mind might be brought to a higher intuition. On this level the vanity of human existence would become apparent, and the desire to strive for individual accomplishments would be gone. Such intuition would make possible reabsorption in the cosmic Will. The re-semblances of Schopenhauer's philosophy to beliefs held by Eastern philosophers is obvious and, in fact, Schopenhauer was widely read in Buddhism. However, his original contribution and the one impor-tant to us was his linking of intuition to Will. Schopenhauer's under-standing of intuition goes beyond Kant's in its ethical implications and motivational connections, but it is still derived from the Kantian notion of intuition as a source of knowledge using sensory impres-sions. Schopenhauer clearly stated, however, that intuition can re-veal a cosmic truth, a position the more cautious Kant would never take. Schopenhauer's connection of intuition to motivation, and especially to the individual's quest for meaning, is one that we shall emphasize later.

Throughout the nineteenth century, intuition's respectability in the eyes of many was damaged by the continued interest of religious writers in the subject. In an increasingly secular age, the interest in intuition manifested by clerics trying to resurrect Scholasticism did little to recommend the concept to those who favored a new rationality when approaching questions of the human mind. And although the Romantics, led by Rousseau's followers, also acclaimed the value of intuition, the new science of psychology did not take the Romantics' views too seriously. Intuition was seen by these scientists as little more than another name for uncontrolled imagination. Yet while philosophy tended to ignore intuition, another discipline was developing ideas for the fostering of this faculty.[32]

At the same time that Schopenhauer was developing his theories of intuition, continental pedagogy was drawing on Kant's definition of the intuitive experience. The heart of Johann Heinrich Pestalozzi's object lesson was the belief that education is essentially a process through which sense impressions acquire meaning. The conversion of sense impressions into knowledge involves a realization of deep structure which corresponds closely to Kant's conception of the com-plementary functions of intuition and understanding. Pestalozzian pedagogy stood in stark contrast to the heavily moralizing, conventional religious views and structured pedagogy of many nineteenth-century schools, which suppressed creativity and intuitive thinking. Although Pestalozzi did a good deal of moralizing himself, he realized the importance of relating objects to one another in order to make their understanding clearer. Lessons involving such direct observation and experience Pestalozzi called *Anschauung* lessons, using the same word by which Kant had denoted intuition.

F. W. Froebel (1782–1852) built on Pestalozzi's ideas and also emphasized a curriculum flexible enough to include the development of intuition. Although he is best known today as the founder of the kindergarten movement, Froebel was also an educational philosopher deeply concerned with symbolism and the mind of the child. One of the play activities recommended by Froebel in his kindergarten program involved the use of certain concrete objects, presented to the child in a definite sequence, to convey essential truths about the universe. For example, one of these symbols, a ball, would convey the idea of the basic unity of the universe. Another object, the cube, represented to Froebel the multiplicity and diversity of the universe. Froebel evidently hoped that these simple concrete objects, if presented to the child at the right moment, would help cultivate an intuitive sense of larger, more difficult concepts in both the physical and spiritual worlds. What is noteworthy about Froebel's theories, aside from their striking originality, is their emphasis on physical context as the stimulator of intuitive thinking. Although Froebel's followers did not make extensive use of his pedagogy of symbols, Froebel's theory remains important as an attempt to foster an intuitive leap between symbol and reality.[33] A century later, Max Wertheimer would once again use geometric shapes to teach youngsters basic truths, this time in mathematics rather than philosophy.

At the end of the nineteenth century there was a renewed interest among philosophers in many activities and experiences labeled intuitive.[34] For Henri Bergson, just as life precedes matter in its reality, intuition precedes intellect. By this Bergson meant that a person, object, or situation may be intuitively perceived, but never completely known, analyzed, or described in intellectual terms. Although psychology (in Bergson's time a very young science) tries to analyze the human mind in order to provide knowledge about individuals, the knowledge it provides is never complete. The poet, prophet, philosopher, and even successful businessman use their intuition to gain a deeper understanding of reality than can be obtained from analyzing data. Bergson's view was that only by entering through feeling into unison with the whole world of reality can one acquire real truth about it.[35]

Bergson relied on his own intuitions in formulating a philosophy which made the life force (*élan vitale*) its centerpiece. Bergson's philosophical ideas have been sharply criticized, partly because of the lack of documentation for his views, partly because his concept of time was rendered inadequate by Einstein. His emphasis on the power of intuition is nevertheless of some value to educators. This is primarily because of Bergson's recognition of what might be called acquired intuitions (e.g., tricks or skills, connoisseurship, "knowing" the weather of a certain place, etc.). These acquired intuitions develop after a long acquaintance with their superficial manifestations, and are exactly the sort of faculties needed to gain a sense of a historical period or literary milieu. They also may aid in the development of mathematical and computer programming skills in young students, and are of obvious value in physical education and manual arts.

To illustrate what Bergson meant by intuition, let us consider the following analogy. A man owns many pictures of Paris, and by looking at them frequently becomes familiar with the major landmarks of the city. Yet, no matter how much the man studies the pictures, his understanding of what the city of Paris is actually like in no way approaches that of a person who has lived in Paris. His understanding is cognitively mediated; it is not a product of "being one" with the streets of Paris. This contrast between mere cognitive acquisition of facts and a deeper, more vivid understanding of a situation is analogous to what Bergson perceived as the difference between superficial familiarity and intuitive understanding.

As the nineteenth century drew to a close, the Western intellectual world presented a secure, confident image. Many agreed with A. A. Michaelson, the renowned American physicist, when he asserted:

> The more important fundamental laws and facts of physical science have all been discovered, and these are now so firmly established that the possibility of their ever being supplanted in consequence of future discoveries is exceedingly remote.[36]

The universe, it seemed, had been deciphered, and all the ways of knowing it had been catalogued. Few imagined the tremendous changes that the twentieth century would bring in almost every field, and even those who advocated a serious approach to questions of intuition could not have foreseen the revitalization and transformation the concept would undergo at the hands of such men as C. G. Jung, Max Wertheimer, Eric Berne, and others. Intuition was about to emerge from the doldrums of intuitionist speculation and rationalistic scorn to occupy once again a position of somewhat more respect and credibility, and this vindication was to come largely from a discipline that was barely recognized in the 1890s: psychoanalysis. At the same time, a counter-blow would be struck that would further weaken intuition as a respectable scientific concept, and this blow would come at the hands of a very different sort of analysis: philosophical analysis.

SUMMARY

We started this chapter with a discussion of the various meanings and uses of the term "intuition." We have noted that the term is widely used in commonsense language but also in mystical, theological, aesthetic, and technical discussions. Although we certainly have not presented a comprehensive history of the concept, we have attempted to lay out a picture of intuition's development as a concept.

As we examine what happens to our concept in the twentieth century, we shall see three main trends extended. As a technical concept in philosophy and psychology, intuition will undergo refinement and acquire new emphases; as an everyday concept, it will continue to be used as a synonym for a host of other terms; as a term always attractive to mystics, it will be employed again as a special source of truth.

With this brief history, we have provided little more than a hint, a flavor, of the rich and complex past of intuition. There is, clearly, some risk in doing this. Other authors might select different high points or dwell at greater length on particular episodes. Our purpose has been to provide a background for the analysis, elaboration, and application of the concept in education.

Chapter 2

THE TWENTIETH CENTURY

> The role of intuition in research is to provide the "educated guess," which may prove to be true or false; but in either case progress cannot be made without it and even a false guess may lead to progress.
>
> Raymond L. Wilder,
> "The Role of Intuition"

THE TWENTIETH CENTURY has been the era of the explosion of knowledge and of the multiplication of directions of inquiry. One cannot speak of *the* school of philosophy or psychology during the present century, for both have split into many different branches. The same is true of mathematics and the natural sciences. Many of these new fields have concerned themselves with nonrational ways of knowing, and a few intellectual leaders in these disciplines, such as Einstein and Jung, have taken special pains to emphasize the intuitive component in their own thinking. This chapter will review some of the contributions made by individuals in various disciplines during the past eighty years toward a better understanding of what intuition is and how it operates. We consider, first, psychoanalysis.

JUNG AND BERNE

Psychoanalysts as well as philosophers drew upon intuition in their explanatory theories. Although Freud apparently did not concern himself directly with intuition (even though the notion may be inevitably implicated in reference to the "unconscious"), his one-time disciple, C. G. Jung (1875–1961), did, including a definition of the term in *Psychological Types*.[1] Jung characterized intuition as a function that transmits perceptions meaningfully but unconsciously. Other writers, from Aristotle on, had hinted that intuition operates in an unconscious manner, but Jung was the first to articulate the fact clearly. Jung divided intuition into two forms, subjective and objective. Subjective intuition is a perception of unconscious "psychic facts" of subjective origin; objective intuition is a perception of facts deriving from what Jung called "subliminate perceptions of the object" and the thoughts and feelings generated by the subliminal perceptions. We, too, shall find a notion of internal and external intuition useful, but the terms *subjective* and *objective* will prove misleading. With Schopenhauer we shall insist that all intuition has a subjective aspect, since it is driven by the Will. Further, we shall not allow our own pains, feelings, and the like to be objects of intuition. Rather, we shall consider these part of being-itself, directly felt rather than directly known or seen. For us, internal intuition will be intuition turned inward upon cognitive objects and schemata. These, too, must be *seen* in order to be understood.

Approaching intuition from still a different angle, Jung distinguished between what he called concrete and abstract intuition. His explanation of these two terms is not entirely satisfactory, since he defines abstract intuition as deriving from Will rather than circumstances. We, too, shall put an emphasis on "Will," but we shall insist that *all* intuitions are called forth and guided by the Will. Further, there is a subjective aspect to the determination of what an individual calls "concrete" and what for the same individual is "abstract," and this gives rise to difficulties that make the terms inadequate for the definition of kinds of intuition. Some of Jung's other remarks on intuition are important, however, and worth noting. Intuition, he wrote, is a nonrational function.* "Like sensation (q.v.) it is an *irrational* (q.v.) perceptive function. Its contents, like those of sensation, have the character of being given, in contrast to the 'derived' or 'deduced' character of feeling and thinking contents."[2]

In the same work Jung also described the *intuitive type*, an individual who is guided by the intuitive principle or perception through the unconscious. Jung's insistence on intuition's unconscious nature and his separation of intuition from other thought processes influ-

---

*Jung used the German word *irrational*, but it is clear from his discussion of this word in *Psychological Types* that he did not mean *irrational* as the word is used in English, but rather *nonrational*.

enced modern understanding of intuitive thinking and paved the way for the contributions of other psychologists, such as Eric Berne. Jung's contribution to the development of a serious notion of intuition also includes the respectability he gave to the concept after decades of neglect. The wide popularity of *Psychological Types* and others of Jung's works also helped inform a large lay audience of the existence of intuition as something separate from a spiritual or mystical experience. For this, Jung deserves recognition as the first modern psychologist to investigate and publicize the importance of intuition.

Clearly, we have no argument with Jung's assessment of intuition as a nonrational function. We must, however, divorce ourselves from Jung when he insists on the unconscious character of intuition and its lack of "direction." For us, intuition is better thought of as a form of nonreflective consciousness, one in which focus on the object is so intense that there is no possibility of our observing our own intuitive processes. This does not make intuition "unconscious"; only its *structure* is unknown. Hence we reject Jung's characterization of intuition as lacking direction and his consequent devaluation of the intuitive capacity. Indeed, it is likely that this compromise of intuition is linked to Jung's well-documented devaluation of the feminine, which is strongly related to the intuitive.

Jung's discussion of intuition poses several other problems. His characterization of the "intuitive type" seems too rigid and exclusive. His identification of such historical figures as Schiller, Goethe, and Nietzsche as intuitive, extrovert, introvert, or combinations thereof is, on the face of it, somewhat simplistic. Finally, it is not clear in *Psychological Types* whether Jung acknowledges the potential of every individual to be, at least at times, an intuitive type. The closest he comes to this position is to assert that intuition is "a basic psychological function."

More troubling is Jung's desire to force intuition into a rational mold. Even if the elusive "laws of reason" into which intuition can supposedly be broken down could be clearly defined, one should ask of what value such an analysis would be. Jung himself is not explicit on how this analysis would be accomplished, or whether it should be done by the intuiter or the psychoanalyst. In saying this, we do not deny the importance and feasibility of verifying intuitions through reason or experience; however, we do deny the value and feasibility of subjecting the intuitive experience itself to such analysis. It thereby becomes something altogether different from the immediate contact with objects of knowledge.

In fairness to Jung, we should remember that his primary concern was analytical rather than educational. The fostering of intuition as an aid to learning and knowing was not on his agenda. It is enough that Jung approached intuition as an important concept and included it in his catalogue of psychological functions. It remained for others, including some other psychiatrists, to develop further the notion of universality and importance of intuition. Jung's interest in intuition and the parapsychological encouraged both European and American psychologists to pay more attention to these subjects. The generation of psychiatrists that followed Jung were able to build on his theories, which, although controversial, did not invite the ridicule that spiritualist or other mystical notions had. A new world of possibilities was opening up, although at this point educators had little awareness of this world.

During the 1950s and 1960s, the American psychiatrist Eric Berne formulated a detailed and fascinating analysis of intuition. Berne recognized that many philosophers, theologians, and others had defined intuition in different ways, and he sought to articulate a limited, precise meaning for the concept, which could be useful for the psychiatrist. Drawing on Jung, Berne defined intuition as an unconscious source of knowledge, distinguishing it from three other ways of rendering judgments. Specifically, the type of intuition in which Berne is interested relates closely to observation and is called by him "clinical intuition." Clinical intuition, described in Jungian terms, is objective and concrete. It is knowledge (notice that Berne does not say "truth") based on experience and acquired through the senses. Once again Kant's emphasis on the aesthetic (i.e., sensory) aspect of the intuitive process is repeated in a later theorist's writing, with the difference that Berne is vitally concerned with the feelings of the intuiter, something that Kant ignored.

Berne points out that not only does the intuiter not know *how* he knows something, but that sometimes he does not even know *what* it is he knows. Instead, the intuiter reacts in a certain way as if his actions reflected something he knew. This suggests a distinction we shall later find important, namely, the difference between intuitive knowledge and intuitive feeling. It is characteristic of intuiters that they perform most effectively when they are not conscious that they are in fact intuiting. This fact is important for educators trying to foster intuition or heuristic thinking in their students, for the intuitive experience does not thrive in an overly structured, self-conscious setting.

Berne's book *Intuition and Ego States* credits Aristotle with being the philosopher whose views come closest to his own conclusions about intuition. According to Berne, the Greek thinker described "intuitive induction" as being based on three abilities: (1) sensory, (2) organizational, and (3) systematic. Aristotle also recognized, Berne notes, the systematic functioning of the nervous system, describing it in ways resembling Norbert Wiener's discussion of cybernetics. Berne's combination of new theories, coupled with recognition of his debt to other thinkers, makes his book particularly appealing to anyone beginning a study of intuition.

The most important single contribution of Berne's theory of intuition is the description of the "intuitive mood," a state in which intuitive thinking is most encouraged. It is best characterized in Berne's own words:

> The intuitive mood is enhanced by an attitude of alertness and receptiveness without actively directed participation of the perceptive ego. It is attained more easily with practice, it is fatiguable, and fatiguing. Intuitions in different fields do not seem to interfere with one another. Intuitions are not all dependent upon extensive past experience in the given field. Extraneous physical stimuli, both external and internal, appear to be irrelevant.[3]

In later chapters we will develop the notion of the *intuitive mode*. The intuitive mode is similar in many of its characteristics to Berne's "intuitive mood" but differs in several important ways, as we shall make clear.

Intuition consists of two processes, says Berne. The first is a perception registering in the subconscious. The second is a conscious verbalization of that perception. Here we demur. We must point out that there seem to be many intuitions, for example in mathematics, that are only with some difficulty put into words. Berne does not address this issue, nor does he deal with the question of how the limitations of language might influence our intuitions. If verbalization is a fundamental part of the intuitive process, would not all sorts of intuitions for a Chinese speaker be understood very differently from similar intuitions for an English speaker?

There is a further problem with Berne's distinction between the verbal and perceptual aspects of intuition. For intuitions that are fundamentally verbal, the separation into perceptual and verbal components is by definition impossible. For intuitions that are nonverbal, on the other hand, the verbalization (if it can be accomplished at all) often involves laborious nonintuitive processes. We shall see later that Albert Einstein testified to this. Finally, there are intuitions that simply cannot under any circumstances be verbalized, e.g., kinesthetic intuitions, musical intuitions.

In his conclusions, Berne makes several penetrating observations concerning intuitive thinking. He asserts that the intuitive function can be studied empirically and that this function is a series of perceptive processes working in an integrated fashion. He recognizes that "what is intuited" is different from what the "intuiter" verbalizes as his intuition. Finally, Berne states that the intuitive function is "useful and worth cultivating."[4] This endorsement of intuition by a contemporary psychiatrist underscores the continuing importance of the study of intuition today and the great possibilities in the future for the understanding of these processes.

Unfortunately, Berne does not treat earlier philosophical and aesthetic theories of intuition and the Gestaltists' approach to intuitive problem solving. His ideas, though original, do not build upon the important work of his contemporaries. By making verbalization a part of intuition equal to perception, Berne clearly overlooks intuition in the fine arts. He also largely ignores spirituality, in which one of the typical characteristics of intuitive experience is its ineffable quality. Later we shall say more about the action of intuition with respect to both the verbalizing intellect and the Will.

Finally, Berne shows no interest in or awareness of intuition in other cultures, something Jung pursued with obvious interest. Berne's view remains narrow and linear, shackled to the notion of intuition's debt to verbalization. Yet Berne's recognition of the difference between intuition and recollection of past experiences is important and a distinction too often overlooked. His serious approach to questions concerning intuitive experience lends needed support to those who desire further investigation of intuitive processes.

PHILOSOPHICAL CONTRIBUTIONS

During the same period when Jung was beginning his investigation of intuition, there was a revival of interest in the idea of intuition as an artistic faculty, rather than a primarily analytical or investigative one. Benedetto Croce was the most prominent of the aestheticians to deal with this aspect of intuition. In his *Aesthetic*,[5] Croce attempted to give a history of aesthetics and also propound his own theories of knowledge, perception, and creativity. For Croce, knowledge exists in two forms. The first is intuitive and works through the imagination to reveal what is real. The second is logical and, drawing on the intellect, organizes and analyzes systematically.[6]

Croce's *Aesthetic* represents an attempt to bring together widely disparate views of perception, beauty, and intuition in order to formulate concepts of art and aesthetics that include the leading philosophical trends of his day. Probably the scope of such a project was too great. Croce's synthesis fails largely because it lacks a convincing position on creativity, and his rhetorical style sometimes obscures his intentions. However, Croce's recognition of the expressive and creative aspects of intuition will be valuable in our own analysis.

A much more rigorous definition of intuition was put forth by the phenomenologists. Foremost in this movement was Edmund Husserl (1859–1938), who had been greatly influenced by the work of Franz Brentano, Gottfried Leibniz, and Kant. His motto, "to the things themselves" (*Zu den Sachen selbst*), summed up the phenomenologists' position on how to investigate the world around us. The phenomenologists insisted that phenomena must be investigated as they are directly experienced, without intervening theories or causal explanations. They strove to conduct their examinations of phenomena as free from unexamined preconceptions and presuppositions as possible. Relations and values, as long as they present themselves intuitively, were also acceptable objects of examination for the phenomenologists. Naturally, it was impossible to have an actual situation devoid of theories or interpretations that would completely satisfy the phenomenological school, but the ideas they established pointed toward a more objective way of evaluating experiences. The situation became primary and the example, methodologically supreme. Separating intuition from the realm of preconceived notions also emphasized the potential of intuition to provide knowledge not encountered through other experiences and raised the status of the intuitive experience to equality with other sources of knowledge. Intuitive experience now had the status Kant had intended in his narrow definition of intuition and the status accorded intuition in the days of the ancient seer.

Phenomenology has also contributed a dynamic quality to the notion of intuition. When meaning-intention without intuitive content is fused with a sense-related intuition, what Husserl called static "covering" or coincidence results. This "covering" is, in effect, the goal of the original intention; that is, that sense and meaning be joined. Significantly, the sense-fulfilling intuition has brought about this transformation. The holistic approach of phenomenology, including both intention and intuition, is of great value to educators; it shows how essential intuition is to the acquisition of knowledge, and that intuition (at least in Husserl's definition) is central and not peripheral to the learning process. Husserl specifically calls intuition

> a source of authority (Rechtsquelle) for knowledge, that whatever presents itself in "intuition" in primordial form (as it were in its bodily reality), is simply to be accepted as it gives itself out to be, though only within the limits in which it then presents itself. Let our insight grasp this fact that the theory itself in its turn could not derive its truth except from primordial data.[7]

We shall not find formal theories of phenomenology useful in our later discussion, however, because the phenomenologists, including Husserl, developed phenomenology into a detailed analysis of the structures of consciousness. With Piaget we also reject the phenomenologists' claims to a suprascientific form of knowledge. Nevertheless, Husserl and his followers form an important link between Kant and contemporary thought on intuition.

Among twentieth-century philosophers, existentialists share many of the concerns of the phenomenologists. Although some existentialists call themselves phenomenologists, there appear to be significant differences between the two groups. The phenomenologist Husserl, drawing on idealist traditions, affirmed Berkeley's "to be is to be perceived" (Esse est percipi) and wrote of a "transcendental ego" that directed consciousness. For the existentialist Jean-Paul Sartre, such constructs were unacceptable.[8] Sartre saw no need for the transcendental ego and was not convinced that one's existence depends on being perceived. For Sartre, consciousness, a concept used almost synonymously with intuition, was central. Sartre's concept of nonreflective consciousness is similar to the generally accepted concept of intuition. His idea of reflective consciousness focuses on the observer, not the object, and relates the observer's knowledge of the world to his own quest for meaning.[9] We shall return to the distinction between reflective and nonreflective consciousness.

Our discussion of twentieth-century philosophical contributions to intuition would not be satisfactory without some mention of two philosophers whose contributions are of interest to educators: Whitehead and Russell. (We shall also have to discuss briefly the contributions of analytic philosophers, but their contribution is largely destructive and we shall put off its discussion until the end of this chapter.)

Alfred North Whitehead (1861–1947) was interested in mathematics, epistemology, speculative philosophy, and educational reform. He constructed a complicated theory of knowledge involving intuition.[10] On one occasion Whitehead spoke directly to educators about a topic closely related to intuition. In "The Rhythm of Education," he described three stages of acquiring knowledge: romance, precision, and generalization. The stage of "romance" as described by Whitehead has much in common with what we shall call the "intuitive mode," and it is also reminiscent of the "anticipations" of Epicurus. In Whitehead's own words:

> the subject matter . . . holds within itself unexplored connections with possibilities half-disclosed by glimpses and half-concealed by the wealth of material. In this stage knowledge is not dominated by systematic procedure.[11]

Whitehead also recognized that intuitive judgment may differ very little from conscious perception, that is, when indicative feeling and physical recognition are the same feeling. This more unified approach to intuition is, from an educator's point of view, Whitehead's most significant contribution to the theory of intuition. Unfortunately, the highly abstract organization of Whitehead's ideas and his sometimes difficult language have kept his concepts from being widely read or understood by most educators. Whitehead nevertheless deserves recognition as one of the most important intellectual figures of the twentieth century to write on intuition.

Whitehead's famous colleague, Bertrand Lord Russell (1872–1970), took a somewhat different attitude toward intuition. His investigations in mathematical set theory led him to the conclusion that our "logical intuitions" (i.e., those concerning notions such as truth, concept, class, etc.) may include some that are contradictory. Russell went on to develop two avenues whereby these mathematical entities could be made to exist without contradiction. Ultimately, he relied on extensions of propositional functions of these terms, which seem to resemble intuitions. Although Russell claimed to reject mathematical and Platonic intellectual intuition, as Philip Wiener has noted, a certain sort of Platonic idealism remained in Russell's philosophical thought.[12] An enthusiastic campaigner against Christianity and other beliefs he considered "superstitious," Russell did not include spiritual or mystical experiences in his discussions of intuition.

Russell's own attempts at educational reform, in which he, too, was deeply interested, must be considered failures, but his notion of "knowledge by acquaintance"—a form of prelinguistic knowledge of concepts—is of some interest to educators. We shall put considerable emphasis on the role of intuition in acquiring familiarity with objects and, again, on how that familiarity enhances intuitive activity.

The popularity of spiritualism and other pseudosciences and their subsequent loss of credibility during the latter half of the nineteenth century caused some scientists, philosophers, and educators to regard intuition with some suspicion. As phrenology, spiritualism, and other fields filled with quackery were partially or totally discredited, the value of intuition was questioned by those willing to trust only the "provable" physical sciences. In addition, the rise of Darwinism, "scientific" psychology, and social and economic theories that tried to explain human behavior discouraged the investigation of concepts, such as intuition, that are difficult to isolate and define. As we have seen, intuition's association with Christian spirituality caused it to suffer as the influence of organized religion among intellectuals continued to decline.

However, the nineteenth century was also an era when intuitionist ethics, long a poorly defined region of philosophy, matured and grew. The views of the intuitional ethicists varied, but all agreed that humans possess a special faculty or capacity for recognizing moral distinctions. Beyond agreement on this general point, three forms of intuitional ethics can be distinguished. Aesthetic (in the Kantian sense) or perceptual intuitionism maintained that the moral value of a particular action is apprehended or understood intuitively and that a sort of moral hierarchy is formed by motives to action derived from intuitions. Dogmatic intuitionism, as espoused by Bishop Butler and later James McCosh,[13] claimed that it is possible to know intuitively the rightness or wrongness of whole classes of notions or motives. This point of view has been largely discredited in technical circles during the twentieth century, although, as we have noted, the notion that anyone can "intuitively" determine the difference between right and wrong persists in our culture. Dogmatic intuitionism, at its peak in the eighteenth and nineteenth centuries, may be seen as an attempt to preserve the ethics of Protestantism without demanding belief in its theology. This philosophical theory was more than this, however. It was a response to the apparently nonrational sources of ethical values that have always been felt to exist by human beings. Several schools of psychology, most recently the behaviorist school, have sought to explain away such influences on moral decision making by emphasizing the impact of the environment on the individual. Yet such arguments do not seem to dispel completely the sensation that something within us is the source of these moral directives. It is this sensation that keeps alive the belief in ethical intuitionism among the great majority of laypersons and provides much of the impetus for the discussion of intuition in popular literature. Philosophical intuitionism, another form of intuitional ethics, tried to synthesize a set of practical rules into one universal, immutable precept that distinguishes good from evil. This last system is in effect a search for an articulation of Kant's categorical imperative. In each case intuitionists believed that moral truth is an existing essense that intuition can discover, but not create. All forms of intuitional ethics claim intuition as a way not simply to knowledge, but to truth. At the present time, intuitional ethics has been largely displaced as the insistence on intuition leading to truth has fallen from favor. Intuitionism is discussed in ethical debates, and there are still ethicists who call themselves intuitionists, but the view no longer dominates the field as it once did.

It is fair to say, however, in favor of intuitionism that no moral philosophy is entirely independent of intuitions. What is the source, for example, of the basic principle of Utilitarianism? Whence the notion that pleasure is to be promoted and pain diminished?[14] We might, however, reject the notion of intuitive knowledge and substitute in its place the concept of intuitive feeling. This would involve the direct and immediate arousal of feeling in an individual as a result of some external happening. We feel pain intuitively, for example, when a feeling akin to pain arises in us as a response to another's pain. Our own direct bodily pain we shall not call "intuitive," but this is an argument we shall pursue a bit later.

THE GESTALTISTS

For the educator concerned with finding ways to foster intuition, the work of the Gestalt psychologists is among the most useful and challenging offerings of this century. Central to Gestalt psychology is the notion that a unified psychological, physical, or symbolic configuration (*Gestalt*) has properties that cannot be derived from its parts. The Viennese psychologist Max Wertheimer (1880–1943) explored the educational implications of this idea in his book *Productive Thinking*,[15] which represented the product of many years' research on mathematical problem-solving approaches. Wertheimer believed that humans tend to join together and complete "disturbing" or incomplete figures in search of a "good Gestalt" which will possess properties of wholeness, balance, and unity. Logic itself may not hold the key to the solution of some problems. Instead, association, recollection, and an intuitive sense of "rightness" frequently lead to successful problem-solving strategies. By conducting experiments with children and adults using blocks or geometric figures, Wertheimer amassed evidence that convinced him that the ability to solve a problem often depends on an understanding of the problem's deep structure. This spontaneous, nonrational understanding may rightly be called intuition. Although Wertheimer never calls this experience or process "intuition," he writes often of "seeing the light" while working on problems. Thus Wertheimer returns to the visual metaphor that has been associated with intuition since the time of the ancient seers. This experience of insight involves the reordering of elements already visible (perhaps for a long time), grasping what Wertheimer calls "p-revelations," and simultaneously setting aside "blind" or fruitless procedures.

Unlike Kant, Wertheimer recognized the role of subjective experience and emotion in thought processes. Even so, his debt to Kant is obvious. Although Wertheimer de-emphasized logic (which Kant valued) as a sterile and inadequate tool for many problem-solving procedures, his concern with form, unity, and the importance of relating sense impressions to frames of time and space clearly have their antecedents in Kant and even Plato. Wertheimer personalized and redefined Kantian concepts, and provided a link from philosophical theory to the problems of classroom teaching.

One of the most interesting chapters in *Productive Thinking* recounts an interview that Wertheimer held with Einstein. Einstein, a truly intuitive thinker, arrived at his revolutionary concepts of the universe in sudden flashes of insight. Later he worked out the mathematics of his theories, but the mathematics itself was never the vehicle of discovery. Interestingly, Einstein was considered dull as a child because he did not respond well to the conventional pedagogy of the day. It was only after his parents placed him in a Pestalozzian school that the child began to make visible progress. Einstein's experience is a powerful argument for the development of programs that encourage intuitive thinking among school children.

FURTHER PSYCHOLOGICAL CONTRIBUTIONS

In the almost four decades since *Productive Thinking* appeared, a number of books relating to intuition in education have appeared. One of the most influential is Jerome Bruner's *The Process of Educa-*

tion.[16] As was noted earlier, Bruner failed in this book to give a workable definition of intuition, but he did make a number of valuable observations about intuition in the classroom. In mathematics, he noted, there are apparently two kinds of intuition. One involves being able to "make very good guesses whether something is so, or which of several approaches to a problem will prove fruitful." The other type of intuitive mathematical thinking, Bruner claims, provides a solution to a problem without a formal proof. Intuitive thinking occurs in many other fields as well. Bruner cites the example of poets producing successive drafts of a poem until the "right" version appears.[17] The intuitive sense of "rightness" is apparent to the reader examining various drafts of a poem, Bruner asserts. Yet he recognizes that it is very difficult to say what makes the "right" version of a poem superior to the other drafts. In a later chapter we will take a closer look at what this sense of "rightness" is. Nevertheless, once one's artistic intuitions are recognized and valued, something that Bruner calls "courageous taste" can be developed. The possessor of "courageous taste" is willing to resist the uniformity and lack of style that the mass media emphasize. He or she seeks individual expression without banality or willful eccentricity. Bruner maintains that such a commitment to what one believes to be beautiful can be a direct product of intuition. It is certainly one of the most important contributions that a recognition of intuition can make to our society.

Bruner is deeply concerned about the denigration of intuition that occurs constantly in the classroom. Since it often produces the wrong answer, the intuitive approach is sometimes ridiculed in competitive academic settings where giving the right answer and giving it first are very important. Ironically, disciplines such as mathematics and pure science, whose histories reflect the breakthroughs of intuitive thinkers, are ones where intuition receives scant encouragement in schools and where a rigid formalism survives. Bruner protests against this approach and urges students to guess "when the cost of guessing is not too high." He also recognizes the close relationship that exists between intuitive thinking and heuristic procedures. Although making students overly aware of heuristic rules can sabotage genuine heuristic thinking, by making students too self-conscious of the problem-solving process, the presentation of heuristic methods along with encouragement of intuitive problem solving can help youngsters to rely on intuitive thinking with better results, suggests Bruner.

Bruner carries his interest in nonanalytical thinking further in a later book entitled *On Knowing: Essays for the Left Hand*.[18] His conception of intuition is similar to Wertheimer's. Bruner writes:

> Intuition implies the act of grasping the meaning or significance or structure of a problem without explicit reliance on the analytic apparatus of one's craft.[19]

In *On Knowing*, Bruner comes closer to isolating and identifying intuition, but he still cannot provide a concrete definition for the classroom teacher or curriculum designer. In the following chapters, we will try to bring intuition still closer to educators who need to understand more clearly what these experiences or processes are.

One of the most important creative figures of the twentieth century, one of interest to both psychologists and inventors, is R. Buckminster Fuller (1895–1983), who long championed the cause of intuition. He believed it to be a principal tool of humankind in all of its endeavors. It is fitting that Fuller should be the last individual mentioned in this psychological account of intuition, for his concept of intuition combines and integrates many of the ideas of earlier writers. Fuller sees intuition as a positive force that can benefit individuals and society as a whole, and he believes intuition has spiritual content. These views echo the optimistic writings of Schleiermacher, but put an emphasis on the material future of the human race which the German philosopher's writings did not.[20] At the same time, Fuller holds on to the notion of intuition as a source of truth, an idea that has generally been discarded by modern philosophers. Finally, Fuller seems close to medieval mystics or Eastern philosophers in his conception of the intuitive experience. Indeed he extols intuition as the "key to humanity's scientific discoveries."[21]

Fuller's optimism and personal history of success in implementing his own intuitive ideas undoubtedly colored his attitudes about the value of intuition. Yet his ideas should not be dismissed as the naive and overly optimistic dreams of an ivory tower intellectual. Buckminster Fuller recognized that many of the major scientific breakthroughs from the time of ancient Greece onward were the result of what he identified as intuitive insights, and he predicted that such insights would continue to contribute to future conceptual and technological advances. No doubt he is right, but the realization of Fuller's vision of the future requires that intuition be taken seriously in society, and especially that it be accorded the respect and attention it merits from all educators.

WOMEN AND INTUITION

Throughout history, parallel to the evolving religious and philosophical notions of intuition, there has existed a distinct and persistent notion of a specific kind of intuition that women alone possess. At present it is impossible to separate the influences of woman's biological role as nurturer, the greater degree of emotional expression typically allowed women in our society, and traditional folklore stereotyping on the shaping of the concept of women's intuition. Nevertheless, the widespread belief in this phenomenon and its historical durability require that it be mentioned in this study of intuition. If it is merely a superstition, then feminine intuition should be discarded as meaningless to a serious study of intuition. If, however, the concept cannot be proven to be only an artifact of folklore, then exploring and defining some of its functions and characteristics will be of use to educators and to women generally.

The reported manifestations of feminine intuition are many and varied.[22] They range from the sibylline pronouncements of ancient Greece and Rome to modern folklore about women who perceive aesthetic or social subtleties more readily than their male counterparts. The common theme of the folklore of feminine intuition is that many, perhaps all, women can understand the deeper structures or real meanings of certain objects or situations without resorting to conventional logical processes. Also, women are credited with hunches concerning future events that frequently prove correct. A related phenomenon is the exceptionally high percentage of women among those who claim to be mediums or psychics, as well as the prominent place of women in many pre-Christian religions and cults. The commonly held notion that intuition and artistic ability are linked suggests that woman's traditional role in our society as the artist or seeker of beauty may have allowed the intuitive faculty to be developed more completely in women than in men. It is obvious, however, that most of the great artists in history have been men, a fact due at least in part to the social position of women through the ages.[23] This observation will encourage us to look at the link between intuition and experience. It is likely that what is called feminine intuition is at least in part a product of women's social position, that is, their special function as nurturers and caretakers.

Unfortunately, we cannot adequately resolve the question of feminine intuition at present. Undocumented folklore and sexist stereotyping still obscure the real nature of what is popularly called feminine intuition. The educator interested in the special intuitive abilities of women must wait for the psychologist, the historian, the anthropologist, and others to illuminate this potentially important aspect of intuition.

Since, as we have noted, women in our society have often been cast in the role of mediators of social relations, they may have developed abilities making them especially suited to the task of recognizing and bringing out intuitive abilities in others. If such an ability were definitely identified in women, it would be of particular use in elementary education, where the overwhelming majority of teachers are women. However, more research in this area is needed to determine the nature and scope (if any) of women's abilities in this field.

CHILDREN AND INTUITION

Another question worth raising is whether young children, who have presumably less exposure to linear, logical thought processes, are more naturally inclined to intuition and can be more easily trained to be intuiters than their older counterparts. It would be valuable to know, in particular, if there is any relationship between a child's native tendency to use intuition to solve problems and his Piagetian level of intellectual development. If, for example, evidence were to suggest that the natural tendency to use intuitive approaches decreases when the child enters the stage of concrete operations, curriculum designers and instructors could concentrate efforts to establish and retain intuitive patterns of thought in the period immediately before the stage of concrete operations. On the other hand, if it is determined that at some point students actually become more likely to use intuitive approaches, other types of curriculum could be developed to integrate these approaches into the child's other activities and experiences, both in and outside of the classroom.

Investigation of intuition in children can take many other directions. A study of the connection between early evidence of talent in music, mathematics, writing, and other fields and intuitive patterns of thought would obviously be of value to educators and parents alike. Among other possible valuable areas of study are the influence of cultural background and religious training on children's tendencies to use intuitive processes and the impact of heredity on successful intuition. Clearly the field of study involving children and intuition is rich with possibilities.

INTUITION IN CONTEMPORARY LITERATURE

During the last few decades, a new body of literature dealing directly or indirectly with intuition has appeared. This is the work of popular writers appealing to the general public. While many of these books border on the bizarre and deal with unconfirmed claims of psychics and others, some are responsible and sincere efforts dealing with society's values, such as *The Aquarian Conspiracy*[24] by Marilyn Ferguson, while others, such as *Gödel, Escher, Bach — An Eternal Golden Braid*[25] by Douglas Hofstadter, address more philosophically sophisticated issues and draw upon current high technology. These new books are significant for two reasons. They reveal the continuing and even growing public acceptance of the possibility that knowledge can come from nonrational processes and experiences. This acceptance is partially due to a growing disillusionment with science and its accomplishments in an age of nuclear weapons and environmental pollution. It is also the result of a growing awareness of other systems of knowledge, among them Zen, Native American, and Buddhist epistemologies. Public interest in this subject can be exploited by unscrupulous purveyors of paperback horror stories and irresponsible producers of movies dealing with the occult, or it can be refined and developed by educators demonstrating the success of intuitive techniques in the classroom. We shall say more about some useful popular works on intuition in chapter 8.

This dangerous crossroads in the history of intuition is the second reason why increased interest in intuition is significant. Intuition can become simply one more sensational, unconfirmed phenomenon lingering at the borders of educational respectability, or it can be a validated and useful part of a skilled educator's repertoire. Which direction the investigation and utilization of intuition will take depends on the conscientious efforts of teachers to encourage intuitive thinking, become familiar with its strengths and uses, and defend intuition from critics who deride it as merely sloppy or inaccurate thinking.

Finally, intuition is at a point where its study can no longer be the exclusive province of theologians, philosophers, or even psychologists. In a world filled with difficult decisions at all levels, the powers of the ancient seers are as badly needed now as they were thousands of years ago. Students must come to recognize the potential of becoming a "seer" in dealing with the problems of school and life. Just as importantly, teachers must recognize their role in fostering intuitive processes in students so that an important source of knowledge will not be ignored by future generations.

At the present, no philosophy embracing intuition contains a direct link to a practical theory of knowledge or education. It is worth asking why this is so. Lack of clarity in defining intuition is part of the explanation, but it is not the whole reason. In the West, the tendency of intuition to work closely with reason has caused it to be overshadowed by the latter or downgraded by those who mistrust nonrational processes. The rational bias of Western thought has made intuition seem questionable whenever it has received attention. This bias must cease before intuition can be fully appreciated and utilized in the classroom and elsewhere. Intuition cannot and should not be placed higher than other thought processes. But the wide range of thinkers mentioned here who were concerned with intuition cannot be ignored.

Before turning to our own analysis of intuition, we shall consider briefly the work of analytic philosophers on this concept.

ANALYTIC PHILOSOPHY AND INTUITION

Philosophers have, according to Richard Rorty's account, identified four principal meanings of "intuition."[26] The first is unjustified true belief—or belief not preceded by inference. The existence of such intuitions, or "hunches," is, according to Rorty, "uncontroversial." But, as we shall see, the source, nature, and limitations of such intuitions are far from uncontroversial. A good part of our own analysis will be devoted to these questions. The second is immediate (noninferential) knowledge of the truth of propositions. On this issue, we shall line up with Kant, insisting that propositional knowledge involves both intuition and reason; we do not directly apprehend truth, although when a notion strikes us with the clarity of perception we may want to claim it as an "intuitive truth." Such truths, we shall claim, always bear further inspection and stand in need of some form of verification. The third meaning is associated with immediate knowledge of a concept. Educators are familiar with this sense in the often-heard student protest, "I know but I can't explain it." Philosophers of the linguistic and behaviorist schools reject both the student's protest and the basic claim to prelinguistic knowledge, but we shall see that this rejection leaves many things unexplained—and resorting to "unconscious inference" is not much improvement. The fourth and final sense identified by Rorty is nonpropositional knowledge of an entity. This form of intuition includes sensory intuitions (the holistic sense accompanying perception), intuitions of universals, and mystical or inexpressible intuitions.

In our own treatment, we shall avoid narrow rationalist or empiricist views, largely because we do not want to get bogged down in matters that are irrelevant to the analysis of intuition. With empiricists generally, we shall accept sensory intuitions; with rationalists generally, we shall insist that mind must contain the forms of pure intuition that make experience possible. Finally, we shall adopt an agnostic position on mystical intuition. Certainly there is testimony to the existence of such "intuitions," but accepting them as bona fide cases of *seeing*, of direct contact, involves postulating the existence of some domain other than empirical reality and the inner reality of individual cognition and memory. We leave that exploration to others. Most importantly, we explore a relation largely ignored by both rationalists and empiricists: the relation between Will and intuition or, put differently, the connection between our individual quest for meaning and our immediate apprehensions. This is where our analysis begins.

SUMMARY

In this chapter, we have reviewed the work of several individuals who have contributed to the development of intuition as a philosophical and psychological concept. We have also discussed very briefly the uses of intuition in a variety of contemporary activities. In philosophy, we have noted a complete range of attitudes toward intuition—frank dismissal, implicit or reluctant acceptance, analytical curiosity, and identification of intuition as a fundamental concept in both epistemology and moral philosophy.

Some aspects of intuition that we have discussed so far will now disappear from our investigation. Women's intuition, intuitive types, and the direct intuition of moral truth are all fascinating topics and worthy of further treatment, but we cannot undertake their study here. We shall, however, make extensive use of Gestaltist concepts, the intuitive mode, and the relation between intuition and the dynamic center of self or "Will." Special attention will be given to the personal use of intuition (as described by Buckminster Fuller) in learning and creating.

Chapter 3

WHAT IS INTUITION?

> Here we touch the enigmatic two-fold nature of the ego, . . .
> namely that I am both: on the one hand a real individual which
> performs real physical acts, the dark, striving and erring
> human being that is cast out into the world and its individual
> fate; on the other hand light which beholds itself, intuitive
> vision, in whose consciousness that is pregnant with images
> and that endows with meaning, the world opens up.
> Hermann Weyl, *Mind and Nature*

IN OUR HISTORICAL account of intuition, we have seen that
certain features of the concept have persisted across centuries of
thought and that others have been discarded, modified, or specula-
tively amplified. The notion of intuition as some form of direct contact with objects — as a form of "seeing" — has persisted. Indeed,
without this notion, the concept would deteriorate to a word denot-
ing an ellipsis of sorts; we would be suggesting a mere speeding-up
of analytic processes in which the steps become blurred and difficult
to identify because of the speed itself. Clearly, this is not what a
serious user of "intuition" intends and, as serious users ourselves,
we shall retain the central notions of direct contact and "seeing." At
the same time, however, we should recognize and accept progress
that has been made in developing a concept of intuition. In particular, we consider it a gain and not a loss that intuition is no longer
tightly or pervasively associated with the truth of propositions.
Clearly, an intuition may come to us in propositional form, that is, in
the form "p is the case," or so very nearly so that we cannot distinguish the intuition proper from its verbalization, but its *truth* is not
guaranteed by its coming to us *as* intuition. Insistence upon that

connection led to the near demise of intuition as a respectable concept in the study of knowledge. In an essay entitled "The Crisis in Intuition," Hans Hahn goes so far as to dismiss intuition as merely "force of habit rooted in psychological inertia."[1] According to his view, we wrongly sanctify that with which we are familiar by calling it "intuitive truth." We, too, reject dogmatic views of intuition, but we shall argue that critiques such as Hahn's have not destroyed the usefulness of intuition as either a philosophical or psychological concept.

Keep in mind that our characterization of intuition is intended for use in education. We want to consider how intuition contributes to learning, creating, expressing, and problem solving, and we want to ask how education may enhance intuitive capacities. Our purpose will not dictate our definition, of course, but it will guide us in matters of emphasis and elaboration. When we discuss intuition's function in contacting objects, for example, we shall not become deeply involved in ontological questions; that is, we shall not become entangled in questions concerning the ultimate nature of reality. One might easily put all of one's effort into attempts to describe what is *real* and, while we cannot avoid such questions entirely, this is not our goal. Similarly, epistemologists might be concerned primarily with intuition as a ground for truth or as a mode of evidence, but, again, although these matters are of great interest, we are more deeply concerned with how intuition functions in knowing and understanding. Even here, our interest is most clearly focused on how intuition functions in whole human beings—in real, striving, fallible, feeling people. Our interest is not that of the phenomenologists, who take as their task a meticulous identification and elaboration of the structures of consciousness. Rather, as educators, our interest must move us outward in both directions from the central phenomenal contact—toward the *object* so that we may know more about the things that capture the interests of learners and toward the *subject* so that we may learn more about individual learner propensities involved in intuition.

We will, however, discuss some problems and concepts that arise in the aforementioned areas of philosophical investigation in order to arrive at a defensible and useful concept of intuition. Certain concepts have long been associated, and sometimes confused, with intuition. Among these are perception, representation, receptivity, understanding, will, and consciousness. Each of these must be placed in proper connection to intuition. From what was laid out in the first chapters, it is clear that the view to be presented here has its roots in the Kantian conception. Hence it seems reasonable to start with that notion of intuition and to discuss related terms, their revisions, and connections as we need to do so.

THE STATUS OF KANTIAN INTUITION: SPIRIT AND LETTER

A view that is fundamentally Kantian posits a receptive capacity —an object-oriented faculty—that makes initial schematic sense of perceptual material. It is that capacity of mind that presents objects to reason, that sees configurations to which verbal symbols have not yet been assigned, and that detects rightness or accuracy without using rules in conscious analysis. This last is not yet a departure from Kant for, while he claimed that the understanding operates on *rules* and reason with *principles,* the rules guiding the understanding are not claimed to be rules used in conscious analysis. We shall depart from Kant, however, on several counts. First, we shall allow intuition to look inward, to *look at* the representations of reason and to convey an affective representation—"I see!"—to the dynamic or motivational center of self. In this, we are in agreement with Croce. With Schopenhauer and later phenomenologists,[2] moreover, we shall put greater emphasis on intuition's contributions to the *creation* of representations and to understanding but, at the same time, we do not want to repeat the fundamental error of idealism (as some phenomenologists do) by moving so far from Kant's conception of receptivity that the world becomes a mere construction, or "correlate," of mind.

Some writers, including Hahn, have claimed that intuition (at least Kant's intuition as a ground for knowledge) was effectively destroyed by the discovery of non-Euclidean geometries. It may be, however, that only the letter and not the spirit of Kant's claims has been destroyed. As D. W. Hamlyn has observed: "If this discovery is a refutation of Kant's formal position, however, it is not so clear that it is a refutation of its spirit."[3]

The difficulty is that Kant *did* claim that geometry (Euclidean) comprised a body of necessary truths anchored in pure intuition:

> Geometry is a science which determines the properties of space synthetically, and yet *a priori.* What then must be the representation of space, to render such a knowledge of it possible? It must be originally intuitive: for it is impossible from a mere concept to deduce propositions which go beyond that concept . . . . That intui-

tion, however, must be *a priori,* that is, it must exist within us before any perception of the object, and must therefore be pure, not empirical intuition.[4]

The discovery that Euclid's fifth, or parallel, postulate (through a given point not on a given line there is exactly one line parallel to the given line) could be replaced by alternative and mutually contradictory postulates without loss of consistency shattered Kant's claim that geometry was a body of necessary truth grounded in truths of intuition. Each of the geometries consists of necessary truths in the sense that its propositions follow necessarily from its axioms, but any claims to "truth" must be restricted to this internal sense. Euclidean geometry does not, apparently, state a truth concerning the empirical world.

Hamlyn points out, however, that it is "no coincidence that Euclidean geometry was the first to be developed; the system somehow fits experience more obviously than do the alternative geometries later developed."[5] We think the case can be put even more strongly. If experience itself is dependent upon intuition, it may be the case that only Euclidean geometry could have been developed first. Non-Euclidean geometries developed as products of reason but are still dependent on intuition both for their existence and for proof of their consistency. Intuition supplied the first set of representations; analytical reasoning then had a set of objects to think upon, rearrange, and recast. But intuition played a role again in creating or discerning objective models that could be used to test the consistency of the postulational systems. Here our emphasis is on the claim that intuition plays on the domain of intellectual constructs as well as on objects in the physical world. Even as a ground for knowledge, then, it is by no means clear that Kant's conception of intuition has been refuted.

We are not so concerned with intuition as ground for knowledge, however, as we are with intuition as a *way* of knowing. Indeed, we shall see that every view of mathematics relies in some way on a conception of intuition. Even when the philosophy of mathematics rejects intuition as a ground for knowledge, it must grant that mathematics can be known "intuitively," and it is reasonable to ask what is meant by saying this. Rudy Rucker points out, for example, that mathematicians are not simply reasoning or theorem-proving machines:

> In the initial stages of research, mathematicians do not seem to function like theorem-proving machines. Instead, they use some

sort of mathematical intuition to "see" the universe of mathematics
and determine by a sort of empirical process what is true.[6]

This is one of the functions of intuition in which we shall be
particularly interested: perception turned inward upon the objects of
conception. A view of mathematics as a "sort of empirical process"
carried out inwardly was expressed by Charles Sanders Peirce when
he described mathematics as activity carried out on "schemes built in
the imagination."[7] His position contrasted with that of his father, the
mathematician Benjamin Peirce, who described mathematics as "the
science which draws necessary conclusions."[8] In the elder Peirce's
statement, we see a view of the mathematician as theorem-proving
machine. It is as though mathematical thinking begins with the *manipulation* of mathematical objects. In the younger's, we see an emphasis on the constructive, iconic, and diagrammatic nature of
mathematics. He suggested looking beyond the conclusions drawn
to both the process of drawing them and to the world of objects on
which they are drawn and how that world is created.

This discussion of the Peirces' contrasting views of mathematics
raises questions about the nature of mathematical objects and the
role of intuition in contacting, representing, or discovering them.
Philip Davis and Reuben Hersh discuss the ways in which various
philosophies of mathematics rely on intuition.[9] Platonists, they note,
believe that mathematical objects exist in a universe of ultimate reality, that of ideal, eternal forms. This domain, they believe, is open to
discovery, and it is intuition that connects us to the world of universal forms. A difficulty with this view is that the domains of intuitive
activity are multiplied. We have the universe of ideal forms, the
empirical world, and the internal world of mind, and difficulties
arise in describing the connections among these worlds. Even if we
consider the world of mind as part of the universe of eternal forms
(Rucker's "mindscape"), we need to explain how the objects of this
world combine with those presented to reason through empirical
intuition in order to form configurations that are so often verified in
perception. Further, since intuition is posited as the mechanism by
which we come to know the real objects of a nonperceptual world, we
have no means of describing intuition through reference to the ordinary and familiar objects of external and internal experience. We
shall not adopt this view, although if what we say is interpreted
metaphorically, our discussion of intuition should still be useful for
those who *do* hold a Platonic position. Clearly, we have not refuted
Platonism nor even greatly disturbed its surface in this brief account.
Our interest in education pushes us to find a view of intuition that is

explicable under the least strenuous metaphysical conditions. Note, however, that the Platonic view is a *serious* view of intuition; intuition is an absolutely essential faculty for those who believe in ideal forms.

Another philosophical position on mathematics, formalism, may be regarded as holding a *nonserious* view of intuition. Formalists locate the entire meaning of mathematics in its form and insist that, empirically, mathematics is a meaningless game that yields no "truths" concerning the empirical world. They are, however, hard put to explain how people "know" certain mathematical objects and relations before the formal names, concepts, and proofs are available. They attribute "intuitive knowledge" to those who reveal a grasp of mathematical relationships capable of proof and as yet unproved, but it is not clear what they mean by "intuitive knowledge." Such knowledge might be described in terms of hunches or guesses, but this description evades the issue. How does the mind put together conclusions that are "seen" but not worked out? The only hope here is to describe intuition as an accelerated, or even unconscious, version of analytic thinking. We have already noted that linguistic and behavioristic philosophers lean toward explaining intuitions as unconscious inferences. This view, however, does damage to a reasonable view of inference. To draw an inference is, precisely, to make conscious connections between prior statements (premises) and conclusions (inferences). The view is particularly unsatisfying when we consider the *affect* that accompanies intuitive accomplishment. Why should the intuitive conclusion come to us with the surprise, clarity, and beauty of perception if it is merely a rapid version of reasoning? Why should we so often find ourselves inarticulate when the intuition comes to us?

Formalism suffers still another difficulty. The mathematician is, once again, mainly a theorem-proving machine. The connections between the mathematical world and empirical world are portrayed as happy accidents, and the relation between mathematics and meaning is simply denied. Again, as in the elder Peirce's statement, it is as though mathematical thinking begins with deduction, with the manipulation of mathematical objects. Even though formalists insist that mathematics is totally a human creation, meaning nothing in itself for the empirical world, they give peculiarly little attention to the *origin* of mathematical objects. Where do these objects come from, and how do we make contact with them? To say that these objects are "created" by human beings is not much more—if any more—satisfactory than to say that they are discovered by an intuition that probes a universe of eternal forms.

So far we have followed Davis and Hersh quite closely. It is appropriate to say, however, that their exposition may not be entirely fair to formalism on a nonmetaphysical level. There is considerable evidence that formalists have taken seriously the constructivist attitude both toward the step-wise production of dependable results from demonstrably nonempty beginnings and toward a recognition of the concrete in their use of models.[10]

The philosophy of mathematics most obviously indebted to intuition is constructivism. Its basic position, that mathematics begins with the intuitively given natural numbers and the intuitively given process of iteration, is clearly compatible with the Kantian view of intuition. We do not begin with self-evident truths but with given *objects* and clearly discernible *acts* we can perform on them. The attention of the mathematician is on the construction of mathematical objects. Hermann Weyl, for example, advised aspiring mathematical thinkers to "think concretely."[11] Indeed, he challenged the elder Peirce's description of the mathematician's work even more strongly than did C. S. Peirce, insisting:

> The business of the constructive mathematician is *not* to draw logical conclusions. Indeed his arguments and propositions are merely an accompaniment to his actions, his carrying out of constructions.[12]

In this view, we see two important features of intuition: its object-giving function and its experience-enabling function. When we speak of intuition as an experience-enabling function, we mean that it precedes and makes possible the experience from which knowledge is constructed. Without intuition, "experiences" would consist of a simple series of occurrences without direction or meaning. Experience would be something merely "had," not something anticipated, organized, chosen, evaluated. Clearly, the constructivist view of intuition makes a claim about the structure of that capacity of mind we call intuition. In agreement with Kant, it posits a pure intuition of time in the form of iteration; this is our ability—given a first occurrence—to mark the next, and the next, and the next. But it also ties in firmly with the pure intuition of space. The form of iteration that we call counting depends not only upon our capacity for noting a "next occurrence" but also upon our ability to pick out discrete objects, locate them in space, and separate them from their backgrounds. It is in this sense that the natural numbers are "given." This view is clearly different from that of the Platonists, for the natural numbers need not be posited to exist in an intuitively apprehended universe of forms. Rather, they come into existence, are given, in the interaction between mind and object made possible by the pure intuitions of time and space.

The *forms* of pure intuition are prior to experience and make experience possible. It is this claim that most clearly separates mathematical intuitionists from radical empiricists, who, like intuitionists, also rely heavily on perception in their theory of knowledge. A second area of general agreement between these two groups, intuitionists and radical empiricists, is the claim for openness in the body of what can be known intuitively. Those who adopt this view reject the Kantian program insofar as it posits a mentality entirely fixed with respect to the synthetic *a priori* at the outset. The mechanisms of mind are for Kant completely described as an inherent structure. An alternative is to allow mind to grow developmentally. This growth occurs *in* experience but is not necessarily a result of—something caused by or tested in—experience; rather, a developing intuitive capacity makes increasingly sophisticated experience possible. In this, those who make intuition primary differ from radical empiricists such as Richard von Mises, who says:

> In agreement with the empiristic conception of science, intuitionism holds that the source of mathematics is the insight which we intuitively comprehend from experience of the external world, but which cannot once and for all be collected in a closed system of axioms.[13]

We must, of course, modify von Mises' statement about insight. For us, insight is not comprehended *from* experience but, rather, is that which makes experience comprehensible. It results from a complementarity in the quest for meaning and subsequent experience. This difference will be fundamental for us when we suggest ways of taking intuition into account in our teaching. Our mention of "insight" reminds us, also, that we must discuss the connection of intuition to understanding, and we shall return to this matter shortly.

Let us complete our defense of the Kantian view of intuition as ground for knowledge. Along with his insistence that the discovery of non-Euclidean geometries destroyed Kant's claims for a pure intuition of space, Hahn also claimed that pure intuition as a foundation for arithmetic was equally mistaken. He extols the

> vehement and successful opposition to Kant's thesis that arithmetic, the study of numbers, also rests on pure intuition—an opposition inextricably bound up with the name of Bertrand Russell, and

which has set out to prove that, in complete contradiction to Kant's thesis, arithmetic belongs exclusively to the domain of the intellect and logic. [14]

Here, again, the case is not all that tidy and closed. The logicist program, Russell's program, took for granted the important notion of iteration that we have already discussed. In constructing the whole numbers, for example, the empty set, { }, was made to correspond with zero; then 1 became the name of the property belonging to all sets *containing* the empty set, { { } }; and 2 was constructed as we might now expect, { { }, { { } } }. The basic marks, braces, used to denote "set," are repeated as the construction takes place. Indeed, the notion of iteration is so fundamental (so, we might say, "intuitive") that we scarcely notice when it is being used. Braces and other "marks" used by Russell and Whitehead to indicate certain logical acts were, after all, *repeated*. What justifies, or even suggests, this repetition? In opposition to Russell, G. Spencer Brown has shown that it is possible to "arithmeticize" logic;[15] that is, it is possible to construct logic from the basic intuitive act of making a distinction and two fundamental arithmetical acts: (1) making a mark to signify the distinction and (2) repeating the mark. Hence, it is not at all certain that Kant has been refuted with respect either to geometry or arithmetic.

INTUITION AND REPRESENTATION

Our discussion so far has been in defense of a Kantian position. We indicated earlier, however, that we would move closer to Schopenhauer in identifying understanding as a function of intuition. One very important reason for doing this is that Kant failed to connect intuition to the dynamic or motivational factors influencing intellectual activity. For him, even though he insisted that reason is insufficient for knowledge of the empirical world, reason still reigned supreme both in intellectual and moral life. In the former, intuition merely supplies representations from which objects are extracted for thought; in the latter, affect must be submitted to the rule of reason.

Schopenhauer castigates Kant for failing to investigate the content of our intuition. He notes that we are led to expect such an investigation. Having described the forms of our intuitive faculty, Kant was in a position (Schopenhauer says) to tell us something about the empirical content of our intuition and how it reaches us. Kant's repeated "it is given" draws special criticism from Schopenhauer. To say of perceptual content, "It is given," is to deny the creative aspect of intuition. Further, Kant's separation of understanding from intuition and his equivocation concerning the definition of this "understanding" are almost incomprehensible to Schopenhauer. For him, it was clear that perceptual knowledge—the center of an empirical intuition—comes to us with meaning, that it "is given" because, in an important sense, we seek it. Further, even abstract knowledge, which he agreed was fundamentally the work of reason, stands in need of the intuitive light in order that it may be understood. Schopenhauer's complaint thus centered on Kant's neglect of the understanding that accompanies perception itself and on the final need, met by intuition, for understanding abstract knowledge. Further, Schopenhauer would insist that both internal (ideational) and external (perceptual) intuitions involve direction, "an act of will or purpose."[16]

For Schopenhauer, it is clear that the content of all intuitions is partly determined by dynamic factors (what he calls "Will") and, hence, by our quest for meaning. Since this is so, it cannot be the case that intuition simply receives representations and that something called the "understanding" extracts objects from these representations to pass along to reason for "thinking." The search for meaning must pervade the entire sequence. Intuition must provide not just an organized set of sensations aroused by what is there and developed pictorially through its forms, but it must also be *affected* by the quest for meaning and understanding, and, therefore, provide at least a first layer of meaning. It is clearly not synonymous with perception, if we mean to restrict perception to what is gathered by the senses, for it includes an influence from within and not merely from its own form. Further, it can be turned inward as an "inner eye" or "inner ear," watching and listening for what is within as well as for what is without. Allowing intuition to look inward in a search for the meaning of analytically derived conclusions will allow us to connect the two domains of intuition, internal and external—logical and empirical—and thus escape the need for a universe of eternal forms. When we permit intuition to look inward, intuition does become—as Husserl insisted—intellectual,[17] but this does not mean that intuition springs from reason, as Husserl claimed. It means only that intuition may *look at* and *see clearly* or understand intellectual objects. The intentionality that Husserl associates with intuition does not come directly from reason but, rather, directly from the dynamic capacity.

This intentionality is influenced by reason — what we know influences what we seek — but is not originated by it.

That understanding should be associated with intuition itself is reasonable when we consider the clarity and certainty with which intuitive knowledge (perceptual knowledge for Schopenhauer) affects us. Understanding is not properly attributed to the recitation of steps in a proof, no matter how perfectly the steps unfold from premise to conclusion, but to the "seeing" that occurs when the products of reason are re-examined — looked at — by intuition for the purpose of discerning or creating meaning. This sense of meaning, of having something at hand, pervades intuitive phases of thinking. Max Wertheimer quotes Einstein on his remembrance of this feeling:

> During all those years there was a feeling of direction, of going straight toward something concrete. It is, of course, very hard to express that feeling in words but it was decidedly the case and clearly to be distinguished from later considerations about the rational form of the solution.[18]

A defensible view of intuition must take into account the affect that impels it and accompanies it, but it must not confuse the intuition itself with the feeling of certainty that often accompanies it. What seems intuitively correct or obvious may, indeed, turn out to be wrong. But that feeling of excitement, of anticipation, of certainty is in itself an indication that the quest for meaning and understanding is part of the intuitive function. Things are not simply "given" to us in accordance with fixed and limited intuitive forms; rather we capture them in our search for understanding.

This capturing, however, does not imply that our intuition or consciousness creates the objects of thought totally. It constitutes them in the sense that it composes them, but we must be careful not to interpret "constitute" in the stronger sense of founding or supplying completely the elements of composition. The elements are both given and received by perceptual processes; the intuition *composes* them. There is some question, on the stronger view, whether we can avoid the trap of idealism; even Husserl, who claimed to have avoided it, finished up by labeling the correlates of mind (*noema*) "unreal."[19] We prefer to view intuition as a capacity that *reveals*, and we shall insist that what-is-there and our revealing intuition play equal, if different, roles in producing what is "given" to us. Intuition's ability to initiate meaning, then, is partially dependent upon the thing to which meaning will be attached. There *is* a sense in which "the world is my world," as Wittgenstein said, but there is, equally, a sense in which *I* am the world's. Sartre recognizes this dual possibility when he discusses how emotion occurs:

> Thus, there are two forms of emotion, according to whether it is we who constitute the magic of the world to replace a deterministic activity which cannot be realized, or whether it is the world itself which abruptly reveals itself as being magical.[20]

We suggest that this notion, which attempts to avoid the extremes of both idealism and realism, may be extended from emotion to *knowing* as well. We can *let* reason dominate even in our contact with the empirical world. It cannot operate alone in this domain, of course, but it can dominate. We can lay assimilatory schemes on the world repeatedly in accordance with what we hope to find or accomplish. We can even defend these schemes against perceptual knowledge that resists them. Or we can put aside the urge to control and impose; we can become intentionally receptive. Intuition seems to have the special function of allowing us, after we have decided in a reflective conscious mode, to submit ourselves to the world and to be, nonreflectively or directly, spoken to, grasped, and moved by it.

Now, in this use of "reflective" and "nonreflective" consciousness, we are following Sartre. In reflective consciousness we are aware of ourselves as subjects, as thinkers, as actors; reflective consciousness is consciousness attempting to look at itself. All it catches sight of, of course, is a memory, something fleetingly there and then gone — as a shadow disappears when light is cast directly on it. Nonreflective consciousness, on the other hand, is consciousness of objects. When we are in such a mode, consciousness is fastened upon the object. This bond between subject (ourselves) and object is ruptured when we turn consciousness upon ourselves-looking. For the most part, we shall use "consciousness" in its ordinary sense of awakeness or awareness but, with Sartre, we shall reject the association of intuition with the "unconscious." No mental mode could be more fully conscious than the intuitive mode. Indeed, for Sartre "consciousness" and "intuition" are very nearly synonyms. We, of course, want to distinguish between analytic and intuitive modes. But, if we speak of intuition operating "unconsciously," we shall mean only that we cannot catch ourselves in the act of intuiting; intuition itself is consciousness supreme and unanalyzable. In the intuitive mode, we *are* subjects, but we are unaware of our subjectness. Paradoxically, we experience enhanced subjectivity (we are affected) while, at the same time, we seem to have lost ourselves as subjects. In such states, possible objects in the external world do not appear to us as objects, because (in a sense we shall have to describe more fully) we have yielded our role as subject voluntarily to the *other* as subject. This seems clearly to be the case when we empathetically receive another human being—one who is properly described as "subject." But it is at least metaphorically an accurate and powerful description of what occurs when we submit ourselves to the inanimate other. It does not mean that we are simply and inevitably acted upon or stamped with impressions. On the contrary, we *choose* this condition; we allow it and even strive for it.

As we examine intuitive modes, modes which are dominated by intuition rather than reason, we shall see that creative artists often give testimony of this passive-receptive state that is entered so willing by and with such anticipation. Mozart, as we shall see, described himself as hearing melodies in his head, Gauss was "seized by mathematics," and Joan Miró spoke of himself as "like drunk"— in an altered state of consciousness. The fear of losing one's creative powers comes across, also, and provides further evidence for the felt loss of control or lack of subjectness in such states. It is as though things are accomplished *through* one and not by one.

Have we departed so far from Kant that our view is no longer properly even "neo-Kantian"? The essential elements are still there: Intuition is a capacity that makes contact, that participates in the creation of representations, that is capable of "receiving" representations when the Will is disposed to this intense form of receptivity. But we have departed from Kant in suggesting that intuition provides a first understanding or meaning along with its representation and that the search for meaning influences the empirical contents of intuition. We have suggested that intuition creates representations in response to the Will's demand for meaning, but we want to preserve the possibility of something close to true "receptivity," and we shall discuss this further. We have also insisted that intuition *looks at* the representations of reason and instigates the familiar "I see!" affect. We must say more about both the domains on which intuition acts as it creates representations and its range, that is, the realms to which it *sends* representations. Further, if the search for meaning influences or is somehow part of intuitive functioning, can we properly defend our claim that intuition is a form of direct or immediate contact?

INTUITION AS IMMEDIATE

We mentioned at the outset that anyone who takes the concept of intuition seriously retains a notion of intuition as direct contact, as a form of "seeing." For Kant, "immediate" as a property of intuition referred to the nonintervention of cognition. We affirm this, but we do not mean to imply by this affirmation that perception cannot come under the influence of cognition. Everything that can be thought, the entire content of cognitive workings, is either directly or derivatively a product of intuition, deposited for thought by intuitive representation. But in a particular act of perception, cognitive schemata may obscure what-is-there. Our perceptions may, then, under certain conditions, be mediated.

Many cognitive psychologists insist that *all* of our knowledge is mediated. Ulric Neisser, for example, says: "We have no direct, *immediate* access to the world. . . . Whatever we know about reality has been mediated."[21]

Now, obviously, there is a temptation to move in this direction when we postulate an active subject in human perception and cognition. But we should be cautious for, if *everything* is mediated, one of two consequences follows: if by "mediated" we mean simply that our contact with the world is restricted to phenomena, then we must postulate, with Kant, a world of *noumena* behind the world of appearance that is somehow more real than the world of phenomena but which must remain unknowable and reached only by speculative inference; if, however, we mean by "mediated" that everything we know in the phenomenal world is itself mediated, the very notion of "mediate" loses its force. Postulating a world of *noumena* raises philosophical problems, and we shall consider some of these, but it does no damage to the serious notion of intuition. Intuition makes direct (noncognitive) contact with objects as phenomena, and these are the real objects of knowledge. (The thing-in-itself, Schopenhauer's "Will," is known, or we would prefer to say "felt," in an entirely different way.) If we insist that we have no direct access to the phenomenal world, intuition has disappeared.

Consider an analogy. Suppose I am wearing gloves to work in my garden and, drawn by its beauty, I reach out to touch a rose. What do I feel? Well, it yields even to my gloved fingers, but I cannot feel the silky texture of the petals; the thickness of my glove mediates what I feel. So I take off the glove. Shall I now say that my touch is mediated by my skin? Or is the very meaning of "touch" so bound up with "skin" that I should more properly consider the touch of my ungloved finger to the rose petal as unmediated contact?

If we take this latter course, which we believe is reasonable, we enrich the meaning of "mediate" and we retain the essential characteristic of intuition. We see, also, that what is immediate passes swiftly into the mediate and, in practice, the passage is often impossible to detect. We agree with Neisser that any discursive knowledge we have of the world is mediated, but we reject his claim that we have no direct access to the world. That perception *can* be mediated, that there are "perceptual sets," for example, we do not deny, but we deny that it *must* be so mediated. Training in many Eastern religions, we observe, is designed to eliminate systematically the cognitive mediators that all of us use unconsciously. In intuitive modes, as we shall describe them, such mediators are kept relatively inactive. The hallmark of the intuitive mode is seeing without glasses, hearing without filters, touching with ungloved hand. The immediate character of intuition does not imply accuracy, rightness, or moral goodness. It does imply commitment and clarity.

There are many examples in the history of creative work that suggest practical, as well as theoretical, reasons for maintaining the distinction between constructing an object conceptually and seeing it, or contacting it immediately. Jacques Hadamard, for example, recounts incidents in which he and other mathematicians actually constructed certain mathematical products of great importance but failed to see that they had done so.[22] This is not merely a matter of not seeing certain applications but a matter of not seeing to the heart of the construct itself. "It" was there, but its essential nature was not revealed.

Our position, then, is as follows: Intuition is that function that contacts objects directly in phenomena. This direct contact yields something we might call "knowledge" in that it guides our actions and is precipitated by our own quest for meaning. As we shall see, some things that are intuited, for example, feelings in others, may be represented first and most directly to the dynamic faculty, thereby inducing an "I must do something!" response. We might call this form of representation "intuitive feeling." When the intuitive representation is created primarily for cognition (but, of course, a report goes also to Will), we may properly refer to that which guides us as "intuitive knowledge."

That this position may leave us with Kant's unknowable realm of *noumena* is, it seems to us, not only acceptable but unavoidable. We can perhaps achieve fleeting glimpses (feelings) of that world but no definite knowledge of it. Powerful mathematical results, in particular Gödel's theorems, suggest that we as *systems* cannot possibly know our own functioning entirely and certainly not that of a system beyond us. Therefore, our view of intuition is conceived in this phenomenal world and meant for application within that world.

INTUITION AND WILL

Schopenhauer regarded the Will as thing-in-itself. This *Will* that is in us all can be felt; indeed, it is felt as ultimately and basically real, as that which is more directly known than anything else. But the "knowing" of which we speak here is different from intuitive knowing. Intuitive knowing comes to us through representations created in phenomenal contact and, indeed, we can know the Will-as-manifestation, say as motive, in just this way. But this is not *the Will*. Similarly, when we regard the force that drives a growing plant through stone or concrete as the plant's "Will," we err, says Schopenhauer, for the Will is beyond the force, and force is its mere manifestation. Schopenhauer says further:

> Therefore, if we refer the concept of *force* to that of *will*, we have in fact referred something more unknown to something infinitely better known, indeed to the one thing really known to us immediately and completely; and we have very greatly extended our knowledge. If, on the other hand, we subsume the concept of *will* under that of *force*, as has been done hitherto, we renounce the only immediate knowledge of the inner nature of the world that we have, since we let it disappear in a concept abstracted from the phenomenon, with which therefore we can never pass beyond the phenomenon.[23]

We prefer to regard an individual's relation to the Will as neither knowledge nor pure affect but something clearly beyond either. In its manifestations it comes to light through intuition as feeling or sensibility or insight. Sometimes it comes to us as pure feeling, as a sure sense beyond knowledge that we *are* and that we are in relation to other forms of being beyond their manifestations. We shall not be concerned with this fundamental being-to-being contact, for it must by its very nature belong to the mystical. This does not mean that we deny such contact but only that we cannot be concerned with it in the present context. We are concerned, rather, with occasions that approximate such pure contact: when we feel what the other feels, when we are on fire with inspiration, when we see with breathtaking clarity. Each such situation occurs in the phenomenal world; what happens guides us and seems properly a form of intuitive knowledge or of intuitive feeling; the understanding that flashes upon us may be used to trigger activity in the instrumental world. We accept such occurrences as real not only because people say that they have experienced them but, also, because there are products resulting from them: tender acts of human love, symphonies, paintings, mathematical theorems. Now, of course, both analytic thinking and physical activity have also been involved in producing products that can be observed by others. But we are here concerned with that intuitive activity that, under the influence of a Will striving to manifest itself, presents us with vivid representations. We shall continue to use the term *Will* as a shorthand designation for the dynamic center of self—the heart of being.

The Will in manifest form must be considered, then, as we discuss intuition. Its appearance as force—directed toward understanding, feeling, expressing, creating—sustains and promotes intuitive activity. It subordinates analytic and algorithmic activity to its needs, quieting the continual humming of the internal logic-machine. It provides the intuition with supportive affect: "Go ahead, go ahead!" it seems to say.

Now, clearly, we have begun to discuss intuition in terms of its function and potential contents and not just in the fixed form that makes experience possible. It may be that the intuitive capacity, fundamentally necessary to experience and so alive and vital in early years, works less often in a dominant role as we acquire more and more concepts and routines. Indeed, the loss of creativity that we so easily blame on schooling may be more properly traced to reading. When we learn to read, we accept a preformed representation that is assimilated rapidly to reason. Words themselves too often become the objects of our attention, and the organ of understanding, intuition, is made subservient to the logical demands of decoding. The intuition no longer plays on the objects picked out naturally by Will in a quest for meaning but, rather, it is either made to slumber or reawakened by a Will aroused to the symbol. The affects—curiosity, awe, excitement—that accompany intuitive activity quite naturally disappear when the intuition is placed in a subordinate and automatic role. How do some of us avoid this? By creating vivid representations? By remaining in intense contact with something other than the code and the literal translation that our machine-mind can produce? These questions will be vital for us as we explore intuition in education.

Here it is important for us to repeat that our use of "Will" is meant to connote the dynamic or motivational mechanism at the center of our being. In an important sense this central mechanism *is* "us." It is that which feels directly, moves us directly, gives us the "I am" directly. Schopenhauer, with his great interest in Eastern philosophies, was concerned with showing that the Will is *one*, that it manifests itself in various ways at various levels of objectivity. A serious metaphysical examination of intuition must consider whether ultimate reality is many or one (in mathematical philosophy, Rucker discusses this question), but we are not primarily concerned with metaphysics and will not consider this question in depth. Our description of intuition turned inward, however, implies a view of reality as *many*, many Wills and many minds, for we have not provided for intuitive contact with a realm of eternal forms, and our "mindscape" is an individual one even though it is socially constructed. Our use of "Will," therefore, differs importantly from that of Schopenhauer.

THE DOMAINS OF INTUITION

We have been striving for a description of intuition and its relation to Will, perception, understanding, and reason. We still have to say a bit more about the domains with which intuition makes contact. Being-to-being contact we have assigned to the mystical, but this is not to say that our contact with the thing-in-itself is unimportant in our quest for knowledge. As we have seen, this thing-in-itself, this Will, struggling to become manifest, impels us to look, and listen, and touch—to encounter from as many aspects as possible so that we can understand.

But what is it that we contact when our intuition functions? Certainly, we must include everything in the perceptual world and, in a Kantian sense, this is the function for which "intuition" was created — to explain how it is that we can have knowledge of the external world. This seeing capacity, however, may be turned inward; it may look at the products of reason as well as the products of perception. When we look at it this way, we see another reason for insisting on an understanding function of intuition itself. Reason uses the objects provided in intuitive representation, combines them, transforms them according to its own rules; but the conclusions of reason must be looked upon by intuition in order to be seen and understood. Often we have a result right before us, a result we have ourselves produced, and we still do not understand it. Our cognitive schemata form a cloud between "us" and the material we are thinking about. In such situations, we literally need to stop thinking and look at the objects of reason. Clearly, reason is not complete in itself so far as our understanding is concerned. Saying is not equivalent to understanding.

Now, allowing intuition to look inward upon the results of cognition gives us another advantage: It permits us to discard a realm of ideal forms. Allowing intuition to turn inward, we can describe mathematical objects as the products of a series of intuitive acts starting from the concrete representations of empirical intuition. Hence, two domains — the perceptual and the conceptual — must be organized and understood by the intuition. For us, the "phenomenal" world will include subject-object contacts in both perceptual and conceptual domains.

Should sensations such as pains, twinges, aches, and the like be included in the domain of intuition? We think this would be a mistake. First, these sensations do not seem to be objects of knowledge; at least, "having" them does not seem to be a case of having knowledge. We do not mean by this that we cannot think about pains and aches. Of course we can, and in that context, they are objects of knowledge. But the pain itself is something we *have* directly—not through representation. The thing we call pain was not first in the perceptual world and then in us. It is part of that which, as Kierkegaard pointed out, cannot be reduced to knowledge.

Conceptually, this decision is of great importance. The Will—our own Will in its entirety—is not a domain for intuition. Rather, the Will controls and directs intuition. As we shall see, the Will is a primary *range* for the intuitive function; intuition creates representations for or in the Will, but it does not—cannot—provide us with that which exists prior to itself. We should pause here to explain that we are using "domain" and "range" in the standard mathematical way: the domain is the set acted upon; the range is the set of images resulting. What we are claiming, for the purpose of keeping our conceptual machinery in working order, is that intuition *looks upon* and creates representations from two domains, the perceptual and the conceptual. It carries its representations (or creates them in) two ranges, the cognitive-intellectual and the Will. The Will is always a range for intuition; whatever it sees, it reports to the center of meaning and life; but the Will, being the thing behind intuition, cannot itself be acted upon by intuition. There is no element of mysticism in our use of intuition. Throughout our discussion, we shall be careful to separate our concept of intuition from alternative concepts that associate intuition with being-to-being contact or with knowledge of being-itself.

We have so far considered the domains of intuition — those worlds on which intuition acts to create representations. We must also consider the range of intuition, those regions to which representations are carried. So far, it is clear that intuition as function or mapping carries perceptual material into the cognitive domain. It seems right to say that it also carries perceptual material to the Will, to that central self that cannot be a domain of intuition. The representation that reaches the Will must, of course, be congruent with the purposes manifested by the Will. If understanding is the quest, then what reaches the Will is, "Here it is," "This is what it means," and the Will responds, "Eureka!" If quiet receptivity is the quest, then what reaches the Will takes the form, "Remember this. Delight in this. Submit to this." If feeling with the other is the quest, then what reaches the Will is oddly like the pain or pleasure that reaches us from within. It motivates us to act in behalf of the other as we would for ourselves.

Are we saying, then, that we see what we want to see, hear what we want to hear, feel what we long to feel? No. Such a position is clearly wrong. We are often deeply shocked and disappointed by what we intuit. But what is reported matters to us; it is reported in the interest of our quest for meaning, for physical and mental and emotional survival. A representation goes to cognition so that matters may be thought about and to Will so that they *will be* thought about.

When we consider both reason (the operative conceptual domain) and Will as ranges of intuition, we achieve a conceptual mechanism for explaining the feeling of certainty or sense of knowing that accompanies intuitive functioning. At the first moment of knowing, one in which perceptual material is carried both to reason and Will, we have that initial flash, the sense that this is the way to go or that something is the case. Later, when our analytic and conceptual work has yielded a solution, intuition carries the new representation to Will as a final flash of clarity, as clear understanding.

The intuition carries images from the perceptual world into both reason and Will or, in more familiar but not entirely accurate language, into cognition and affect. While our own pain and feeling reach us directly, arise *in* the Will, without representation, that of the other must reach us through intuition. When intuition is dominant, that is, when the connection to Will is very strong, we have the sense of being-to-being contact. There is a resistance to thinking the other. If the activity is intellectual, it seems to be primarily perceptual — things are seen, and what is manipulated conceptually is observed. It is the observing and seeing that dominate. If the activity is nonintellectual (directed not to the conceptual world but to the world of persons and their affective responses) it seems to be all-being, all-feeling. If what is received is pain or fear, the feeling aroused is a direct, "I must do something!" One's motive power is enlisted in behalf of the other as if for oneself. This feeling, this primary moral impulse, precedes thinking on *what* should be done and directs it.[24] Moral intuition construed as moral feeling is clearly very different from the intuition of moral knowledge or truth as postulated in moral intuitionism. It involves no direct apprehension of the "morally good" but, rather, provides the initial impulse to act in a caring fashion toward the one with whom contact is made. Such contact made with the other may be described as Martin Buber describes the *I–Thou* relation:

> This human being is not *He* or *She*, bounded from every other *He* and *She*, a specific point in space and time within the net of the world; nor is he a nature able to be experienced and described, a loose bundle of named qualities. But with no neighbor, and whole in himself, he is *Thou* and fills the heavens.[25]

This sort of relation may be experienced, also, with nonhuman objects in the perceptual world and with objects in the conceptual world. One may have an *I–Thou* relation with things or ideas. This sort of contact is, of course, momentary; *Thou* must become *It* in order to be thought and acted upon in the instrumental world. We are here concerned with interpreting what is expressed so beautifully by Buber as the *I–Thou* in terms of intuition's capacity to approximate being-to-being contact.

What seems crucial in all this is that our Will must allow intuition to make such contact; it must, in a sense, be more concerned with subject-to-subject relation than with subject-to-object contact. Traditionally, we have conceived intuition as our capacity to contact and represent objects for reason. We have neglected its dynamic or motivational connections and its affective connections. We are suggesting that this object-contacting function may well behave as though, *willingly*, the roles of subject and object were reversed. We may, in a sense, become willingly *object* to the other in such a way that our subjectivity is shared. We have a sense of we-ness or even of being acted upon by the other. Things are accomplished through us, as it were.

At this stage, we have a conceptual mechanism that should

prove fruitful in a discussion of teaching and learning. Because it is clear that intuition as function operates momentarily and intensely, we shall be interested not so much in products of intuition (which are rarely unmixed with conception) as we are in intuitive modes, those modes that seem to be dominated by intuitive rather than conceptual or analytic activity. We have tried to answer the question, "What is intuition?" by describing its function, its domains, and its range. To get at a conception particularly useful for education, we shall find the move to intuitive modes productive.

Before we make this move, however, it may be wise to consider the role of *familiarity* in producing intuitions. Even the nonserious user of "intuition" recognizes intuitions as "educated guesses." We, too, need to account for the increase of intuitive activity that seems to be induced by familiarity.

INTUITION AND FAMILIARITY

Suppose for a moment that we are skeptical about the whole business of intuition. As positivists or behaviorists we might say: Look, this is all nonsense. *Intuition* is just a term we use to name certain kinds of happenings. When a person is deeply familiar with a domain of knowledge, some things which seem difficult to novices are so elementary that they are taken for granted. They are labeled "intuitive." Or, sometimes, we think so rapidly and are so concentrated on our goal that we fail to keep track of the steps we use; then we label our thinking "intuitive" because we cannot recall the analysis. Similarly, we sometimes pull promising ideas from a vast store of potential knowledge and, because we cannot trace the analytic procedures by which we did this, we label the result "intuitive." But one must admit that people do not produce "intuitions" in subject areas where they are ignorant. Educators should concentrate, then, on building up stores of knowledge in their students. What we call "intuition" will then take care of itself.

Now, of course, there is some truth in all this. Intuition, whatever it is, does seem to manifest itself often in familiar domains. Generally, the people most knowledgeable in an area are those who have the most frequent and the most reliable intuitions. We have already acknowledged this fact by including the individual mindscape or cognitive domain in the domains of intuition. Clearly, those who have more information on a topic have a larger domain for intuitive exploration. But this is by no means a complete account of intuition. First, familiarity is certainly not sufficient for the production of intuitions. Many who are well informed on particular subjects seem to be singularly lacking in insight. Second, familiarity does not seem to be necessary, although it obviously increases the possibility of sophisticated guesses. We sometimes encounter people who exhibit a marvelous intuitive grasp of subject matter in which they are relatively untrained. As we shall see, the intuition may operate effectively through metaphorical domains. Therefore, while we shall discuss ways in which familiarity may enhance intuitive activity, we shall also want to explore how intuition may be exercised to develop familiarity. Clearly, if intuition follows, it also leads, and, indeed, we have claimed that it provides the very foundation for experience.

But the nonserious view is very much with us. Consider Linus Pauling's suggestion that intuition is best thought of as application of knowledge, as "reaching some conclusion on the basis of what you know. Not perhaps by a simple logical step, but a complicated logical step."[26] This description is in line with the skeptical comments above, but consider now Pauling's response when a student asks, "How do you go about having good ideas?" Pauling answers, "You have a lot of ideas and you throw away the bad ones." Perhaps the student should have asked, "How do you get *ideas*?" How is the essentially closed system of logical reasoning invaded by events in the external world? What connects empirical object and reason? What connects the store of analytical results with the problematic situation? What separates good ideas from bad prior to empirical test?

In a similar problematic vein, consider, illustratively, the topic of mathematical induction. Students, even those quite appreciative of the method's power, ask: "But how do you *get* the formula in the first place?" An easy answer, and one put to use somewhat uncritically by advocates of "discovery learning," is, "by experimenting." Bright students see that the reality is not nearly so simple as the verbal response. "But how do you think to experiment in this way?" they protest. "How did anyone hit on the problem? How did he or she proceed?" Some of these questions can be satisfied by including a historical account in our instructional procedures and some by discussions of mathematical motivation, but there remains the intriguing nucleus of the problem. How did experiment and reason come together in this particularly happy result? What made meaningful experience possible?

In attempting to answer these questions, the emphasis on Will or affect will be very useful. Our answer, in essence, is that the things considered matter deeply to us, that they appear to us as responses to our quest for meaning and are therefore embraced with delight. Henri Poincaré, in his discussion of mathematical creation, emphasizes the role of affect in producing intuition:

> Among the great numbers of combinations blindly formed by the subliminal self, almost all are without interest and without utility; but just for that reason they are also without effect upon the esthetic sensibility. Consciousness will never know them; only certain ones are harmonious, and, consequently, at once useful and beautiful. They will be capable of touching this special sensibility of the geometer of which I have just spoken, and which, once aroused, will call our attention to them, and will bring them into consciousness.[27]

Thus, we see again that intuitive functioning involves dual representation and that the representation sent to Will plays a crucial role in understanding.

We are not suggesting that we have solved the problems under discussion when we agree to label what is going on "intuition." Rather, we are suggesting that one will not illuminate the problems at all by labeling something "intuition" and then denying that anything deserving that name is going on. The first step, then, is to take intuition seriously, to ask what characterizes the activities, moods, and events that we agree to label in that way. Our initial step in analysis has been an attempt to answer the question, "What is intuition?"

SUMMARY

We began this chapter with a defense of Kant's basic description of intuition's role in knowing. In particular, we accepted the concept of intuition as that capacity of mind that reaches objects of knowledge directly. But, with Schopenhauer and later phenomenologists, we recognized that Kant failed to give an adequate account of the role of motivation and the quest for meaning in intuition. It was further suggested that understanding is properly associated with intuition itself, and that intuition provides both Will and reason with representations. This interpretation makes it possible to account for the characteristic affect that accompanies intuitive activity.

We explored the domains and range of intuition, identifying two domains—the perceptual and conceptual—and claiming that understanding always involves the activation of intuition in seeing what-is-there. This seeing involves a representation from one of the domains into the range we labeled "Will," that central self or being that manifests itself as motive, desire, feeling, and the like. This Will, we claimed, could not itself be an object for intuition, although, of course, its manifestations might be.

We concluded our initial analysis with a brief discussion of the role of familiarity in intuitive activity. Here we suggested that, while familiarity seems often to enhance intuitive activity, intuition is essential to the development of familiarity. We shall say more on this topic when discussing intuitive approaches to curriculum and instruction.

We are now ready for the second phase of our analysis, an exploration of intuitive modes and their enhancement. In this phase, we shall distinguish intuitive from analytic modes.

Chapter 4

INTUITIVE MODES

I have found you an argument; I am not obliged to find you an understanding.

Samuel Johnson,
in Boswell's *Life of Johnson*

I am not for imposing any sense on your words: you are at liberty to explain them as you please. Only, I beseech you, make me understand something by them.

Bishop Berkeley,
"A Dialogue Concerning the Principles"

IF OUR PRIMARY INTEREST in intuition were epistemological, we would very likely follow up the initial analysis with an examination of intuitions, the products of intuitive activity. We would be concerned with the validation of such products. If our first concerns were metaphysical, we would build upon our discussion of the domains of intuition and argue more strongly for the abandonment of ideal realms. Or, of course, we might argue against such a position and adopt a stance that could be argued only from a metaphysical standpoint; we might undertake an explication of mystical realms. If our central interest were phenomenological, we would launch an investigtion into the structures of consciousness. If our main interest were religious or spiritual, we would concern ourselves either with an extension of intuitive domains beyond the perceptual and conceptual or with a description of how the spiritual might arise within the conceptual itself. Our great interest, however, is in education and how intuition is involved in its processes.

Clearly, there is no way to take an episode of mental activity and carve it up in such a way that we can properly label the first six acts "intuitive," the next eight "analytic," and so on. As we have described it, the intuition acts in complementary fashion with reason, and it is impossible to isolate the two meticulously and discretely. We can, however, identify episodes that are dominantly intuitive and contrast these with episodes that are primarily analytic or algorithmic. The latter, at least in the algorithmic pattern, are characterized by step-wise procedures. We are occupied in executing certain chosen operations. When we are involved in such episodes, we can sustain interruptions without loss of continuity; we simply pick up where we left off, because it is perfectly clear where we left off. Interruptions of intuitive activity, however, are devastating; we cannot say where we left off or, even, *why* we were at the level at which the interruption occurred. The great labor of reaching such a level of concentration must be undertaken afresh, and our dispositions may suffer as a result.

In this chapter, we shall suggest a characterization of intuitive modes that involves four major features: involvement of the senses, commitment and receptivity, a quest for understanding or empathy, and a productive tension between subjective certainty and objective uncertainty. As we discuss each aspect, we shall be careful to connect it to our initial analysis, to give examples to support and illustrate our description, and to describe the relation of the aspect under scrutiny to the other three features of intuitive modes.

INTUITIVE MODES AND THE SENSES

Intuitive activity involves immediate contact with the objects of knowledge or feeling. Cognitive or conceptual schemes do not intervene or mediate the interaction. When we contact objects analytically or conceptually, we lay structures on them, or we move away from the objects under study to other objects, operations, or principles that we relate conceptually to the original objects. When we contact objects intuitively, however, we continually return to the objects themselves: We look, listen, touch; we allow ourselves to be moved, appeared to, grasped. If there *is* a structure that we are imposing on what we view, some sort of "reality frame" or inherent structure for, say, language, we are unaware of it and have no control over it; indeed, we may be unable to explicate it even upon request.

An example may make clear the contrast between intuitive and analytic (conceptual) modes. Consider a variation on a popular test for creativity. Subjects are presented an ordinary brick and asked to list as many uses for it as they can think of in a limited time interval. A subject operating analytically might first associate a brick with building. What can I build with it? he might ask. His list would be constructed from his consideration of the concept "build": Use it to level a short table leg; use it to support a shelf; build a tower of it and other objects; prop a broken chair with it; prop a broken dresser with it. A subject operating intuitively would reject the temptation to be diverted by a conceptual line. She might look at it: It's red—hang it on the wall where I'd like a bit of red; it's rectangular and solid—use it to demonstrate a rectangular solid. She might touch it: It's hard—use it for a robot's pillow; it's grainy—use it as an abrasive. She might lift it: It's heavy—use it as a doorstop or paper weight; use it as a weapon. She might strike it: It crumbles—dissolve its grains and make a red liquid. She might think of expressions she could coin from contact with it: "brick red," "he's a brick," "hard as a brick." She might listen to it: It's quiet—make a good companion for a pet rock.

Now it is clear that subjects operating in an intuitive mode are using concepts. They must in order to communicate. But they return again and again to the object. They allow contact with the object to direct their thought, whereas analytic thinkers are directed by concepts they have attached to the object. In regarding a postulate, for example, the analytic thinker moves away from the postulate toward what can be derived from it. The intuitive thinker may return to the postulate itself and ask: What am I doing? I'm *accepting*. This is a *postulate*. Need I accept it? What are my alternatives?

So far in this discussion, we have been using analytic and conceptual synonymously. When we refer to concepts, we shall consistently intend reference to the objects constructed by reason through abstraction. When these concepts are themselves involved in a conceptual mode, they are employed deductively, hierarchically, and serially. They are submitted to the machinery of logic. A concept under treatment in this mode is subjected to operations. A concept may, however, be the object of intuition. We may look at the conceptions of reason, play with them, combine them in visual, auditory, or tactile patterns. Generally, we associate concepts with language, but concepts need not be cast linguistically, and language itself may be the object of intuition. Consider Lewis Carroll's "Jabberwocky":

> Twas brillig, and the slithy toves
>   Did gyre and gimble in the wabe;

> All mimsy were the borogoves,
> And the mome raths outgrabe.[1]

How do we make sense of "Jabberwocky"? We can take the position that it is exactly the *lack* of sense that appeals to us, that "Jabberwocky" is literally a non-sense poem. But that position does not hold up well under attack. We *do* make sense of the poem; reading it is entirely unlike reading a set of nonsense syllables for a memory test. Further, it is not just the going forth, the slaying, and the hurrahing that make sense to us. Even the verse quoted above makes sense of a sort. Perhaps we bring to bear on it some inherent (or tacitly learned) syntactic machinery but, as we do, we need not be aware of it, nor need we be aware of nouns, verbs, adjectives, etc. As Martin Gardner points out:

> Alice herself, in the paragraph following the poem puts her finger on the secret of the poem's charm: ". . . it seems to fill my head with ideas—only I don't know exactly what they are."[2]

If we consider the number of commentaries, science fiction stories, imitations, and applications that have grown out of "Jabberwocky," we can say with some confidence that it has, indeed, filled heads with ideas. To say that we encounter this bit of language intuitively seems accurate. We encounter it, we feel something as a result of the encounter, and we understand something from it. It is worth emphasizing again the important results of our earlier analysis: Intuition involves sensory encounter, subjective response, and compliance with the Will's quest for meaning.

Consider, further, this fragment from e. e. cummings that violates even syntax:

> what if a much of a which of a wind
> gives the truth to summer's lie;
> bloodies with dizzying leaves the sun
> and yanks immortal stars awry?[3]

How do we approach "what if a much of a which of a wind"? With auditory delight? With cognitive dismay? With both? Both are necessary: The first supplies the typical affect of intuitive activity— keep going, there is something here! The second readies us for a new look at eternal verities. It is essentially hopeless to come at the poem conceptually, although, of course, one may try to describe its techniques conceptually.

It is obvious that the senses are involved when intuition is turned toward things in the external world, but they—or something very like them—are also involved when intuition is turned inward. In reflection, I turn my internal senses upon particular episodes of consciousness. I do not simply state a belief and defend it; I see and listen to the "I-believe" that accompanies it and, seeing it *as* belief, I become aware of my subjective role in accepting or rejecting it. In deliberation, I scan the conceptual programs that are available to me in the formulation and solution of problems. In imagination, I turn the internal senses upon intellectual entities. I do not simply define a "unicorn" as a mythical beast of such-and-such description, but I *see* a unicorn munching in my garden.

What sort of seeing and hearing is this? Is the notion of "internal senses" simply a metaphor? There is reason to believe that something other than metaphor is involved. When we are in an intuitive mode, we quite literally do not see or hear things that are outside the present domain of intuitive concentration. It is as though the senses were already occupied; we are totally present to the object of intuition. While a mother is thus engaged with her writing, a child may gain permission for all sorts of things: "Mother, may I go downtown to buy film?" "Yes," comes the answer in robot-like tone. Later, when the child returns, the mother may demand, "And where have you been, young man?"

Bertrand Russell described such an incident in the life of his teacher and collaborator, Alfred North Whitehead. Russell dropped in on Whitehead to present a guest who had expressed a desire to meet him. As Russell and the guest stood in the garden where Whitehead was working at a table, it became obvious that Whitehead was unaware of their presence. His eyes seemed to be upon them, yet he did not see them. He was not a rude man and would not, certainly, have deliberately ignored his guests. It was clear to Russell that Whitehead could neither see nor hear them and that it would require a perceptual event very much like a physical blow to wrench him free from his present domain of concentration. Russell and the visitor considerately left.

Much of what we say in discussing the involvement of internal senses will be metaphorical, but the use of convenient and vivid language should not obscure the clear fact that physical events of an important kind are taking place. Mozart, for example, described himself as *hearing* melodies in his head:

When I feel well and in a good humor, or when I am taking a drive or walking after a good meal, or in the night when I cannot sleep, thoughts crowd into my mind as easily as you could wish. Whence and how do they come? I do not know and I have nothing to do with it. Those which please me, I keep in my head and hum them; at least others have told me that I do so. Once I have my theme, another melody comes, linking itself to the first one, in accordance with the needs of the composition as a whole: the counterpoint, the part of each instrument, and all these melodic fragments at last produce the entire work: Then my soul is on fire with inspiration, if however nothing occurs to distract my attention.[4]

Here we have personal testimony that hearing may be turned inward, that "another melody comes," that it presents itself in accordance with a holistic representation of the entire future work. And we hear also that nothing must occur to distract the attention of one who is thus listening. It is as though one might miss something actually said or played if one is distracted by auditory or visual stimuli from without. Interestingly, we also hear confirmation of Pauling's contention. Pauling claimed to have lots of ideas and to have thrown away the bad ones; similarly, Mozart finds that thoughts crowd into his mind, and he keeps those that please him.

We shall see that this sense of wonder, this sense of receiving something, of being spoken to, is an important feature of intuitive modes. Martin Buber's description of the *I–Thou* relation has already been mentioned. In such an encounter, the object—whether human or nonhuman—"is *Thou* and fills the heavens."[5] No objective result has yet occurred: The impulse to aid the injured other has not yet been acted upon, the art-object has not yet been "led across" into the observable world, the proof of what is seen so clearly has not yet been formulated for public examination. Yet there is both an intellectual (or cognitive) representation and an affective one. If the activity is mainly intellectual, the intuition gives over its representation to reason, and objects are thought. If the activity is mainly moral, the intuitive representation is nearly pure feeling striking the motivational center with the force of its own being. In neither case is the second representation unimportant; the intellectual representation is supported by an affective one, and the feeling representation is supported by an intellectual one. But we are inclined to think of the first as a form of intuitive knowledge, whereas it may be more appropriate to think of the second as a form of intuitive feeling. We shall return to this distinction in a later chapter.

Throughout our discussion on the involvement of external and internal senses in intuitive modes, we have alluded to the sense of vivid passivity that accompanies intuitive activity. Caught up in such activity, we are peculiarly alive and fully engaged, and yet we have the feeling that we are not in control. Mozart went so far as to say, "I have nothing to do with it." What is this receptivity that induces such humility in its subjects?

RECEPTIVITY AND COMMITMENT

Receptivity of the sort we are discussing suggests paradoxes that we must unravel. First, while we are peculiarly engaged in a receptive mode, we experience a reduction of subjectness. The subjective aspect of experience—affect—is dominant, and yet we feel as though we are objects to another acting as subject. We are not, however, diminished, for we have been chosen as objects, just as we ourselves have chosen to be potential objects. The experience is recounted in fields other than music. E. T. Bell describes the mood as it came upon the great mathematician Gauss, whose preoccupation with mathematics is described as involuntary:

> As a young man Gauss would be "seized" by mathematics. Conversing with friends he would suddenly go silent, overwhelmed by thoughts beyond his control, and stand staring rigidly oblivious of his surroundings. Later he controlled his thoughts — or they lost control over him—and he consciously directed all his energies to the solution of a difficulty till he succeeded.[6]

The nature and value of the passive-receptive mood or phase in intuition is too often overlooked. Those who work from a philosophical base that accepts intuition as a faculty generally emphasize the activity of the subject, and that activity is not denied here. But activity must cease in order that what-is-there may exercise its influence upon the intuition. If we agree that an act of Will puts us into contact with the object, there is still the question: How shall I act upon it? One possible answer, critical at many stages of intellectual activity, is *not* to act upon it—at least not to act upon it in a manipulative way. I may watch, listen, feel, undergo, but I refrain from acting upon the object as though I have made a decision about what I have seen, heard, or felt. I let the object act upon me, seize me, direct my fleeting thoughts as I scan the structures with which I may, in turn, act upon the object. My decision to do this is *mine*; it requires an effort in preparation, but it also requires a letting go of my attempts to control. It involves a deliberate giving-over of subjectness.

Such modes are not always intellectually oriented. Sometimes they are almost purely consummatory and affective. I may decide, for example, to hear a recording of *Tristan and Isolde*. I have no intention of analyzing, critiquing, evaluating. I prepare the room: banish dust, clutter, and noise. I prepare myself: glass of sherry, light reading material, comfortable chair, shoes off. I let the music flood all of my being. I am totally receptive. I may remain that way to satiety.

Similarly, a devout Christian may prepare himself for Holy Communion with a rigorous intellectual search of conscience and an active quest for forgiveness. But when he turns to the communion rail, it is with an expectation of being filled. The space purged of willfulness and pride can be filled with grace. The expression, "Be still, and know that I am God," illustrates the ultimate receptivity of the intuitive mode. Because we have taken a position that confines intuition to the domains of physical (perceptual) entities and cognitive or mental entities, we cannot interpret such experiences as direct contact with God or, for that matter, with any mystical realm of ideal forms. If we treat the religious at all, we must consider it as a set of intellectual constructs. We must keep in mind, however, that many writers have used intuition in exactly the way we are rejecting.

The religious aspect of receptivity is, indeed, so often recognized that those who miss it feel somehow deficient. Thomas Hardy, in "The Impercipient," expresses a wistful—if skeptical—longing for what he cannot "see":

> That with this bright believing band
>   I have no claim to be,
> That faiths by which my comrades stand
>   Seem fantasies to me,
> And mirage-mists their Shining Land,
>   Is a strange destiny.
>
> Why thus my soul should be consigned
>   To infelicity,
> Why always I must feel as blind
>   To sights my brethren see,
> Why joys they've found I cannot find,
>   Abides a mystery.
>
> Since heart of mine knows not that ease
>   Which they know; since it be
> That He who breathes All's Well to these
>   Breathes no All's Well to me,
> My lack might move their sympathies
>   And Christian charity!

> I am like a gazer who should mark
>   An inland company
> Standing upfingered, with, "Hark, hark!
>   The glorious distant sea!"
> And feel, "Alas, 'tis but yon dark
>   And wind-swept pine to me!"
>
> Yet I would bear my shortcomings
>   With meet tranquility,
> But for the charge that blessed things
>   I'd liefer not have be.
> O, doth a bird deprived of wings
>   Go earth-bound wilfully!
>
> Enough. As yet disquiet clings
>   About us. Rest shall we.[7]

We see in this poetic account the perceived lack of responsibility for *not* seeing. Hardy is not spoken to by whatever or whoever it is that speaks to the religiously receptive. Indeed, he says that he would welcome some sign that a willful intelligence is meting out our miseries:

> If but some vengeful god would call to me
> From up the sky, and laugh: "Thou suffering thing,
> Know that thy sorrow is my ecstasy,
> That thy love's loss is my hate's profiting!"
>
> Then would I bear it, clench myself, and die,
> Steeled by the sense of ire unmerited;
> Half-eased in that a Powerfuller than I
> Had willed and meted me the tears I shed.[8]

Hardy finds nothing in the religious vision to aid his understanding of life, its miseries and joys. Yet, clearly, he is not deficient in receptivity. In "Afterward," we become aware that the natural world spoke to him: the "May month" flapping "its glad green leaves like wings;" "nocturnal blackness, mothy and warm," "the full starred heavens that winter sees." And in "To an Unborn Pauper Child," we know that the world's human agonies spoke to him: "Breathe not, hid Heart: cease silently," he counsels the unborn pauper child. Better not to be born than suffer the coming miseries. But he knows the child will strive to live and so wishes him "Health, love, friends, scope / In full for thee." Hardy strives to understand but can only confess "an eye for such mysteries" as confront us all in daily living.

As we shall see a bit later, the goal of an intuitive mode is usually understanding rather than some tangible product. But even this goal may be absent. We may, instead, receive images and store them away with the intention, only half-formed, to use them someday. Robert Frost describes this function of the receptive mode:

> The impressions most useful to my purpose seem always those I was unaware of and so made no note of at the time when taken, and the conclusion is come to that like giants we are always hurling experience ahead of us to pave the future with against the day when we may want to strike a line of purpose across it for somewhere.[9]

Frost describes his creation of poetry much as Mozart describes his composition of music—in passive terms:

> The figure a poem makes. It begins in delight and ends in wisdom. . . . It has an outcome that though unforeseen was predestined from the first image of the original mood—and indeed from the mood . . . . It finds its own name as it goes.[10]

He goes on to contrast this "passive" way of operating with the scholar's way in the acquisition of knowledge. Here, too, we simply receive in contrast to the purposeful quest we usually associate with coming to know. Frost casts the contrast as one between scholar and artist:

> Scholars get theirs with conscientious thoroughness along projected lines of logic; poets theirs cavalierly and as it happens in and out of books. They stick to nothing deliberately, but let what will stick to them like burrs where they walk in the fields.[11]

Our contrast, however, is not between scholar and artist but, rather, between conceptual and intuitive modes. Both scholar and artist submit to intuitive modes; both must, obviously, complete their public work in the conceptual mode. We have already mentioned, for example, Einstein and Gauss. Many other examples might be given.[12]

What is this receptivity to which we submit ourselves and over which we then have so little control? The object of intuition seems to be both given and taken, offered and accepted, in one process. If we use a machine analogy, reason may be likened to the totality of programs a machine is prepared to execute. But the programs must have input; capta must be fed into the computer. The intelligent human being (or, for very specific and limited purposes, another carefully prepared machine) supplies objects in a form that the computer's reasoning capacity can use. This capacity to discern and form objects is what we call intuition. It represents the present and perhaps permanent superiority of human being over machine. If the machine were asked about the source of its input, it would have to answer (in whatever terms we made possible), "It is given." This is the way Kant answered, and Schopenhauer criticized him severely for this. While it is certainly useful and almost certainly correct to put greater emphasis on the meaning-seeking activity of the subject than Kant did, we want also to reserve a role for the object in *suggesting* meaning. If the machine were asked about the faulty input it regularly rejects, what could it say? It has no memory of this material, no way ot imposing sense on it. Yet, surely, the inept human being who tries to enter such material has something sensible to convey and wishes to achieve some goal. Current attempts to develop artificial intelligence seem properly to be counted as attempts to develop machine intuition.

Here we must back up a bit. If we acknowledge that attempts to develop artificial intelligence are attempts to develop machine intuition, we have only acknowledged that human beings — the current possessors of intuition — are meaning-seekers. It does not follow from this that beings other than human beings offer meaning. Further, it seems logically impossible to insist either that such a property exists or that it does not. But it seems reasonable to state that beings appear in infinite aspects and that our Will can submit itself to an examination of these aspects. It also seems productive to extend this notion to cognitive or imaginative entities and to take seriously the claims of creative persons who hear music, are seized by mathematics, or see angels in stone. The important thing for our purposes is to take seriously the claim to direct contact. Our knowing is not fully explained in terms of assimilation and accommodation. There is an important process that precedes either of these in which we try nonselectively to discern what-is-there. Before we can ask "What is it?" we must ask "What shall I do?" We shall return to this, but for now it is enough to point out that the intellectual question— "what is it?"—can only be engaged when we have been assured that we are at least temporarily safe enough to ask it. The very acknowledgment of our Will's involvement in the construction of meaning suggests that we see something very like a Will in the object. Hence, even though we turn continually from the motivational question to the intellectual question and back again, the motivational (or action) question is logically first. This is, in a sense that we shall develop, the question that intuition is designed to answer. Intuition links us with the object in such a way that it and Will in collaboration produce the first layers of meaning.

We can now explain, at least in part, why we experience both increased subjectivity (intense affect) and reduced subjectness in intuitive modes. Our Will—so self-oriented, so action oriented—has the power to submit, to objectify itself. In such a mode, it can be acted upon directly by either external or internal stimuli. A common fear accompanies work that is dependent upon intuitive modes, the fear that the other will not reveal itself. As we shall see, those involved in creative work often find ways to enhance their intuitive modes, and some of these methods can be useful in education.

It may be that the well-known phenomena of incubation and illumination represent an extreme case of the passive-intuitive phase. We strive mightily on a problem (the period of preparation), try every trick we can think of, wring the situation dry of all it will produce, and then we give up. It is important to note that we do not give up with the intention of abandoning the topic forever; we give up "for now." At this point, it is possible that the intuition can maintain an unconscious (unaware) openness to a well-defined class of internal stimuli. While we are engaged in routine tasks or half-sleeping, while our senses are merely monitoring and not really engaged, our inward senses are listening, watching. This is the period of "incubation." Illumination, if it occurs, comes dramatically, accompanied by the characteristic "Eureka!" reaction.[13]

This is a good time to note that our contemporary conceptual terms and schemes are inadequate for the description of intuitive-intellectual moods, and this recognition provides added incentive for our exploration. Attempts to use terms that may seem superficially appropriate lead only to gaps and paradoxes. Take, for example, Piaget's *assimilation* and *accommodation*. We are taught by Piaget that all learning is an assimilation to some schema and that every assimilation requires—somewhere in the temporal order—an accommodation. This "adaptation," as it is described by Piaget, may very well be adequate on a grand conceptual level to describe what must have occurred in cases where learning has been successful. But it is obviously inadequate to describe the mental activity that goes on while one is learning. Clearly, in a passive-intuitive state, I am neither imposing structures nor changing existing ones. I leave everything as it is; I observe; I defer decision making. I am in a state described by McCulloch[14] as one of redundancy of potential command; I do not know where to send my problem for the next stage of control. If this stage is "assimilatory," it is so only trivially. The structure (if any) I am using is an executive structure exercising a monitoring, scanning function. I am looking at structures and for structures, not imposing them. We need to examine this stage carefully, and we badly need respectable terms with which to describe it. We have been using terms like *watch, listen, submit,* and *grasped, moved, seized,* and perhaps this is the best we can do. These are respectable English words, and we must argue for their use.

To push the point a little further, consider terms that are thought to be possible neurological correlates of *assimilation* and *accommodation*: *redundancy enhancement* and *redundancy reduction.*[15] In the first state, redundancy is increased—all channels are tuned to the same stimulus; in the second, redundancy is decreased — a variety of stimuli is admitted. Now what sort of state am I in when I am concentrating on a situation and allow all sorts of potential stimuli relevant to that situation to flow in freely? The very question is a mishmash of terminology, hopelessly inadequate and inaccurate.

The language of behaviorist learning theory is, of course, inadequate also. There is no way in that framework to account for the effort of Will by which I control the stimulus class to be admitted, no way to describe the ideas that emerge in the engagement but are not caused by raw stimuli, no way to describe the decision mechanisms through which I select promising hypotheses and heuristics.

We have dwelt on the passive phase at some length because we believe it represents an area of pedagogical neglect and, perhaps, pedagogical helplessness. We see in it something of the unteachable and turn away without considering what we might teach that would enhance it. We quite naturally turn to proof that is complete in itself and away from creating a picture that reveals our seeing; we rely on explanation and shy away from an obligation to induce understanding.

UNDERSTANDING

An intuitive mode that is intellectually oriented is characteristically directed toward understanding or insight. This orientation is contrasted with analytic modes, which are product-goal oriented. The methods we use in an intuitive mode are selected with the hope of reaching a deeper understanding of the situation we are in. Even the algorithms we use are applied heuristically. If this is the right method, we say, then we shall arrive at the right answer. If the result is unsatisfactory, we discard the algorithm as inappropriate. If the result is satisfactory, we still return to the original situation to reflect on the source of this satisfaction. Why did it work? Will it work again? With what limitations? The quest is for meaning, understanding, enlightenment. Success in an analytic mode is realized in an answer: a proof, a numerical result, a sustained hypothesis, a finished poem. Success in an intuitive mode is realized in seeing, creating a picture in our minds, understanding.

The quest for understanding establishes a direction in the intuitive mode, but this direction is at once both sure-and-clear and continually open to change. We know where we are headed but must constantly tack to stay on a course we cannot chart beforehand. Frost's comment about "giants hurling experience ahead of us" seems to describe what we are doing in an intuitive mode: hurling ahead of us the very directional signs that will lead us. Recall Einstein's comment: "there was a feeling of direction, of going straight toward something concrete." This directionality is very like that in motor activity. The psychologist Frederick Bartlett described thinking in such motor terms as "point of no return," "timing," "direction."[16] But, again, the domain of motor activity is not just a metaphorical domain through which to describe this aspect of intuition. When the intuitive quest for understanding is interrupted or the train of thought derailed, real mental trauma occurs. If it happens often enough, the quest for understanding may be abandoned.

It seems obvious that teachers may be involved in either sustaining or destroying directionality, and perhaps this is the proper time to foreshadow some of the problems we shall encounter when we consider intuitive approaches to curriculum and instruction.

Suppose that one of us, as a mathematics teacher, demonstrates the solution to a mathematical word problem for a class of high-school students. I may very well use a set of techniques some of which are labeled "intuitive" in responsible accounts of mathematical pedagogy. I may, for example, attempt to lay out a context for the problem, locating various data at their sources, establishing empirical connections among variables, speculating over an appropriate range of expectation for the eventual answer. An attempt such as this to establish an overview of the "whole picture" is often referred to as an intuitive treatment. What will interest us as we delve more deeply into the topic is the question of just what the intuition is doing as it grapples with such a presentation. Clearly the intuition of the student does not just absorb the holistic structure that I as a teacher present; it must, rather, re-form the objects and network I present into a new internal representation useful to its own cognitive structures and purposes. What kinds of acts does the intuition perform when it is fully engaged in the creation and arrangement of objects? How does it use external objects? What sort of objects are most useful to it?

The mathematics teacher may also draw pictures to accompany the solution. As I talk, I draw; sometimes my drawing is not merely illustrative but constitutes a convincing form of visual proof. Virtually all writers on mathematical pedagogy and on mathematical invention recognize visual displays as part of an intuitive approach. Morris Kline, for example, lists as "intuitive" the following techniques: "pictures, heuristic arguments, induction, reasoning by analogy, and physical arguments are appeals to the intuition."[17] Jacques Hadamard even attempted to differentiate between "logical" and "intuitive" mathematical thinkers on the basis of the number of sketches appearing in their notebooks.[18] But he realized that "visual" cannot be taken as synonymous with "intuitive."

When I produce a drawing or visual proof for my students, I must be aware that they need to encounter what I offer in some meaningful way. My drawing may facilitate their construction of objects and settings or it may represent an additional burden on memory and information processing. What sort of drawing should I produce and how? Are the drawings that I produce piece by piece in front of my class likely to be more helpful than the finished products shown in textbooks?

Besides drawings I may, as part of a conscious attempt to approach the material intuitively, provide concrete objects for my students to manipulate. I may, for example, precede lessons on factoring with certain manipulative exercises on Cuisenaire rods. Now, we have heard Weyl's advice to "think concretely," and we have spoken of intuition as an "object-oriented" faculty. It seems reasonable, therefore, to think of hands-on experience as part of our set of intuitive techniques. But do all hands-on lessons facilitate the work of intuition? This seems highly unlikely, for we have all observed students trying valiantly, and apparently mindlessly, to arrange concrete objects according to instructions given either orally or in writing. Objects, even the delightfully pregnant Cuisenaire rods, may add still another level of bafflement to the struggle for understanding. John

Holt, in *How Children Fail*, observes that the solidly concrete little blocks may, indeed, become "symbols made of colored wood."[19]

It seems clear, then, that while attempts to provide holistic pictures, visual displays, and hands-on experiences are all identified with "intuitive methods," no one of them nor all three together can be assumed as necessarily or universally facilitative for the operation of an intuitive faculty.

It would seem, as we consider each of the intuitive methods offered, that we cannot just look at and listen to a holistic presentation, nor just look at a visual display, nor just handle objects, if our quest is for understanding. Somehow, it seems, we must approach each of these tasks guided by some sense of, or desire for, meaning. Obviously, teachers use these methods in hope of revealing or inducing meaning for their students. But if we look at this situation closely, a problem begins to emerge. If I suggest particular meanings for each facet of the picture I develop for my students, if I give careful step-by-step instructions for each manipulation, I may distract the student's intuitive effort or overburden it so that the student escapes into an input-output, analytic mode. Instead of receiving what-is-there, the student takes input and executes a simple command. After a chain of such executions, he or she may be able to respond correctly to a terminal question. It often happens, however, that the student cannot deliver a response we take to be obvious, given the activity that preceded the question. What seems to have happened in such cases is that what was offered as an intuitive approach was converted into something far less powerful by either our step-wise instruction or the student's choice (perhaps unconscious) of an alternative mode.

Now, interestingly, the problem deepens when we consider why we elaborate our intuitive presentations as we do. At bottom, we want to be sure that our students are not "just" listening and following directions. We want to be sure that they are thinking as well. But this may be exactly the wrong thing to insist upon. It may be that the intuition can pursue its quest for understanding (for objects set in meaningful relationships) only if analytic thinking is suspended or placed in a subservient role. Perhaps the right advice is to "stop thinking" and "just do and feel" or "do and look" with the intention and expectation of understanding. Davis and Hersh, for example, describe the excitement and frustration of acquiring four-dimensional intuition. One of them describes a beautifully executed film designed to reveal aspects of the hypercube, a four-dimensional solid:

When I saw the film presented by Banchoff and Strauss, I was im-
pressed by their achievement, and by the sheer visual pleasure of
watching it. But I felt a bit disappointed; I didn't gain any intuitive
feeling for the hypercube.[20]

Some days later, however, the same author had an opportunity
to manipulate the hypercube at a computer console. He tells us:

I tried turning the hypercube around, moving it away, bringing it
up close, turning it around another way. Suddenly, I could *feel* it!
The hypercube had leaped into palpable reality, as I learned how to
manipulate it, feeling in my fingertips the power to change what I
saw and change it back again.[21]

We do not know, of course, from this account whether the initial
film viewing played an incomplete but crucial role in the eventual
acquisition of four-dimensional intuition. It may have. But we see in
the account of episodic success a concentration on the kinesthetic
and visual coupled with intentionality — that is, with a purposive
quest for meaning and understanding. The author at the console was
not trying to produce the answer to a well-formulated problem; he
was trying to get acquainted with the hypercube. If he had been told
exactly what moves to make step-by-step, would the intuition have
eluded him? If he had been trying to achieve a particular state, defined as the "answer," might he have achieved it without any real
understanding of what he had done to achieve it?

We can begin to identify other problems that we shall encounter.
When we concentrate on an intuitive faculty, we quite naturally use
perceptual language: looking, listening, feeling. But when we move
things about in order to observe them and feel them, what part of our
intellect is operating? Intuition or reason? Deciding this may be very
difficult, and we can see why some investigators just abandon talk of
intuition in face of the problems involved in separating the two
"faculties." But a practical, temporal set of difficulties should not
compel us to abandon a great conceptual convenience. If, in a particular concrete situation, I move the objects of study under guidance
of a conscious hypothesis (if I do X, Y will occur), then clearly analytical activity is involved. Possibly my physical activity is guided by
unconscious operation of analytical schemes, and many writers insist
that this sort of activation is intuition. But under either conscious or
unconscious direction, I may still want to separate the moments of
seeing and feeling; the moments of anticipation, of wanting to see
and feel; the moments of doing; and the moments of deciding what

to do. An interval or episode dominated by "seeing and wanting to see" or "feeling and wanting to feel" may be characterized as intuitive even if it is contaminated inevitably by subintervals of analytic reasoning.

We shall close this section with a consideration of the kinds of tasks intuition undertakes in response to the Will's demand for meaning and understanding.* There seem to be two general situations in which the intuitive faculty can be directly involved in producing intellectual results: In one, we may be confronted with a conceptualization of some sort, say, a verbal description of a phenomenon or a statement of principle and we must, to understand it, find objects that can serve as representatives of the things referred to in the verbalization. In the other, we are presented objects in a hazy context; we "see" the objects, but because we do not understand their possibilities, we can say nothing about them nor predict the result of anything we might do with them.

Let us start with the first problem. I am faced with a statement of principle or conceptual definition; for example, "every group is isomorphic to a permutation group." Presumably this statement is not thrown to me out of the blue by a sadistic teacher. I have some preparation for it; I have some notion, although it may be vague, what is meant by "group," "isomorphic," and "permutation." Faced with this half-meaningful statement, I ask: What shall I do? This is, we think, important. Too often those interested in the relation between intellect and intuition entirely neglect the initial motivational factor. The Gestaltists, for example, leap immediately to the intellectual question—What *is* it?—and fail to see that a reason for their subjects' frequent failure in intellectual tasks might be that they never asked that question. If one's reaction to the initial internal question is memorize! or fake it! or run! one never really confronts the statement in a search for meaning. So first of all, there must be a feeling that it is safe to move on to the intellectual question, and there must be a will to do so. I must not be pressed for time, I must not be made to feel foolish as I begin my exploration. The intuition in its quest for understanding serves under the command of the Will, which seeks personal meaning and enhancement. As teachers, we must not force students to abandon the quest for understanding in order to preserve their self-image.

I say, What does this mean? and receive, perhaps, a storm of silence in reply. Then I return to the active question, What shall I do to

---

*The next few paragraphs appear largely as they do in Nel Noddings, *Caring*, with permission of the University of California Press.

find out what it means? I need objects I can handle. I construct a simple group. I put beside it a permutation group with the same number of elements. I draw up a correspondence matching identities and inverses. It works. I ask, Is there a systematic way in which I can produce a permutation group from any given group? What does the behavior of these objects tell me? What do I see here?

We are describing here what can be called an intuitive mode of working. I am working; there is effort expended. But I am alternately active (I'll try this) and receptive (What is happening here?). The active phase depends upon my store of knowledge and is partly analytic, but the receptive phase provides that which will be acted upon. I must let things come in upon me. I cannot be interrupted. I am watching, being guided, attentive as though listening. The idea "fills the heavens."

In our example, I was trying to bring meaning to the statement "every group is isomorphic to a permutation group." The purpose of my intuitive quest was to understand, to create meaning. I may or may not succeed in constructing an actual proof. The quest for meaning is itself a creative endeavor and, thus, I must go through much the same process in trying to understand an existing proof as I would in producing my own.

The second kind of problem is one in which perception starts with given objects and intuition must appropriate these in a form useful for cognition. We encounter, now, a quest for background, for contextual structure. But it is important to realize that, again, there is a motivational context that sets the stage for what is to follow. The question "What shall I do?" arises again and must be resolved in favor of an intellectual orientation before meaningful exploration can begin. I must be free to explore and to choose, and I must make a commitment.

Consider what children may struggle with when they encounter a problem such as $\frac{2}{3} + \frac{5}{6} =$ _____ . Their only experience with signs of the form p/q may have been as labels for "parts of things." If so, they may begin immediately to draw pies and color in parts of them. This is usually unproductive unless they hit upon the idea of dividing up the thirds into sixths, and most children do not. A teacher who realizes that students must find a familiar context for new conceptual objects may introduce youngsters to counting by $\frac{1}{2}$'s, $\frac{1}{3}$'s, $\frac{1}{4}$'s. Then they may play with their new objects in a familiar setting, the number line, scaled in both old and new ways. Consider the value of matching objects along the number scales in figure 4.1.

We deprive the intuition of an opportunity to see when we fail to

Figure 4.1

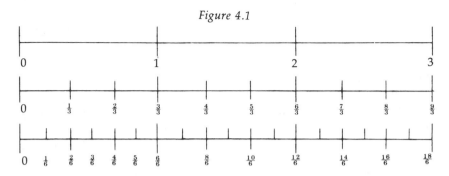

encourage the invention and manipulation of objects in familiar settings. When we have before us—either perceptually or imaginatively —objects whose behavior we can manipulate and observe, we experience the feeling that something is present, something is happening. We want to say, "Hold on. Wait, I am getting it!" Long before the result is ready for public demonstration, there is inner assurance that things are coming right.

SUBJECTIVE CERTAINTY AND OBJECTIVE UNCERTAINTY

A successful receptive phase ends in a decision to act that is accompanied by a feeling of certainty and a question about the form of public demonstration by which that inner certainty can be communicated. Together, subjective certainty and objective uncertainty maintain direction and effort. The intuition presents true data to both Will and cognition, for its representations are the "givens" with which intellectual and interpersonal life must begin. The intuitions initially given are, of course, taken tentatively (they may be wrong or inappropriate) but they are given with the power of certainty. We often find ourselves saying, when an intuition has proved faulty, "but I was so *sure* . . . ." Thus, while the Will rejoices in what is given and the joy of "knowing" (better, of "seeing"), the intellect must remain properly skeptical. This is the state of mind with which the intuitive phase proper begins. If the intuitive mode ends successfully, skepticism with respect to the result or incipient product vanishes and only questions concerning execution remain. Answering these questions may, of course, trigger new phases of intuitive activity.

The intuitive phase proper to which we have just referred begins and ends in an intuition. It is sustained by the dynamic force of its

motivational aspect; the intuitive representation given to the Will
suggests that its quest for meaning, for personal enlightenment, will
be satisfied. But there is a stage that may precede the first clear
intuition. During this stage the intuition is *looking*, but as though in
a darkened room or at a great distance. The feeling that accompanies
this stage is discomfort. We are impatient, uncertain that anything
will be accomplished, afraid that interruptions will occur, edgy,
doubting our own capacities. We may find all sorts of reasons to
break off work: There is a droopy plant that must be watered; the dog
wants out; the mail is due; student papers should come first on the
work list; what about dinner, recreation, the state of one's soul? We
would like to avoid this looking that may or may not result in seeing.
As we discuss ways in which to enhance intuitive modes, we must
give considerable attention to this first stage, this stage of mental
torture, in which no subjective certainty sustains us.

It may be that what we label "genius" is an easy ability to enter
the intuitive phase proper, that is, to secure an initial intuition. Some
creative artists, Mozart for example, seem to have obtained their
intuitions so freely that they have been led to disavow their own
roles in producing them. Others, as we shall see, suffer the pains of
that first stage, and they often formulate patterns to aid them in
establishing intuitive modes. Still others seem to proceed in a relaxed
fashion, "letting stick to them what may," in the comforting belief
that something in all that now is merely enjoyed will eventually flash
upon the mind as bright vision. These are the happy artists, neither
consumed by vision after vision demanding immediate execution
nor haunted by the fear that the Muse will desert.

We can see in this account that there are three crisis or danger
points in the course of intuitive activity. The first, obviously, comes
and remains throughout the initial stage of establishing the intuitive
mode. The second arises with the first clear intuition. This initial
intuition may be faulty; what stands out *as given* may be wrong.
Trained scholars and artists know that they are just entering a period
of feverish activity, and they cultivate the intellectual uncertainty
needed to sustain effort. But young students may simply accept the
initial intuition and rejoice in the satisfaction it brings to them.
Teachers, then, quite naturally fear that their intuitively bright students will become lazy or intellectually sloppy. Indeed, this may
often be the case. Such students wonder why they should bother to
prove or to investigate what they already *know*. Enormous teacher
sensitivity is required in guiding students through their analytic

"mopping up." Students must be provided with the necessary skills so that this process is not inordinately burdensome. They must not be pushed to boredom by having to repeat the process for innumerable results all of a kind. They must be encouraged to see the possibilities for elegance and simplicity in their finished products, and they must understand that power resides in their ability to communicate their knowledge effectively.

The third danger lies partly in intuitive activity itself and partly in how its results are received by others. A perfectly sound insight may not be shared because the work is perceived as unfinished. Gauss's notebooks, for example, were filled with beautiful and accurate intuitive results that were never published. Gauss published only those results for which he had rigorous proofs. Had he shared his intuitions, others might have devised proofs and forged ahead in mathematics. For students, the danger is that their intuitive results may be disparaged by the teacher. If such disparagement is frequent or caustic enough, students may come to devalue their own insights and to avoid the grueling labor involved in attaining them. They may, instead, resort to weird strategies by which they can legalistically (or even illicitly) produce answers to satisfy the teacher and abandon their own quest for understanding.

We see, then, that there is an effort required to enter the intuitive mode, that the subjective certainty accompanying an initial intuition must be counterbalanced with a skeptical, objective uncertainty, and that the entire activity must be handled with pedagogical sensitivity and respect.

SUMMARY

In this chapter we have laid out a characterization of intuitive modes. Such modes are characterized by involvement of external and internal senses, by a relaxation of subjectness into receptivity, by a quest for understanding or insight, and by a continuing tension between subjective certainty and objective uncertainty. Building on the conceptual framework established in chapter 2, we have tried to show how the senses are concentrated on an inward form of looking and listening, how the Will must direct intuition in order that receptivity may occur, how the Will and reason strain against each other in the productive tension between subjective certainty and objective uncertainty. We have discussed, also, how instrumental goals are set aside in favor of understanding, enjoying, embracing. Finally, we have re-emphasized our decision to confine our conception of intuition to perceptual and cognitive domains.

We want to consider next how such modes can be maintained and enhanced.

Chapter 5

ENHANCING INTUITIVE MODES

> The healthy understanding, we should say, is not the logical,
> argumentative, but the intuitive; for the end of understanding
> is not to prove and find reasons, but to know and believe.
>
> Thomas Carlyle, "Characteristics"

IN THIS CHAPTER we shall consider ways in which we can
enhance intuitive modes. We are interested in how we can enhance
our own intuitive modes and, as teachers, in how we can help others
to enhance theirs. We shall not, at this time, discuss specific arrangements of subject matter or modes of presentation that might be
labeled "intuitive," but those matters will occupy us fully in the next
chapter.

ACKNOWLEDGING INTUITION AND INTUITIVE MODES

The first and most obvious thing we can do to encourage intuitive activity is to acknowledge intuitive capacity and the reality of
intuitive modes. As teachers we can share with our students information about intuitive activity, our own intuitive experiences, and
biographical accounts of intuitive thinking that has produced admir-
able results. This sort of discussion should become part of the psychology of learning and teaching. It is odd that we so seldom engage
our students in dialogue about learning, thinking, and understanding, when we profess to be deeply concerned about these matters.
We urge people to study, to listen, to apply themselves, but we fail to
acknowledge impediments to full engagement and, indeed, we often
consider discussion of how we learn or why we hate certain subjects
to be "off the track."

Accounts such as those we have already mentioned—of Gauss, Mozart, Miró, Frost, Einstein — are fascinating in themselves and may induce students to explore their own receptive capacities. Under what conditions do they accomplish their best work: morning or evening? well-fed or hungry? with or without music? before or after physical exercise? It may be helpful, also, for students to know that all sorts of odd "enhancers" have been tried by creative thinkers and that no guarantees for the general population are associated with any of them. Commenting on Hadamard's investigation into the psychology of mathematical invention, James R. Newman notes:

> Hadamard . . . considers whether scientific invention may perhaps be improved by standing or sitting or by taking two baths in a row. Helmholtz and Poincaré worked sitting at a table; Hadamard's practice is to pace the room ("Legs are the wheels of thought," said Emile Angier); the chemist J. Teeple was the two-bath man. Alas, the habits of famous men are rarely profitable to their disciples. The young philosopher will derive little benefit from being punctual like Kant, the biologist from cultivating Darwin's dyspepsia, the playwright from eating Shaw's vegetables.[1]

But the student may, out of such discussion and ensuing experimentation, find his own means of enhancing intuitive modes. At least he will become aware of the common search for aids to creativity, productivity, and serenity. If we establish such discussion early, if we consider the serious and the humorous, the spiritual and the intellectual, we can help to prepare our students for intelligent encounters with the esoteric psychologies and exotic religions which abound in our culture. The idea is to acknowledge the legitimacy and universality of the quest for meaning and to induce reflection on ways of pursuing it.

We should also discuss with our students the possibility that intuitive modes may be enhanced by mind altering substances. Engaging in such conversation honestly and as opportunities present themselves paves the way for eventual open discussion of those "aids" we may fear and distrust. If we defer the discussion until something, say, marijuana use, arouses our concern, we have no frame of reference—no previously established questions nor acceptable pattern of investigation — in which to conduct a rational dialogue. Instead, we moralize. But human beings have always sought methods by which to induce certain valued states of consciousness. Old Testament prophets fasted. Members of some religious orders deliberately suffered self-humiliation and self-flagellation; some it should be noted, still engage in such practices. Some meditate to increase awareness; others meditate to escape certain forms of awareness; and still others meditate to concentrate awareness. People have for centuries sought increased health, vigor, and serenity of mind through the magical powers of herbs and various diets. It seems odd that we spend so much time in schools on such matters as simplifying radicals, learning about the War of 1812, and identifying the parts of speech and so little on the personal quest for meaning.

In an earlier chapter, we mentioned the phenomena of preparation, incubation, and illumination. It might be helpful for students to know that their struggles with subject matter may yield a delayed profit—that what is so difficult and elusive today may be crystal clear tomorrow. Here, too, we often work against ourselves by maintaining modes of evaluation that emphasize mastery on schedule and a continuous forward motion in conceptual development. Rarely do we encourage circling back, looking at old material with fresh vision, trying anew problems or questions that stumped us in the past. When students hear the story of Poincaré and his marvelous moment of enlightenment on the streetcar,[2] they often realize that they, too, have had such experiences—not with Fuchsian functions, to be sure —but real, vivid, memorable experiences all the same. Acknowledgment of such phenomena prepares the way to consider changes in assignment, evaluation, modes of instruction, and ways in which we try to facilitate understanding. In particular, we might explicitly advise students to work hard on a particular problem, to try all sorts of potentially useful techniques on it, to reflect on their lack of effectiveness in the event of failure, and then to leave the problem for a while: Run around the block, have a snack, listen to some music, read the comics. Then come back to the problem or let it run through your head as you fall asleep. Keep paper and pencil by the bed in case illumination comes.

The well-documented phenomena of preparation, incubation, and illumination can be contrasted with far more doubtful techniques that are periodically touted: learning in one's sleep through recorded lessons or learning unconsciously through subliminal messages or making great discoveries in dreams. Reading about such methods (used both in actuality and in fiction, e.g., Aldous Huxley's *Brave New World*), discussing their validity, experimenting where it is responsible to do so all add to both self-understanding and cultural sophistication. How better to increase motivation than to engage students in reflective examination of their own learning process?

GETTING STARTED: THE PREINTUITIVE MODE

The preintuitive mode is often characterized by an agony of
indecision and avoidance. It is not just school boys and girls who
consider their lessons with a mixture of fleeting interest and dread,
but most of us who engage in creative activity. How many reasons
might I find for not writing today? for putting it off for an hour or
even for ten minutes? From one perspective the dread is entirely
understandable. As I descend into the utter absorption of the intuitive mode, I lose myself as subject; I submit control to the inanimate
other, the ideas that will soon appear to me, entice me, move me
about in their special world. Entirely engaged, I am lost to the world
—unhearing, unseeing, unfeeling. Indeed, I may emerge hours later
numb with cold I had been unaware of and remarkably surprised by
information that had earlier been conveyed to me but not noted.

When one is seized involuntarily, the intuitive mode simply
happens. It occurs without prior agony. But it seems to be a fallacy
that creation occurs often in this painless fashion. Many, many creative thinkers have to cultivate the Muse, force themselves through
the pain of that preliminary descent. Here we shall consider three
ways of getting started: deliberate warming-up exercises, the judicious use of routines, and a head-on plunge into doing and looking.

Deliberate involvement in warming-up exercises takes a variety
of forms. Church-goers are familiar with the effects of religious
music, special costumes and ritual articles, communal silence, and
shared recitations. All of these exercises tend to ready participants
for religious intuitive modes—the experience of coming into contact
with religious ideas or entities. Zen masters introduce their students
to the koan as a special warming-up exercise. D. I. Suzuki says:

> In modern days the *koan* is used as a starter; it gives an initial
> movement to the racing for Zen experience. More or less mechanical
> in the beginning, the movement acquires the tone needed for the
> maturing of Zen consciousness.[3]

Similarly, physical exercises may be employed to reduce the strain
and stress of the instrumental world and make it more likely that the
world of relation will open up.

Clearly, schools, with their emphasis on classes and group activities, provide a poor environment for engagement in intuitive
modes. Intrusive stimuli must be suppressed if one is to enter the
almost trance-like state characteristic of a deeply intuitive mode. One
must be able to give attention to the object of knowledge without

interruption. While schools cannot provide supportive environments for deeply intuitive modes, they can provide instruction and discussion on intuition, on the working styles of artists, mathematicians, and others, and on the sort of experimentation that might help students find their own methods of enhancing intuitive modes. And, as we shall see later, teachers can help students in getting intuition started; they can take account of the intuitive faculty in planning lessons and in giving instruction.

Setting can be vital to an intuitive mode. We saw that the mathematician Gauss could be gripped by mathematics even during conversation with friends. But most people must entertain the Muses in order to retain their company. Aloneness is necessary. (Gauss, we might point out, was alone even in a group.) Silence, or sound which enhances communion with the self, is necessary. Once the mode is established, it can be impervious to potentially intrusive stimuli, but it must be established. We need to talk with our students about the vagaries and idiosyncrasies that characterize this initial period and, also, about the reality of the established mode. Students have so little experience with the intuitive mode that many doubt its existence and some laugh uncomfortably when they first hear accounts of intuitive concentration. But they *should* hear, as we have noted, the story of Whitehead in his garden, so deeply in contact with his mathematics that he failed to see or hear visitors passing through.

One must find a place to work, and the place must be congenial. Pearl Buck needed fresh flowers on her desk and a view of peaceful countryside. Frost prospered in the hills of Vermont and New Hampshire, while a poet later occupying his old New Hampshire house got no feeling of support from that environment and did her best writing in New York City. Similarly, Sartre preferred manmade surroundings and clearly got no inspiration from"nature." Some are wholly irrepressible. Alexander Borodin could, apparently, engage either his music or chemistry in near-chaotic conditions. Even when his apartment was filled with visitors and his wife used his newly written music to wrap fish, he could separate fish and visitors from music and concentrate on the music.

The story is told that Descartes did much of his best thinking lying abed late in the morning. Did he use a form of mental exercise to get started? Some people do: a few stretches, a cup of coffee, a deliberate slowing down of time, letting thoughts run idly through the mind—all may help establish a mood. It is reported that Pablo Casals started every day by playing several Bach fugues on the piano. Others walk on the beach, or run in the hills, or stroll about the garden, or read psalms. What is done must reduce noise and disorder, set the mind at peace, and induce the feeling that time is irrelevant—relative and controllable.

Is all this too exotic and luxurious for modern living, something to be indulged in only by an elite actually free of instrumental demands? It hardly seems so; on the contrary, deep and universal longing seems evident in the contemporary revival of ritual procedures, secret societies, and cult memberships. Sensuous delight, which might properly be encouraged in education, is so little acknowledged that it must be sought in illicit settings and often becomes a pursuit of the merely sensual. Yet sensuous delight is often the prelude to deep and productive thought.

Can schools provide warming-up exercises to set a tone of intellectual and social communion? "Morning exercises" — a ritual of Bible reading, prayer, and flag salute—once served such a function. We do not recommend their resumption because they clearly violate principles of religious freedom, and we do not suggest that substitute exercises be instituted. But alternatives might be considered. The consideration of alternatives might in itself help individuals invent and practice warm-up exercises of their own and induce teachers to explore ways of setting tone and getting things started.

So far we have suggested that intuition and intuitive modes should be topics of rational discussion in classrooms, that teachers and students be encouraged to share information and experiences concerning intellectual intuitive activity, that biographical materials be used frequently, and that the historically documented quest for enhanced meaning be openly discussed. All this seems reasonable and unworrisome. But our last question, the one concerning ritual warming-up exercises in schools, raises a warning flag. Although we have suggested neither that teachers and students should exchange deeply personal or emotional experiences nor that teachers should engage in forms of emotional therapy, there is clearly affective involvement in any form of intuitive activity. According to our definition, affect is at the very heart of the intuitive. It is likely, therefore, that in a free and rational interchange of information and speculation, beliefs will come under scrutiny and feeling will be aroused. This, it seems to us, is entirely desirable. Such discussion, conducted in the safety and freedom of the classroom, would be a mark of vital engagement with those matters that concern human beings deeply and universally. Classroom talk would cease to be a charade playing around the edges of intellectual and spiritual questions and become more nearly a fully human dialogue.

But there are clear dangers. A strong bond of community trust must exist between teachers and parents if teachers are to be free in conducting dialogue on controversial matters. Teachers must be able to protect the privacy of students, to encourage an appropriate level of discussion and critique, to promote an affectionate respect for those sharing the dialogue. We have placed great emphasis on discussion—on talking *about*—in the classroom setting. Each individual is then set free to explore his or her own mental and spiritual nature. If warming-up exercises are tried, they should be undertaken voluntarily and *as techniques,* not as signs that participants are part of some group that requires commitment to beliefs underlying the rituals.

The use and examination of rituals as techniques leaves many people uncomfortable. Is there nothing, they may ask, to which we are committed? There was a day when many communities felt that their members had a universal committment to God; that day is past. At the same time, most communities expressed a commitment to nation; even that commitment is in some doubt today. Many who have no subversive leanings at all have come to question the wisdom of having established and of maintaining nation-states. They see the need for a commitment to all human life, and this commitment is clearly in potential conflict with the traditional demands of the nation-state. The lack of nearly universal public commitment to clearly stated beliefs and goals is surely one of the root causes of decay in public education. With the rise and recognition of many competing publics, what we present in schools has become increasingly wishy-washy, bland, and often peculiarly beside the point, meticulously avoiding questions of great human importance. Many people see the only solution to this pervasive malaise in the promotion of private schools, schools that can be frankly and fully open in their commitment to stated values.

Is there a way to revitalize public schooling, to revive both intellect and spirit in a public domain that includes very different public subdomains? One possibility is to state and promote a commitment to free, rational, and responsible dialogue and to institute a firm commitment to each individual and the confirmation of his or her growth as a thinking, feeling human being. Do we not already have such commitments? It is clear that we do *not.* In everything from the structure of schools, to the subjects we teach, to the questions we discuss, to the ways in which we evaluate students, it is vividly clear that we do not. We shall discuss these matters more fully in appropriate and specific contexts. Our main purpose in this section is to acknowledge and make readers aware that any program of suggestions aimed at "awakening the inner eye" must tackle difficult and controversial questions if it is to avoid triviality. Otherwise the predictable result, optimistically anticipating *some* result, will surely be a page here and there in mathematics texts devoted to some "great intuitive thinker" and perhaps a unit in one of the social sciences on "intuitive thinking." This is not what we have in mind. The awakened inner eye roves over everything of interest: over thorny conceptual problems, over promising methods and techniques, over domains and objects of sensuous delight, over love and faith, over delight, horror, pain, and pleasure. Once awakened it will not willingly return to slumber.

We began this section with a discussion of ways in which to get intuitive modes started. Following the logic of our program, we were led into an investigation of the problems faced by any educators who recommend changes in schooling that involve affect. Intuition necessarily involves affect, and we are thus committed to thoroughly open investigation of affective questions.

Now it is time to talk about routines. Routines are different from warming-up exercises and rituals. What we are concerned with here is the way in which structure and routinization may contribute to creative freedom. Students often perceive creative thinkers as free-wheeling people who live wildly interesting and unstructured lives. This seems to be untrue. On the contrary, a careful structuring of the routines of life seems to contribute to the ability to find and direct energy toward the objects of knowledge. The poet Heinrich Heine wrote of Immanuel Kant:

> He lived a mechanically ordered and abstract old bachelor life . . . .
> Rising, coffee drinking, writing, reading college lectures, eating,
> walking, all had their fixed time, and neighbors knew that it was
> exactly half past three when Immanuel Kant in his grey coat, with
> his bamboo cane in his hand, left his house door and went to Lime
> Tree Avenue.[4]

Gauss left Gottingen only once in the last twenty-seven years of his life and kept his surroundings and appointments there simple.[5] Bach led a spartan existence and summed up his own life by saying, "I worked hard."[6] The notion that intuition and creativity go hand-in-hand with lack of organization and structure seems, then, to be a half-truth: The freedom of intuitive thinking may be supported and enhanced by structure and organization in the ordinary routines of life.

It seems sensible, then, to recommend an examination of daily activity in classrooms. A comfortable, steady structuring of the routines of school life might well be an enhancing factor in school performance not only in algorithmic work, which is itself a form of routine, but in the complementary mode, which seems to require enormous energy and capacity to live with novelty, change, and ambiguity. The idea is simple: Reduce change, opportunity for choice, and unpredictability in routine, nonintellectual matters and save stimulus-control energy for intuitive encounters. Now this recommendation does not mean that some subjects, e.g., mathematics, should satisfy the need for structure and routine and that others, e.g., art, should be used to open up the world of choice and creativity. Nor does it mean that the day should be separated into a routine half (the morning) and a creative half (afternoon). It means, rather, that careful attention should be given to the smooth operation of procedural matters and that meticulous attention should be given to the features of *all* subject matter that might best be handled by means that lead quickly and surely to routinization.

It seems entirely reasonable to reinstate rote learning as respectable and efficient for some purposes. A good test for its appropriateness might be this: Any skill or set of information that is certain to be used again and again in either school learning or life at large will automatically be "reinforced" repeatedly; it, therefore, makes sense to routinize such material. It will not be forgotten, since it will be in continuous use. But should we not prefer that children "understand" multiplication rather than memorize something called "times tables"? The two options are not mutually exclusive and, indeed, it is likely that children who know their multiplication facts will be more interested in the underlying structure supporting multiplication algorithms than those who do not know these facts. We have in many cases put the cart before the horse, thus making it improbable that some youngsters will ever move along to facility and at least functional understanding.

We should recall, also, the significant correlation of familiarity and intuitive activity. Intuition is by its nature a highly focused and intense function. Even when it is broadly receptive, say to natural sights and sounds on a field hike, it is still intense and suffers dramatically from interruption. Picture yourself collecting images in a lovely meadow suddenly invaded by roaring bulldozers. Clearly, distraction spells doom for intuitive activity. But the distraction need not be as overtly noisy as bulldozers. It can arise entirely on the internal scene. How can one concentrate on the solution of, say, a mathematical word problem, if one must constantly give focal attention to subproblems such as the answer to 7×8, the formula for time, rate, and distance, how to convert miles to feet or centimeters to inches?

We are not suggesting that the subject matter to be routinized should become an end in itself nor that demands be made for exactly one way of doing things. We are not suggesting that youngsters be taught to add horizontally and that they be marked wrong for adding vertically. Sometimes teachers do behave this way, in order, they say, to teach children "to follow directions." Nothing could be further from the spirit of our recommendations. The idea is to free students for productive engagement with subject matter. We are not suggesting that penalties be assigned for names written on the wrong side of a paper (or left off entirely), for missing dates, for an odd arrangement of headings. Routinization should serve thinking, not become its end. Obviously, the same principle should guide the routinization of procedures in the classroom. No penalty needs to be assigned for, say, lateness. It is simply and properly an *expectation* that people will usually be on time because things run ever so much more smoothly when they *are* on time.

Teachers should be entirely open and honest with their students in matters of routinization. Prior to a significant theorem in geometry, for example, a teacher might inform her class that certain skills will prove useful in working with the theorem. Before tackling the Pythagorean Theorem, a teacher might provide practice in simplifying radicals, in memorizing the squares of numbers from one to twenty-five, in extracting square roots. Incentives may be provided for learning these subskills, but the greatest incentive remains the freedom and competence with which students can approach the theorem itself.

The last topic that we shall consider in this section is "doing and looking." A distinguishing characteristic of the intuitive mode is continual direct contact with the object of knowledge. This direct contact is exactly what is missing in the approach many students take to learning and problem solving. Further, our highly analytic curricula and systems of instruction contribute to even greater gaps between student and object of knowledge. The student is taught, perhaps only implicitly, to respond with an *answer*, a definite algorithm, a learned approach. A math student is likely to be affronted by the occurrence of a problem which does not "belong" in a given problem set. "What is *that* doing here?" he will ask. He has been taught to approach mathematical problems through chains of well-defined concepts and so dreads facing a conceptually naked problem.

> Sartre has said that every student must fight against being absorbed
> into the gluey, the sticky, the hazy . . . . His very learning involves
> a struggle against inertia, resistance to the blank contemplation of
> brute fact.[7]

The teacher can help by encouraging or even gently forcing intuitive contact. Consider the following illustration. Ms. Adams, a math teacher, is moving about her new classroom giving help to individual students who are all working at their own rates. When she responds to a call for help, she is told the difficulty: "I can't do these word problems," says the student. "Oh, that's too bad," says Ms. Adams sympathetically. She starts to move away. "Hey, wait!" exclaims the boy, "I need help." "Well, you haven't asked me a question," Ms. Adams explains. "You must ask me a specific question about a particular problem. Then I can really help you." The boy considers, "I can't just ask, 'How do you do these problems?' can I?" Ms. Adams smiles. "No, the question must be directed at a specific point in a specific problem." The student grumbles about the uselessness of teachers as Ms. Adams moves away. Toward the end of the class period, the teacher returns. "Well, Carl, how are you doing?" she asks the student. "Oh, those dumb problems? I finished them. They weren't so bad after all."

The fact that the illustration is a true story adds nothing to its logic but, perhaps, adds something to its potential impact. The boy, Carl, was very bright; he simply did not want to make direct initial contact with the given problems. He wanted to be told what to do and in what order. Ms. Adams wisely forced the necessary contact. It is important to realize that the teacher, in another situation, might have had to answer actual questions or to exercise more leadership in forcing initial contact. There is no script for conducting this sort of teaching, and we are hesitant for that reason even to report such events.

Ms. Adams worked with another youngster who requested help with this problem: $2x - x^2 = 8$.

Ms. Adams:	What's the trouble?
Nancy:	I can't do it.
Ms. Adams:	Well, *look* at it.
Nancy:	How will that help? I can't do it.
Ms. Adams:	Surely, you can say *something* about it.
Nancy:	(Grumbling) . . . Well, it's an equation.
Ms. Adams:	Good. That's a start. Have you ever seen one like it?

Nancy:	I've seen some little 2s like this one. What do you call them, coefficients or exponents?
Ms. Adams:	Exponents. Right. How is this one different from other equations you've seen—ones with x-squares in them?
Nancy:	Oh, I don't know. Wait a minute. Oh, am I dumb! Never mind. I see . . .
Ms. Adams:	Want more help?
Nancy:	No, I'm embarrassed. It's so simple. It's ridiculous!

In our illustrations, both Carl and Nancy were pulled out of Sartre's "gluey haze" by a teacher who invited them *to see*.

The sort of dialogue we have been describing differs from, say, inquiry training in both its pattern and purpose.[8] We are not trying to sharpen students' question-asking skills when we insist that they ask specific questions. We are trying to force them into making conscious contact with the objects themselves. Further, our responses to their comments and questions are not programmed. Once a train of thought is started in the student, we are quite willing to answer any specific question with a specifically helpful response. Neither are we aiming for *discovery* in the usually accepted pedagogical sense; that is, we are not aiming to have the student discover a generalization.[9] We are helping students to look at their own conscious states and put themselves into the presence of the object. We say such things as the following: Look at it. How is it like other things you've seen? How is it different? What are you thinking? Let me hear you think. What could you do to it to make it look more familiar? Listen to it. Touch it. Do you believe this? Describe your believing. Are there soft spots in your believing? Do you need information?

We invite students to examine, alternatively, the object and their own conscious states and cognitive equipment. When they profess a cognitive lack—for example, "I need that formula . . . what is it?"—we supply the necessary information—simply and completely. The idea is for the teacher to complement the student's thinking by maintaining its direction: supplying information, making minor algorithmic corrections, turning the quest inward when things are at a standstill. The teacher does not establish the direction of thinking, does not direct thought at or through concepts, does not wrench thought away from a faulty approach. He or she supports students in their quest for understanding. We are not looking for the discovery of a generalization, nor a particular pattern of investigation, nor the mechanical application of a procedure, nor any glib response. We are aiming at a "Eureka!" response: I see! So that's it! Now I know!

In an earlier chapter, we described a mathematician's experience in acquiring four-dimensional intuition through manipulation of the hypercube. We recognize that intuitive capacities grow; this is not at all to deny that a fundamental intuitive capacity precedes experience and makes it possible. But experience that involves "doing and looking" exercises the intuition and extends the domain of objects over which it ranges with insight. An important form of doing and looking is found in model building. Describing the function of model building in decision analysis, David Kreps first lists the steps in construction:

> The first thing to do when you have a decision to make is to try to get a picture of what strategic options you have, and what are each of their possible consequences. Often the act of simply enumerating your options will allow you to discover very attractive options that you hadn't originally thought of.
>
> The next step is to look at the sources of uncertainty, the things you don't know about, and to quantify how likely the various eventualities are. There is a lot of technique involved in trying to get probabilistic, quantitative statements about respective likelihoods.
>
> The third step is to try to get some feel for how you view the various consequences. It is not enough to judge them separately— you should rate them roughly in the relative ways you feel about each consequence and its relation to the others. In other words "A would be preferable to B because. . . ." This step includes the quantification of how you feel about the risks involved.
>
> The fourth step is a mechanical procedure—take the judgments you made in the first three steps and put them together to get the "answer." And then comes the fifth and hardest step—reexamine all the judgments that you made, to see why you got the "answer" that you did. Ask yourself what important factors you have omitted or glossed over. In other words, try to reconcile what you have put down on paper with reality.

He then notes:

> The models we are capable of building for decision-making never do justice to reality, which is always much more complex, involving so many factors it had not been possible to build into the model.
>
> Therefore, although there are certain types of mistakes that tend to be made, the main function of a model is to try to engage your intuition, so that you can make better intuitive judgments.[10]

What Kreps describes is a method of using analytic work heuristically as a prelude to seeing reality more clearly through the strengths and weaknesses of the model generated. We shall discuss other techniques a bit later. At this point it is important to emphasize again that the techniques suggested in this section for getting started, for engaging the intuition, are not ends in themselves but means to the significant end of enhancing intuitive activity.

ENCOURAGING RECEPTIVITY

When we go to a play or the movies, when we settle down with Hercule Poirot or Miss Marple to enjoy vicarious murder, even when we switch on the evening TV news, we are not usually conscious of exactly what we wish to learn. Certainly we are not preparing ourselves for some performance that will be demanded of us when the story is finished. Indeed, learning does not seem to be the point of such encounters, and yet we do learn from them. Often we find ourselves completely engaged, caught up, in whatever is being presented. We are, clearly, receptive in such intervals, but our receptivity is not necessarily passive or mindless. While we accuse ordinary television watchers of being "passive spectators" and even "mindless boob-tube watchers," we rarely apply such epithets to one watching *Hamlet* or listening to a Mahler symphony. The point here is that we should not confuse a state of active receptivity with mindless passivity.

In one respect, however, a deeply receptive mode *is* passive. There is a relaxation or giving up of subjectness. But this passivity, the giving way to the other as subject, is willed or acceded to by the receptive agent. The mind remains, or may remain, remarkably active, but instrumental striving is suspended. In such modes, we do not try to impose order on the situation but, rather, we let order-that-is-there present itself to us. This is not to say, certainly, that purposes and goals play no role in our submitting ourselves to a receptive state. Clearly they do. We may sit down with our mathematics or literature because we want to achieve something—a grade, a degree, a job—but if we are fortunate and willing, the goal drops away, and we are captured by the object itself. Even if we attack our task initially with some reluctance, we may look back on the session and find to our surprise that it was characterized by a positive affect. The philosopher Husserl commented that, when he looked back over years of work on his phenomenology, he could see that the affect which accompanied his work was joy.[11]

While it is clear that receptive engagement plays an important role in learning and, especially, in coming to understand, it is not clear what role the external world plays in securing our engagement. If we were to equate receptivity with passivity, there would be no problem. We would merely assume that the world imprints itself on us. But we do not accept that view and, therefore, we need to ask what role is played by the world (objects, teachers, peers) and what role is played by the agent. The agent, we have said, embarks on a quest for meaning. The object attended to enters the phenomenon as a manifestation of its nature, of its possibilities. The agent does not create the phenomenal object but transforms it through his or her purposes and knowledge. Michael Bennett writes:

> Given that each "thing" has its nature, and that there are natural laws governing its relationships with other things; it is obvious that "transformation" can only take place if the agent has some understanding of the properties of the things involved.[12]

We prefer, in keeping with our description of intuition, to interpret "understanding" in the Bennett paragraph as tentative, as a set of beliefs, aspirations, impressions. While some "understanding" is required in order even to attend to the object, understanding is more properly regarded as the product of intuitive encounter, not its precursor. Sufficient understanding, or better knowledge, is needed to promote engagement, but this initial knowledge may be useful even if it proves in the final analysis to be faulty. Because accurate information is useful, however, and is likely to facilitate the quest for understanding, we have recommended the routinization of frequently used skills and responses.

The need for engagement with the objects of study has long been recognized by educators. Alfred North Whitehead, for example, feared that students suffer the acquisition of "inert knowledge" when they are not truly engaged with their studies.[13] He identified three stages in the genuine learning process, which he labeled "romance," "precision," and "generalization." The stage of romance is one in which the learner is intrigued by the material, caught up in it but in a nonspecific and perhaps goal-free fashion. Educators associated with the "Open Education" movement are among those who show their implicit belief in such a stage when they allow students a period of free encounter or "messing about" with the materials they will eventually study more narrowly. Whitehead's three stages reveal something important about the progression of goals and purposes in a learning sequence, but labeling a stage "romance" does not tell us how the state is induced, nor does it warn us to take into account that romance may follow reluctance, a sense of duty, or even active dislike. We found it necessary, therefore, to discuss a variety of ways by which human beings can enter this stage of romance. Some of them, especially the "doing and feeling" techniques, overlap the stage of romance itself; and, of course, we acknowledge that there is no sharp line of demarcation between the preintuitive mode and the stage of romantic engagement.

So far we have considered the fruitfulness of receptivity, the role of subject and object in receptive encounters, and the motivational energy required of the subject. We have suggested, with Whitehead, that a period of romantic messing about with the objects of knowledge is a necessary stage in the construction of understanding. But we have also suggested that a period of ordinary labor, of skill honing, may profitably precede the stage of romance.

Now we want to consider another way in which to encourage receptivity. We have already talked about the consummatory flavor of many intuitive modes, and, in so doing, we have established a justification for including consummatory offerings in our instructional procedures. An experience we construct is consummatory if participation in it is sufficient in itself; it is undertaken not instrumentally, with a specific goal in view, but as something to be enjoyed. Now we want to consider what these offerings might look like in the school setting and what rules, if any, should govern their presentation.

Suppose I decide to read Frost's "The Witch of Coös" to a high-school English class. I may have a variety of reasons for doing this as a consummatory offering: Perhaps I like reading aloud some of the eerie passages, perhaps I enjoy especially the son's description of the skeleton that "carried itself like a pile of dishes up one flight from the cellar to the kitchen,"[14] perhaps we have been reading about witchcraft and this poem popped into mind. Whatever particular reasons I may have, I have a general one: I hope my students will *enjoy* the poem and thirst for more. But, although I am serious in this aim, I am not insistent on it, and I dare not undertake formal evaluation of the effort—for to do so would destroy something vital in it. In particular, quite obviously, such an evaluation would destroy the avowed consummatory nature of the experience. It would say, in effect, "I want you to enjoy this, but I shall test your memory and understanding."

Any recommendation against formal evaluation runs counter to present measure-mad educational practices, but we believe the recommendation is defensible. An intuitive mode that is dominantly or totally consummatory is still an intuitive mode, and we do not want to distract the student from the poem, music, work of art, or performance by promising or threatening some form of evaluation at the close of the experience. When we prod the student to interpret, to define, to analyze, we inevitably destroy the consummatory flavor. We are not saying that every poem, painting, or concerto should be presented as a consummatory experience. We are saying that *some* should be and, similarly, some such experiences should be offered in every subject field, and they should be offered without any follow-up in the form of formal evaluation. We might, at the close, engage in the kind of informal evaluation we sometimes make of an evening's conversation with friends, saying perhaps, "That was great." No one (except a thorough-going boor) demands to know exactly *what* was "great," by what criteria it was so judged, or what number the experience should be awarded on some scale of greatness. It was great, that's all. We shared; we enjoyed.

Other writers, notably Elliot Eisner, have discussed the difficulty of evaluating certain kinds of valuable educational experiences.[15] Eisner has used the term *expressive objective* for a statement that describes an encounter instead of an outcome. It is appropriate, he holds, to describe encounters from which certain desired outcomes *may* emerge and from which other, totally unanticipated but valuable outcomes may also emerge. While we are in some agreement with Eisner's position, we would prefer to drop the term *objective* and talk about *expressive encounters*. This semantic change implies something accomplished in the encounter itself and diminishes the demand for outcomes beyond the experience. If I am pressed for an objective I might say that my objective is to share something I enjoy immensely with my students in the hope that they, too, will enjoy it. Are there measurable outcomes that may emerge from the experience? Of course. The students may learn all sorts of things: Why a certain meter is effective, what criteria I use to judge the poem's value, what certain words mean, how the poet lived . . . . We could go on and on. We do not know at the onset where conversation will lead us. But just because outcomes *are* measureable does not mean that we *should* measure them. In genuinely intuitive contact, each subject's experience is unique. He or she may, in sharing parts of it, enhance the experience for others, but even the shared experience will be unique to each participant. So, if one student asks about and appears to learn something about the poem's meter, should we then try to find out exactly how much he or she has learned and whether other people also learned the same material? The suggestion is absurd and wastes time that might better be used in further exploration.

Another reason for resisting formal evaluation, besides our insistence upon intuitive concentration on the object of knowledge (or appreciation), is our recognition that receptivity is central to an intuitive mode. There is no expected product of the encounter. Whatever-it-is-here is confronted, received, and confronted again. The value of the encounter is in itself. We aim to enhance receptivity by allowing the mood to remain receptive. If it naturally takes a turn to the active or analytic, we allow that, too, but we do not force such a turn. And when the analytic phase has spent itself, we urge a return to the receptive mood: listen, look, touch; be grasped, caught up, moved.

There is a genuine uncertainty principle operating in the sphere of educating for intuitive growth. We might like to observe and measure what is being acquired by way of intuitive growth, but try to measure it—and straightaway it disappears.

Another matter to consider as we explore ways in which to increase receptivity is the timing or directionality of intuitive thinking. We have already mentioned the importance of establishing intuitive contact, of supplying information as it is needed, and of maintaining the direction of thought. Time is crucial. Intuitive thinking, because it is not sharply goal oriented, needs time to establish its direction. Because it is not sequential, it cannot bear interruption. If one is doing algorithmic work—say, solving quadratic equations by formula or filling in blanks on a form—it is easy to pick up one's place after an interruption. This is not so with dominantly intuitive work. Moreover, interruption may induce a sense of trauma very like the physical trauma incurred when stride or swing must be broken in dancing or batting a ball. The trauma shows itself not as a bruise or sprain but in disorientation, in difficulty attending to new conversation, in strange responses, and in family complaints that "you're not listening to me."

The psychologist Bartlett, we noted earlier, described thinking in motor terms, and these seem particularly appropriate when thinking has a dominantly intuitive component. He described thinking in terms of timing, stationary phases, point of no return, and direction.[16] Teachers should consider what they do when they insist upon immediate attention during or after supervised study or when they press a thinking student for a response. Interrupting someone deep in thought is very like shouting "Look out for the baby!" at a swinging batter or golfer. Yet, strangely, we in education have made little use of the potentially rich motor metaphor, and we have done little investigation of the relationship between thinking and directionality.

One reason our students so seldom engage subject matter wholeheartedly is that we take away their opportunities to do so. In our enthusiasm for "direct instruction," we suppose that everything is best taught directly, that explicit statement of objectives will facilitate their mastery, that anything not explicitly "aimed at" will surely be missed. We need to look upon the instructional scene intelligently, asking which goals may reasonably be expected to yield to direct instruction, which are variable with respect to both how they are attained and who attains them, which are utterly dependent upon the freedom of the student who pursues them, and which cannot be attained at all by direct pursuit.

The teacher's primary job is to establish thinking and help maintain its direction. Once a student has chosen a method, he or she should be allowed to follow it through, even if the teacher knows it will end in an unsatisfactory solution or product. It is vital that the student's choice, his or her center of engagement, not be demeaned nor that the thinking generated by it be derailed. One must undergo the consequences of one's planning and implementation if one is to bring any sort of meaningful evaluation to it. The teacher, then, facilitates but does not direct, does not traumatize the student by saying, "That won't work. Try this." Rather, the teacher keeps thinking alive and moving by asking, "What's wrong here? How might we fix this up? What do you think of the result?"

There are, then, two important reasons for considering timing and directionality in our pedagogical planning. First, we want to push the student—gently, firmly, supportively—into intuitive contact with the objects of knowledge and, second, we want to help the student maintain a state of receptivity during the encounter. If the external, teacher voice always silences the inner voice, if external stimuli continually supplant what the inner eye observes on "schemes built in the imagination," our students may indeed become passive, waiting half-mindedly to be told what to do, what to hear, what to see.

THE QUEST FOR UNDERSTANDING

In a genuine intuitive mode, consciousness is fastened upon the object of interest. If the object is an object of knowledge, our purpose is to see it clearly and to understand it, its possibilities, its relations with other objects of knowledge. The quest for understanding and meaning, characteristic of the intuitive mode, needs pedagogical legitimation. We must make it possible for our students to listen, to try out, to enjoy the objects of knowledge without always demanding products that can be assessed as the results of satisfactory performance. This suggests that we should at times assign tasks, such as reading, viewing, interviewing, that are completely open-ended. "Read and see what you think," we may advise.

Here again, our advice is very much against the tide of current thinking. In contrast to the approach that says, "At the end of this chapter, you should be able to do the following," we are suggesting a far freer start. In the next chapter we shall discuss intuitive arrangements of subject matter and intuitive instructional presentations, but here we want to set the stage, to argue for more dramatically interesting, more personally satisfying explorations. Think how Charles Dickens starts *A Christmas Carol* : "Marley was dead, to begin with. There is no doubt whatever about that." Or consider how a Chinese mystery begins: "In the end, as a general rule, no criminal escapes the law of the land." [17] And how is this for a start? "I, a demon, bear witness that there are no more demons left." [18] Contrast these lively beginnings with the start (far better than most) of a biology text: "What is science? Is it a body of facts? Is it a set of theories? Science is like a detective story. Science means action and it is exciting action." [19] We are *told* that science is intriguing, that it is "like a detective story," but we may find that hard to believe in the absence of convincing drama. In the very next paragraph, the authors tell us what we should learn in this chapter. What we are suggesting is that this approach should often be delayed at least until after a free, open, and receptive reading has occurred. "Read and enjoy; see what you think."

It is reasonable, even when a free reading is suggested, for the teacher to foreshadow certain events. "Watch for the subtle invasion of theoretical prejudice," the teacher may warn. "See if you could explain things better. Would you write more or less? Give fewer or more examples? Give more or less context?" The idea, the hope, is to engage the student in this material as he or she naturally engages other material. To signal at the outset exactly what is to be learned is a singularly dull and stultifying way to start a lesson, although it may be a helpful way to circle back for the purposes of routinization. Interested students can accept this sort of practicing and polishing.

Uninterested students will at best acquire temporary responses. It is not to our credit that we find these responses so satisfying when they occur on so-called competency tests. They are no guarantee whatever that any lasting learning has taken place or that any thirst for continued learning has been developed.

If the quest for understanding is the driving force behind intuitive intellect, we need to give more legitimacy to activities that use and reveal basic understanding. In mathematics, for example, we often suppose that the only alternative to rote memorization of formulas is the ability actually to derive these formulas logically. This is patently false and directs us toward an emphasis uncongenial to a majority of students. In every subject, there is something fundamental that, if understood, contributes to our rapid development in that subject. In mathematics, what is once properly established may never be violated; nothing is contingent nor subject to empirical vagaries. We can, therefore, use what we already know to "fiddle around" and produce methods for treating new entities or to reproduce forgotten algorithms. For example, suppose that I have forgotten how to handle $\sqrt{2} + \sqrt{3}$. I wonder momentarily whether I may write: $\sqrt{2} + \sqrt{3} = \sqrt{5}$. Well, now, let me consider some facts I know well. I know that $\sqrt{4} = 2$ and $\sqrt{9} = 3$. If it is legitimate to write $\sqrt{4} + \sqrt{9} = \sqrt{13}$, then $\sqrt{13} = 5$, since I know that $\sqrt{4} + \sqrt{9} = 5$. This is obviously untrue, so I discard my impulse to combine radicals in this illogical fashion. Now such a demonstration does not constitute a proof of *how* to proceed, but it certainly does constitute a proof that the proposed method is false.

There are many mathematical routines and formulas that can be reconstituted from partial memory and "trying out" on known entities. Knowing that a formula looks "something like this" can initiate a series of concatenations that will produce the accurate formula. I might do this sort of thing, for example, in reproducing the formula for $\sin (A + B)$. If all I remember is that $\sin (A + B)$ equals some combination of sines and cosines of A and B, I can play with promising combinations in the context of known values such as sin and cos of 30°, 60°, and 90°, and eventually reconstitute the four formulas involving sin or $\cos (A + B)$. This way of operating is a direct appeal to the inner eye. We look at what is available in our mindscape and construct experiments on these useful objects.

This underscores, of course, our earlier emphasis on familiarity. I must have something in my mind to operate on; I must have some familiarity with the objects under study. But I need not have either complete information or complete understanding in order to achieve a satisfactory resolution of the problems I confront. What I *must* have is a will to try, to risk, to look, to judge, and to stick with the material until it speaks to me. The end result of such an episode is a broader and deeper familiarity, which will tend to enhance the next quest for understanding.

MAINTAINING TENSION

Intuitive activity is accompanied by strong affect; indeed, it is the affective intensity of intellectual activity that constitutes involvement of the intuition. But the subjective certainty of the intuitive mode must be balanced by the skepticism and persistent demand for convincing demonstration that is characteristic of objective uncertainty. "I have my result," said Gauss, "but I do not yet know how to get it."[20]

What is required is such a healthy respect for the products of intuition that we shall insist on their effective translation into public forms. This is not necessary, of course, for those intuitions that are entirely fulfilled at the consummatory level. But effective translation is required for those results that must be communicated convincingly. A mathematical result must be demonstrated, a poetic intuition must be expressed, and a kinetic intuition must be acted out. If the mathematical demonstration is incomplete or flawed by a faulty step, if the poetic intuition is expressed carelessly or tritely, if the kinetic intuition is executed clumsily, we give poor marks to the performer. He or she has not done credit to the art.

It is not an accident that so many creative persons testify that they hated school and did poorly in school work. It is not only because we devalue intuition, its concentration, and its products; it is also because we devalue its transformation into public products. When we give lip service to creative expression, we tend to recommend a deliberate lack of attention to the mechanics of expression. Spelling, punctuation, and grammar are ignored in favor of *ideas*. But good ideas deserve meticulous expression. It is not a sound practice to teach mechanics in sets of dull-witted sentences and then ignore mechanics when real ideas are expressed. Rather, we should stick with things that are worth attention, grooming and revising them until they are as lovely to the beholder as to the creator. This means, perhaps, slowing things down a bit in the interests of understanding and conveying meaning as contrasted with the mere acquisition and production of responses.

It suggests, also, that we might consider doing things in stages. Give intuition free play at the outset. If something is to be written, let it be written; if something is to be read, let it be read. Let whatever-is-there come through, be revealed. After something is in existence, we can undertake the elaboration, revision, analysis, perfection of that first product. Finally, we return to the finished product so that the intuition may contribute a final insight on the problem and complete the quest for understanding.

How is it that we fall into the unproductive pattern so typical of our schools—one in which we undertake a unit of study, complete and evaluate it once and for all, and then abandon it as though it were worthy only of discard? For some students, indeed, failure on a particular topic becomes a relief because it means the end of the hated topic. Of course, failure itself may become ritualized when one hated task is failed, only to be replaced by another just as hateful. In part the answer to this question is revealed in our mode of evaluation. It is obvious that we are, or at least most of us have been, more interested in sorting and grading pupils like so many eggs or apples than in cultivating their particular talents and virtues. Those who can produce the most proficient performance most promptly are "A's" and those who are slower or less interested are graded accordingly. That this procedure shows little respect for the individual talents and projects of our students is embarrassingly clear. On the other hand, many of those who reject conventional grading lapse into little or no evaluation at all, and this represents another, though different, form of gross disrespect.

To help students maintain the productive tension between subjective certainty and objective uncertainty, we must help them remain engaged with the objects of knowledge or appreciation; to convince them that objective uncertainty exists, we must ourselves be interested in what they are trying to accomplish. It is true that people who are deeply interested in a particular field of study may persist in perfecting a work even if no one shows interest in its perfection, but such persons are rare, aesthetic heroes. Most of us need the interest and constructive criticism of well-informed others. The finished work, of course, may bear the marks of more than one thinker and, in schools, we shy away from such results. Each student, we insist, must do his own work. How odd that we should behave so differently in mature academic work. Should Ezra Pound have been forbidden to work so productively on T. S. Eliot's "The Wasteland"?

SUMMARY

In this chapter, we have discussed ways of enhancing intuitive modes. It is important to remember that any serious attempt to enhance intuition runs the usual risks of programs in affective education. Even though our emphasis has been almost entirely on the intellectual uses of intuition, the risk is still present, and only the naive or dishonest would deny it. The quest for meaning involves concomitant searches for dialogue, for sharing, for opportunities to challenge and to wonder aloud. In all of these quests, we see an opportunity to explore with our students the deepest questions concerning human purpose, meaning, intellectual power, and feeling. If it were possible to pursue relevant questions in this open-minded fashion in schools, the result might be vital young people immunized against the mental and emotional diseases that now fall upon so many when they leave school.

We have discussed the use of warming-up exercises and the dangers of instituting these for all students. Our recommendation was that such techniques be discussed and that all students be encouraged to find the practices that optimize their own intuitive capacities. We also discussed routinization, and here, of course, we found an element of universalizability: All students need facility with basic skills so that their "seeing minds" can focus on the objects of knowledge instead of being distracted by the subskills required for completion of their projects. In the same section we put special emphasis on the use of biographies and accurate accounts of real-life occurrences of intuitive activity.

The role of "doing and looking" was explored. Here we emphasized the primacy of the motivational question—"What shall I do?"—over the intellectual question—"What is it?" This emphasis is, of course, consistent with our claim that intuitive activity is driven by the Will.

Next we talked about the nature of receptive powers: the need for quiet, for time to establish the focus of thought; the necessity of maintaining directionality; the uses of consummatory offerings; the role of Will in submitting to what-is-there. We contrasted the intense subjectivity and aliveness of the intuitive-receptive mode with its peculiar felt loss of subjectness. We noted that we as subjects become, willingly, objects for the object-as-subject.

We considered demands of understanding. Without discussing actual methods of arranging and presenting subject matter, we set the stage for such a discussion by recommending the use of no-product assignments, consummatory offerings, and methods such as concatenation in mathematics to reproduce partially remembered formulas and algorithms. It was noted that familiarity with the objects of knowledge was both prerequisite to such activities and enhanced as a result of them.

Finally we discussed ways of helping students maintain the characteristic tension between subjective certainty and objective uncertainty. In this area our discussion foreshadows more specific recommendations for the arrangement and presentation of subject matter and the evaluation of student progress. We turn next to these considerations.

CURRICULUM AND INSTRUCTION: INTUITIVE ARRANGEMENTS AND PRESENTATIONS OF SUBJECT MATTER

What the heart knows today the head will understand tomorrow.

James Stephens, *The Crock of Gold*

SO FAR, WE HAVE attempted to describe and characterize intuitive modes and to explore ways in which they might be enhanced. We have located through this attempt a core of the "unteachable" in intuitive activity. In spite of all the conscious efforts of the student and the corresponding efforts of a teacher or facilitator, and despite doing all the "right" things, the student may yet fail to see, to grasp or to be grasped. This we cannot change or deny. Still, we have seen that there is much that can be done to enhance intuitive activity.

Now we want to turn our attention to curriculum and instruction and ask what might be meant by an "intuitive arrangement" or "intuitive presentation" of subject matter. For the sake of this exposition, we shall define *curriculum* as material prearranged for instruction, such as textbooks, work sheets, and the like. We may begin by giving a very general answer to our question: An intuitive arrangement or presentation of subject matter is one that takes into account the functioning of intuition, of an intuitive faculty. It does not begin with well-defined objectives for the student, objectives that spring seemingly from nowhere into full control of the student's intellectual life. Rather it provides setting, background, multiple paths barely to clearly discernible, and a multitude of objects that may stand out vividly against their ground. Are we suggesting that an intuitive arrangement provides "advance organizers"? Our suggestion is not so simple nor so plainly directive. The arrangement must allow for a direction to be taken, but it must not point like an arrow at the beginning. It begins like a novel or a poem, piquing our interest, asking nothing but that we keep reading or listening or watching. It sets out to familiarize students with a domain. Just as we become familiar with Hardy's "Wessex" in *The Return of the Native* without recourse to a guidebook that describes the place point-by-point, so students become gradually at home in the domain described in an intuitive arrangement. Perhaps they *will* turn to a guidebook (they could, as they read Hardy, study Hermann Lea's *Highways and By-ways in Hardy's Wessex*), if certain features of the domain itself become the objective, but this might properly wait. They must first have a reason, a certain passionate interest in the domain, before they turn to a study of it in detail. The intuition must come alive with images, suspicions, affinities, tensions.

Second, such arrangements and presentations aim throughout at understanding. They incorporate tasks and provide straightforward help to ensure their successful accomplishment, but the tasks function to increase the understanding. An intuitive arrangement does not make a pedagogical curtsy to understanding in order to induce a successful performance; the successful performance is part of a larger struggle to attain deeper insight.

With respect to "understanding," we must be very careful. Understanding involves a fulfilled complementarity of intellect and intuition in an individual. It is not to be confused with an elegantly logical explanation. Further, we should be very cautious about making unwarranted assumptions concerning the relation between explanation and understanding, unless we do this specifically for experimental purposes. Curriculum workers of the sixties made several such assumptions, the most prominent of which was the claim that the fundamental ideas and structure of a discipline furnish the most effective arrangement for instruction. Bruner and many others also assumed that

> there is a continuity between what a scholar does in the forefront of his discipline and what a child does in approaching it for the first time.[1]

These two assumptions, functioning together, tend to obscure what is in plain view, namely, that "understanding" differs in children and adults, in novices and sophisticates. For children in particular, understanding is functional. "See, it works this way," they will tell you. Understanding, for children, requires a working demonstration, and this is what we get from them when we ask for an explanation. Hence, most of the explanatory rigamarole which was incorporated in the "new math" at the elementary level, though it was presented in the service of understanding, was useless and, in some cases, even distracting. A continual emphasis on conceptual explanation leads students steadily away from the objects they should be attending to. It satisfies the logic of the subject matter but not the logic of the child.

We have claimed that an intuitive arrangement of subject matter aims throughout at understanding. But how is understanding in individuals to be achieved through prearranged subject material? Our entire discussion so far describes intuition as a revealing faculty; its products depend jointly upon the objects intuited, which arise on their own ground of being, and the intuiting faculty. Hence all we can say at this point is that the construction of an intuitive arrangement takes into account this faculty and its purpose in intellectual endeavors—understanding. There is no guarantee that understanding will result. Further, no Bruner-like hypothesis concerning a relation between arrangement of material and understanding suggests itself with any degree of clarity or givenness. We move ahead, then, on a faith: that arrangement of material in accord with our characterization of intuitive modes will yield a high probability of inducing understanding.

There are familiar and commonly known elements in an intuitive arrangment. It may make substantial use of metaphor. The idea here is to focus the attention of the student on particular conceptual operations and roles in a familiar domain and then move to a domain of new objects in which moves and roles are sufficiently alike to preserve crucial operations and identities. The best possible metaphor uses isomorphism, a one-to-one reciprocal correspondence, in which roles and operations are entirely preserved as we move from one domain to another. But, outside of mathematics, we can rarely attain this ideal. Then our problem becomes one of differentiation. We familiarize the student with a domain-in-general by associating it with a known domain; then we must begin to pull certain objects in the new domain to the fore and show how they differ from their counterparts in the known domain. We produce, if they exist, elements that have no counterparts in the old domain; we demonstrate, perhaps, operations that can take place in this domain but not in the old. But all of this takes place in a setting that is, roughly and a bit darkly, familiar, rather like one's hometown after a twenty-year absence.

The arrangement includes concrete examples to fill out conceptual definitions and descriptions. It may also require the student to produce such examples. From our perspective, it does not matter much whether we move from generalization to concrete examples or from concrete cases to generalization. Both moves must be made if understanding is to be attained. One must exercise judgment and some aesthetic sense in deciding when to favor one over the other. For example, discovery of the quadratic formula is unlikely to take place unless we first teach the student how to solve quadratic equations by completing the square. If we do this, the formula itself is a major convenience but only a minor discovery. There is no point in making a great fuss over this generalization. It is to be used. So whether we display it and then show how to produce it or induce its production by emphasizing solutions through completing the square makes little difference. The proper emphasis is still on the method of completing squares that has uses beyond the production of this formula. But if we are going to share, say, Pascal's triangle with our students, it would seem a shame to tell the generalization by which it is built. The triangle clearly represents a problem for our second intuitive mode — that of finding an adequately descriptive structure for objects posted clearly against an ill-defined background. As curriculum makers interested in satisfying the intuitive faculty, then, we need not be consistent in the direction we take from generalization to concrete case. Indeed, we would be in error to insist on such consistency.

Appeals to the senses are important in intuitive arrangements. But, again, we cannot lay down hard and fast rules for their presentation. It might be very useful, for example, to show pictures of a heath in Dorset in preparation for reading *The Return of the Native* or to make available copies of *Vermont Life* before reading Frost's poetry. Such preparation might well induce in the student, as he reads, the feeling "I've seen this," or "I've been here before." But pictures as a preliminary in mathematics are rarely helpful. One needs the conceptualization in order to know what to look for in the picture. In our first cases, it would seem that events and characters arise naturally in a setting-that-is. In mathematics, the setting itself is often defined and elaborated to accommodate the objects of thought. The problems are different; hence, the use of pictures is different. For mathematics students, perhaps the most useful pictures are those that show *how to make* pictures. Understanding requires that students make pictures for themselves, and any help we can give them in making useful pictures for various purposes should be valuable. Mathematics curriculum writers might consider presenting a variety of pictures for a particular problem and asking students to judge the usefulness of each.

The same sort of procedure might also be useful in connection with labels and symbols. Symbols are not simply conceptual tools. They become objects for the intuition, and their congeniality to the intuition should be considered. If the context is well defined, an otherwise conceptually ambiguous symbol may be perfectly clear to the intuition; if so, it is to be preferred to a more cumbersome, albeit conceptually adequate, notation. There is little likelihood, for example, that students will identify an angle with a measure in degrees as a result of using the notation, $\angle A = 60°$. The alternative, used ad nauseum in some sixties' texts—the measure of $\angle A$ is 60°—is cumbersome and not nearly so handily used as object by the intuition.

In this same vein, there is little reason to suppose that precise language used in instruction contributes much to the understanding of students. On the contrary, it would seem that such language is a product of understanding and not a precursor to it. The intuition must struggle with language (unless it is itself the object of intuition as is language in rhyme, meter, melody), find objects to replace it, and then reconstruct it as essential insight into the objects it discusses. Yet the assumption that precise language in instruction is somehow importantly linked to understanding was prominent in sixties' curricula. Max Beberman, for example, offered the following in evidence for retaining this assumption:

> Take the prime number 13 in the decimal system. In the octic system this is the number 15. Is it also a prime number in the octic system?
>
> Any hesitation at all in giving an answer to this question is a sign that the answerer's understanding is not all it should be. Of course, if the question is posed in language which shows a recognition of the distinction between number and numeral, the "problem" vanishes:
>
> Take the prime number whose decimal name is "13" and whose octic name is "15." Is it a prime number?[2]

All of our own experience and that of many other teachers of mathematics contradict Beberman in this. It seems as though the problem should vanish, but it does not. Students still respond, No. Reason? Because $15 = 3 \times 5$. The distinction between number and numeral is just too subtle for most students. Insisting upon the verbal distinction does not help. What students need is more extensive experience with actual operations on numbers using a variety of numerals. They must come to see that primeness is invariant across domains of representation. After all, without this essential seeing, why should precise language eliminate the problem? One could easily suppose that primeness vanishes under a notational change.

An intuitive arrangement avoids traumatic changes of direction. As a presentation, which the teacher controls and motivates, it may include material that has the potential to distract, but if the teacher advises the students simply to flow with the material, not to worry about subroutines they cannot yet handle, the presentation may still qualify as intuitive. But an arrangement in which the main point is dependent upon the ability to handle subroutines is likely to be counterintuitive if the student cannot manage the routines. What seems obvious to one skilled in the routines seems enormously difficult and complicated to one who is not. In some modern calculus texts, for example, there is an "intuitive introduction" to derivatives through the geometric notion of tangents. Now this approach could, under proper handling, qualify as intuitive: It refers us to a familiar domain, uses pictures, yields opportunities for concrete construction. But in this particular arrangement, the student is faced with a new use for synthetic division, a need to perform translations, and a requirement that he accept on faith the fact that a good linear approximation can be got by simply deleting higher degree terms. This last is acceptable intuitively if we include just a little experimentation to generate the "of course" reaction, but the first two difficulties are virtually destructive of the intuition's efforts. The intuition is several times badly distracted as the intellect must struggle to remember or to figure out (1) how to perform synthetic division, (2) why it is being used here, (3) what a translation is, and (4) how to perform it. Somewhere in the midst of all this, students will have to ask themselves, perhaps repeatedly, what they are doing, what they set out to do originally, what their immediate task has to do with that initial aim. Now, clearly, students may, despite all this, enter and remain in an intuitive mode as they struggle with the material, but if they do, it is because they have embraced understanding as their project. The arrangement is not itself playing to their intuition. To make this arrangement properly intuitive, we should incorporate preliminary discussion and exercises that would remove the aforementioned difficulties. In this recommendation, as in several others, we admit a congruence with the recommendations of behaviorist educators, but, predictably, our reasons are different. We expect and work for particular performances as evidence of object familiarity within the domain under study. This object familiarity will enable us to build and to fill out an outline structure of the domain.

In our discussion of intuitive arrangements, we shall explore five phases of such arrangements: arranging subject matter for engaging the Will, for receptivity, for the acquisition of object familiarity, for the development of structural representations in which to embed the objects, and for the development of understanding. In the discussion of each phase, we shall give detailed examples of treatments in several subject areas, but most of our examples will be taken from our own fields of expertise: mathematics and social studies. Such detail is necessary to support our contention that intuitive arrangements are both distinctive and explicable.

ENGAGING THE WILL

We have emphasized throughout our discussion the relation of Will and intuition. The Will is in itself unanalyzable, because it is the driving force behind all analysis; similarly, intuition-as-process is unanalyzable because it is the immediate apprehension and organization of material in response to the Will's quest for meaning. We can, of course, look at and think about any particular manifestation of Will, but this hardly constitutes an analysis of Will itself, since we are still left with the question of why we decided to look at this particular manifestation in the first place. Again, we can certainly look at the products of intuition and ask how they may be verified, reproduced sequentially, or used instrumentally, but we cannot answer the question of how we came by the intuition except to describe our phenomenal experience. When we talked about intuitive modes and their enhancement, we attempted to describe that phenomenal experience and what makes it more likely that intuitions will occur.

The first thing that we noticed about intuitive modes was their characteristic receptivity, but when we backed up to see what lay behind the receptivity, we found commitment; that is, we found an act of Will that committed us to the mental mode we have called "intuitive." We commit ourselves to listening, watching, feeling. Thus, although the intuitive mode is often characterized by its lack of firm and specific goals, it clearly serves the purposes of the intuiter. The intuiter has committed himself or herself to a state of such intense subjectivity that subjectness, the sense of I-as-the-one-doing is completely lost. Even when the intuiter is seized involuntarily—as were Gauss and Mozart—there is a moment in which he or she *accepts* the surrender.

Clearly, then, any arrangement or presentation of subject matter that is meant to take intuition into account must somehow function to secure the active participation of the student. The student must be involved in the *construction of purposes*. In the opening of his chapter on "The Meaning of Purpose" in *Experience and Education*, John Dewey says:

> Plato once defined a slave as the person who executes the purposes of another, and, as has just been said, a person is also a slave who is enslaved to his own blind desires. There is, I think, no point in the philosophy of progressive education which is sounder than its emphasis upon the importance of the participation of the learner in the formation of the purposes which direct his activities in the learning process, just as there is no defect in traditional education greater than its failure to secure the active co-operation of the pupil in construction of the purposes involved in his studying.[3]

Martin Buber also warns that "intervention"—direct interference with the student's own purposes—works counter to genuine educational efforts. He puts it this way:

> Yet the master remains the model for the teacher. For if the educator of our day has to act consciously he must nevertheless do it "as though he did not." That raising of the finger, that questioning glance, are his genuine doing. Through him the selection of the effective world reaches the pupil. He fails the recipient when he presents this selection to him with a gesture of interference. It must be concentrated in him; and doing out of concentration has the appearance of rest. Interference divides the soul in his care into an obedient part and a rebellious part. But a hidden influence proceeding from his integrity has an integrating force.[4]

So long as the student is split into an obedient part and a rebellious part, the intuition cannot function. The commitment needed to release intuitive power cannot be made until the split is healed. Clearly, the student cannot receive the material fully while his or her attention is directed at himself or herself thinking: Why am I doing this? Why should I do this? How can I get out of this? The very first task of both curriculum maker and teacher, then, is to engage the Will, to win that initial commitment.

But what can curriculum makers do in this regard? We shall be able to make several powerful suggestions for teachers, but they will be derived from the teacher's ability to *receive* the students: to talk with them, discover their interests, and negotiate purposes with them. Curriculum makers face a very different task; somehow they must engage the Will of unknown and unseen persons.

From the point of view we have taken here, current curriculum making is going at the task wrongly. It makes two very great mistakes: first, it establishes specific learning objectives and then asks, "How can we get people to learn these?" and, second, it unduly emphasizes the general, cognitive, and rational over the concrete, affective, and nonrational.

Let us start with the first problem. The curriculum or text writer does have to analyze tasks. Someone writing a second-year algebra text, say, certainly has to decide what skills are part of that subject matter and what form demonstration of those skills should take. But it does not follow from this that subject matter should be presented in this fashion. Depending on the topic to be introduced, presentations might vary from completely unstructured problems to be tried, to biographical accounts of mathematical struggles, to a frank presentation of particular skills to be learned. Even when this last is properly indicated, it is still possible to precede the specific skill statements with the reasons for their acquisition.

Suppose we were to start a unit on number theory with a set of problems and suppose we were to direct our students to "try a couple that intrigue you." We might follow this free exploration period with an exchange of ideas and methods for solving such problems. Here is one such problem:

> A woman with a basket of eggs finds that if she removes the eggs from the basket either two, three, four, five, or six at a time, there is always one egg left. However, if she removes the eggs seven at a time, there are no eggs left. If the basket holds up to 500 eggs, how many eggs does the woman have?[5]

Now, ask whether you could pass this problem by without trying it. Many people cannot, but the curriculum maker cannot be sure, in the absence of students, whether any material—however carefully it is chosen for relevance—will interest particular students. But curriculum makers can provide both teachers and students with choices. "Look these over and see which ones intrigue you," is an appropriate instruction if we wish to engage the Will. Indeed, considerable work in current psychology tends to show that preferences are not entirely rational,[6] and that people can and do make choices without long strings of cognitions preceding them. We are not recommending that curriculum makers induce people to make ill-informed choices but, rather, that the sort of choice that stimulates engagement be actively encouraged. Obviously, it is necessary to guide teachers in how to direct these choices, because teachers are the ones who will be present when the occasional child says, "I don't want to do any of them."

The form of choice must differ not only from child to child but from subject to subject. In mathematics, some essentially sequential skills simply must be learned, but teachers can be directed to inform their students as to the purposes for which drill exercises are undertaken. Further, the drills should usually be provided *before* some important concept, not as ends in themselves. Before presenting the Pythagorean Theorem, for example, texts should inform students and teachers that certain skills will be very useful in applications of a major result soon to appear. The text writers thus share honestly their conviction that routinization of skills will free the intuition to grapple with and to see what the Pythagorean Theorem means and how it can be applied. Drills presented for this purpose should include simplifying radicals, finding square roots, memorizing the squares of integers from one to twenty-five, and combining radicals. Beyond providing drills for the routinization of essential skills, the text should also provide an overview—a sort of Gestalt picture—of the development of mathematical topics. We shall return to this topic when we discuss the development of outline structures a bit later.

Whereas intuitive approaches can often take a Gestaltist approach, emphasizing balance, wholeness, and closure, they must sometimes take a somewhat different form. In social studies and language arts, for example, intuition may take the form of what Bruner calls "courageous taste," that is, a set of convictions derived from personal experience relevant to the material at hand and seasoned with a sense of aesthetic "rightness." In this use, *aesthetic* conveys not only the Kantian concept (borrowed from the Greeks) of sense expression, but also the later, more developed connotations of balance, taste, and beauty. Courageous taste must be achieved without coercion from teacher or peers, but, clearly, encouragement, acceptance, and constructive evaluation enhance its achievement. It must arise in and be ultimately validated by the subjective process we call intuition.

The word "courageous" also signifies something important that we hope to convey to students about intuition. Intuiting involves taking risks in the public domain but it involves, also, taking an inner risk: What is felt with such certainty may turn out to be wrong. Once an intuitive impression is formed, it must be respected. It cannot be treated like an arbitrary position assumed temporarily for the sake of classroom discussion; it is deeply felt. But this is not to say students should be encouraged to cling defensively to an intuitive insight or to strive arrogantly to force the new idea or impression down the throat of others. Rather, the intuition must be respected as a source of knowledge and insight into an aesthetic, historical, or social problem, while allowing for the possibility that another solution (perhaps not intuitive in origin) may prove just as effective or more accurate. Taking such a position requires courage.

Clearly, courageous taste is not enhanced by starting a unit with the remark, "At the end of this unit you will have learned to display courageous taste." Taste, like understanding and appreciation of the Pythagorean Theorem, requires preparation, a sense of the larger picture, and, most of all, intense involvement. One must both understand the concepts at hand and feel something about them. For today's video oriented children, the key to understanding and feeling something about concepts in social studies is in the use of visual materials. There is nothing revolutionary in this, for teachers have used pictures and posters to aid in teaching for generations. But to foster intuitive responses to questions in the social studies, visual material must be used in particular ways. First, images must be linked to students' existing experience whenever possible in order to provide a background against which to draw conclusions. Second, where it is not possible to draw upon the actual experience of students, the material must be designed to induce affective response that is consonant with what might be actually experienced in the pictured situations.

An example will help to illustrate what we have in mind here. Suppose a junior high-school teacher wishes to teach a unit on the Civil War. A typical approach might be to present textbook causes of the war and follow this with discussion of major battles: Antietam, Gettysburg, Lookout Mountain, and so on. Even with the considerable effort of a talented teacher, many students will take away from such an exposition only fragmented impressions of the events—the names of a few battles and generals and, perhaps, some vague notion of suffering and destruction. If we want them to feel something of the pride, grief, horror, stubbornness, convictions, betrayals, mistakes, pain, splendor, and squalor that characterize war, we need to do a great deal more. Further, we contend that an intuitive treatment aimed at inducing affective response will have the correlative result of producing more lasting learning of facts, principles, and concepts.

Our unit might start, then, with a series of films, photographs, and paintings of the Civil War. After students have viewed such films as *The Red Badge of Courage* and such photographs as those of Matthew Brady showing dead soldiers, army camps, and battle scenes, they might be asked the following kinds of questions: How would you feel in such a situation? What does the straight back and raised fist of the orator convey to you? What do you see in the heavy-lidded glance of Abraham Lincoln? Why does an army need drummer boys and flag bearers? Why would a man seize a falling flag and carry it forward to his own almost certain death? What does the man beneath the bayonet feel? What does the man holding it feel?

What distinguishes the aforementioned approach from others using visual images is the conscious emphasis on building a background of experience from which intuitive responses can be generated. Photographs, films, and the like serve not merely as decorative and illustrative supplements to written factual lessons but are the focus of a process to awaken the inner eye: This really *happened*. How would I feel and act in such a situation? The purpose of intuitive arrangements described here is quite different from the one described earlier. It is not merely to see and understand the roles of mathematical elements and backgrounds. It is to come to grips with material that by its very nature is affect laden; it is to understand, by feeling ourselves, what people may actually have felt and how what they felt influenced how they acted. Intuitive arrangements in social studies take into account that social studies inevitably involve human values and that these values are not mere objective statements of factual preferences.

To go at social studies curriculum development in the way we are suggesting requires several changes. First, texts must either give way to total packages (as some curricula did in the well-financed sixties) or must incorporate special directions for their own supplementation. The latter course is probably more practical in times of financial embarrassment. But text writers should be conscientious about this. Supplementary materials should not merely be listed as optional at the end of traditional chapters. A supplement written for the teacher should direct the teacher at the outset to collect the materials that will provide choice and visual stimulation; sources should be listed as well, as should helpful suggestions for the use of materials. Another possibility is to provide multiple-volume texts instead of the usual fact-crammed single volumes. Each volume should provide choices, visual materials, literary excerpts including poetry, references to or some actual scores of music, excerpts from diaries and letters, and many invitations to react, to see, to feel, to plan for the future of self and society.

Second, the content of texts, as well as their format, must change. Texts have been criticized repeatedly for bias; a pupil studying the Civil War in the South would hardly recognize the same war if he or she moved to a northern classroom. Similarly, our Revolutionary War appears to us as a vastly different enterprise from the British view of the "breaking away of the colonies." Our best texts notice this and attempt to present "both sides" of many questions, but they do this in such a bland and aloof way that students often remain unaware of the heated convictions and awe-inspiring sacrifices that characterized those opposing each other. What is needed, instead of bland "objectivity," is a vivid pictorialization of both sides — complete with music, slogans, and outcomes. Students should know that people in this country during World War II actually sang a song that advised, "We've got to slap the dirty little Jap." In arranging material on the Revolution, text writers should consider including (or pointing to) parts of Kenneth Roberts's *Oliver Wiswell* so that students can see for themselves that, had they lived in 1776, they might have been Tories. One of the present authors had that experience as a high-school student, and she has never forgotten it. What an eye opener to realize that what one espouses in distant principle is contrary to what one would have done in concrete, deeply principled, actual living! It is unlikely that any objective accounts could produce feelings similar to those that arise from hearing opposing, impassioned, subjective accounts.

Third, text writers should take the need to provide choice seriously. There is little reason why all students should read exactly the same books, view exactly the same pictures, discuss exactly the same concrete problems. But there is, of course, reason for some students to tackle similar materials. Discussion, challenge, debate are all conducive to both learning and evaluation. Therefore, the recommendation for choice should not be construed as an endorsement of completely individualized learning. Rather, small-group organization is advised. With the help of written guide materials, small groups of students could meet to discuss the biographical, pictorial, fictional, and poetic accounts that the text makers and teacher make available. During these sessions, the teacher might sit for a while with one group and, later, with another. Ideally, other members of the community might join these groups as one does any reading group. How can we be sure that such people are not undesirable? Some screening might take place of course; we should be sure that interests are legitimate, legal, sane. But beyond this, perhaps the best screening is done in whole-group critiques of what transpired in small-group discussions. We do not recommend screening out people on the grounds of their political, social, or religious beliefs. Where better to encounter "undesirable" belief systems than in an orderly, protective, and rational environment? Fascists, dogmatists, and libertines are best countered in face-to-face confrontation, or, at least, judged on the basis of such encounters.

Fourth, and finally in this area, texts should help teachers to make metaphorical and actual transfers from historical domains to domains of current activity. Are the problems of countries struggling to be free of Soviet or United States domination different from those of the "breaking away of the colonies"? In what ways? Are they different from each other? Is one power importantly different from the other? How? What do we need to know in order to be sure? It must be possible to discuss human problems in terms of today's controversies as well as those of past times. Indeed, if the inner eye is truly awakened, it will look upon these times with both passion and a call to reason.

At the beginning of this section, we claimed that contemporary curriculum making commits two great errors. The first is dictatorial prespecification of learning objectives, together with bland and uniform instruction to achieve them. The second, we said, was emphasis on the general, cognitive, and rational over the concrete, affective, and nonrational. We have, without warning readers that we were doing so, already discussed part of this error and made recommendations to rectify it. But we need to give more attention to the matter of general versus concrete.

There is a long tradition in Western intellectual circles that favors the general over the concrete, the abstract over the particular. Sometimes this preference is even extended beyond the intellectual to engulf the emotional as well. Genevieve Lloyd points to this tendency in Spinoza's work:

> Despite his metaphysical rejection of a plurality of individual substances, Spinoza's ethic is highly individualistic. But the achievement of individuality is at the cost of a detachment from the particular, the specific, the transient, in order to turn one's attention increasingly to the general, the universal, the unchanging, to what is common to all.[7]

She then quotes Spinoza:

> An emotion which springs from reason is necessarily referred to the
> common properties of things, . . . which we always regard as pres-
> ent (for there can be nothing to exclude their present existence) and
> which we always conceive in the same manner. Wherefore an emo-
> tion of this kind always remains the same.[8]

Now, we might have difficulty recognizing something as "emotion" when it appears predictably and "in the same manner." We see
here, repeated, the longstanding distrust of the truly emotional—that
which is aroused not from reason's recognition of "common properties" but from the concrete occurrences of actual living. This difference must be kept in mind as we approach the study of literature
where, in contrast to the traditional treatments of social studies, we
usually expect to deal directly with matters of affect.

Intuitive approaches to language arts will seem to most people
less unusual than those recommended for social studies. Literature,
by its very nature, draws upon intuitive insight in both its creation
and appreciation. As mentioned earlier, appreciation of a poem or
novel can be enhanced by acquaintance with the physical (or
psychological) setting of the work. Subtle and frequently overlooked
aspects of a story, such as the austerity of the Puritan community in
which *The Scarlet Letter* takes place, can be examined visually before
the novel is read. Exposure to the period's clothing and architecture
can be helpful in painting this picture of austerity. As with the social
studies, an ultimate goal of intuitive presentations in literature is to
enable the student to evaluate the soundness or "rightness" of the
author's interpretation and to cultivate "courageous taste" in approaching and criticizing other literary works.

In the language arts, development of students' intuitive
capacities can serve another function. It can foster creative responses
to writing assignments. By learning to feel comfortable with their
own intuitive sense of aesthetics, students will be encouraged to
produce writing that reflects their individual values and feelings and
that does this genuinely with some passion. Whether writing a play,
short story, or poem, a student having awareness of the images he or
she has stored up from other literary works will be more sensitive in
designing a new piece of writing.

Effective intuitive arrangement and presentation of subject matter depends ultimately on the teacher. No prepackaged curriculum
can be completely successful in fostering either the intuitive mode of

thought or any intuitive experiences without the continuous, active, committed participation of the teacher. The instructor must have a belief in the value of intuitive insights and should also have experienced intuitive processes personally. A uniform, prespecified approach to intuition in the classroom is unlikely to work; instead the effective instructor will endeavor to present material so that those who are prepared to make intuitive interpretations can do so. Above all, a tolerant, encouraging attitude is essential. As Bruner has noted, the instructor must also be willing to make his or her own intuitions public, even at the risk of being publicly wrong. Students should be made aware from the start that intuition yields knowledge and insight, not immutable truth. The intuitive experiences of noted artists and scientists can be discussed as examples, and the fact that even acknowledged intuiters make mistakes and profit from them should be stressed. Indeed, it is sometimes felt that occurrence of error is evidence that intuition is actually operating. An error in mere calculating would not be held so tenaciously as the product of intuition. Douglas Hofstadter notes that errors made by the great Indian mathematician, Ramanujan, tended to convince people of Ramanujan's mystical intuitive powers:

> Many of his "intuition theorems" were *wrong*. Now there is a curious paradoxical effect where sometimes an event which you think could not help but make credulous people become a little more skeptical, actually has the reverse effect, hitting the credulous ones in some vulnerable spot of their minds, tantalizing them with the hint of some baffling irrational side of human nature. Such was the case with Ramanujan's blunders: many educated people with a yearning to believe in something of the sort considered Ramanujan's intuitive powers to be evidence of a mystical insight into Truth, and the fact of his fallibility seemed, if anything, to strengthen, rather than weaken, such beliefs. [9]

There are two things to remark upon in this passage. First, Hofstadter himself does not deny Ramanujan's intuitive powers; he merely looks with some skepticism on labeling them "mystical." Intuition may indeed be mistaken—just as perception can be. But, like perception, it delivers its results with resounding conviction. Second, the nature of intuitive conviction is so forceful that it carries the credulous along in its wake. We have been careful to emphasize both of these points: Intuition is to be respected but not accepted as infallible; intuition is not to be identified with the mystical but, rather, with the intense personal quest for meaning—which accounts in part, by the way, for both Ramanujan's mathematical insights and his fans' worshipful appreciation of his pronouncements.

We had been discussing the need for attention to the concrete and particular, and we digressed a bit to talk about the benefits of intuitive development in the student and the teacher's role in encouraging that development. But this is not a serious departure. The teacher, in aiding the development of intuition, pays careful attention to the particular — both to particular students and to concrete incidents in literature that may induce intuitive activity. For this very reason, some people may feel that intuitive presentations sometimes smack of elitism, playing to the boldest and most imaginative (and articulate) students. These fears could be valid if teachers do not encourage intuitive engagement in *all* students or if some students' attempts at "courageous taste" are belittled or ignored. The success of a program emphasizing intuition depends on the willingness of all parties to allow teachers to be generously "partial" in their treatment of students and subject matter. *Of course* students should be treated partially and differently; they are different and unique persons.

An effective way to begin the individual quest for "courageous taste" is to expose students to a variety of particularly evocative pieces of writing, stand back, and wait for the affective responses to occur. Often we encounter in literature a passage or, perhaps, an entire work that conveys a sense of "rightness" well beyond the effects of ordinary clear and accurate writing. For one of us, Pearl Buck's *The Good Earth* is such a piece; for the other, this passage from Hemingway is particularly and convincingly "right":

> Maera lay still, his head on his arms, his face in the sand. He felt warm and sticky from the bleeding. Each time he felt the horn coming. Sometimes the bull only bumped him with his head. Once the horn went all the way through him and he felt it go into the sand. Some one had the bull by the tail. They were swearing at him and flopping the cape in his face. Then the bull was gone. Some men picked Maera up and started to run with him toward the barriers through the gate and out the passageway around under the grandstand to the infirmary. They laid Maera down on a cot and one of the men went out for the doctor. The others stood around. The doctor came running from the corral where he had been sewing up picador horses. He had to stop and wash his hands. There was a great shouting going on in the grandstand overhead. Maera felt everything getting larger and larger and then smaller and smaller. Then it got larger and larger and larger and then smaller and smaller. Then everything commenced to run faster and faster as when they speed up a cinematograph film. Then he was dead.[10]

A remarkable thing occurs when we read this passage. Hemingway describes here something none of us has directly experienced: violent death. Many of us have never experienced anything remotely like it. Yet somehow we are made to feel that this is exactly what the experience would be like. There is something in the final sentences of the paragraph that connects us to this unexperienced event and leaves us with a sense of revelation: Yes, these are things I could feel, would feel; this is how it would be. One cannot expect descriptions of violent death in general to arouse the feelings in us that are induced by lucid, concrete accounts, and this is crucial in arranging subject matter for the intuition. The intuition does not deduce; it does not move patiently through strings of logical propositions. It looks at objects and conveys what it sees to the feeling Will that directs it.

ARRANGING FOR RECEPTIVITY

We have so far given considerable attention to "engaging the Will," because the intuition operates only at the behest of the Will. Once we have secured commitment, however, the task of the curriculum maker and teacher is to encourage and maintain receptivity. We have already discussed the importance of providing consummatory experiences in this connection. Drama, delight, and dissonance keep us listening, responding, trying. Curriculum makers can incorporate dramatic episodes in their arrangements, but teachers must observe delight or its absence, and, clearly, they are the ones who must maintain appropriate forms of dissonance until students arrive at an equilibrium that is sound with respect to the structure of the particular subject matter under consideration.

It is important to emphasize again the difference between receptivity and "reception learning." In reception learning, students simply "receive" what the teacher puts forth didactically. There is some question whether such a phenomenon ever occurs, for even the supposedly passive listener must actively process what he or she hears in order to retain it. But "reception learning" does point accurately to a mode or arrangement of instructor and students: The instructor speaks and the students sit as though attentive and listening. In such situations, receptivity may be actualized or it may not be. We can be intensely active mentally in processing someone's speech; we can also lose ourselves in erotic daydreams or "chasing deer in the wildwood." Hence "reception learning" is not a very useful concept for those of us interested in the inner workings of mind. We neither approve it nor condemn it. What we need to know is what is going on in individuals during the episode.

The observant teacher has a clear sense of what is going on. Because he or she receives the students, takes note of their facial expressions and reactions, and adjusts the tone and pace of lecture accordingly, receptivity can be maintained in didactic lessons. The sensitive, receptive teacher makes use of color, tone, rhythm, modulation, passion, texture, and in so doing "seizes" the student. But this seizing is a gentle offering — one that allows students to accept, to surrender—not a frontal attack that threatens, exhorts, and, finally, overwhelms. It does not do things to students "for their own good," for it recognizes that the ultimate good is located in critical and loving autonomy. Students must not be encouraged to choose against themselves. How often do we hear people declare that they are glad that their parents and teachers forced them to do something? They seem to be saying that they are better persons for the bitter lessons, but those of us listening critically may wonder what has been lost, how much better these people might have been if they had been encouraged to choose themselves rather than to accept cumulative, reflected pictures of themselves. Receptivity, then, is vital to both parties. If teachers and parents would maintain and enhance receptivity, they must themselves be receptive. Indeed, receptivity is the key characteristic of human caring; one who cares for another, receives the other.[11] Hence an important function for the teacher's intuition is to intuit the purposes, reasons, and meanings of the student.

Besides the personal ability of teachers to direct their intuitive capacities toward students, there are definite techniques that may be used in encouraging receptivity. One is the structural lesson, in which curriculum maker and teacher collaborate to lay down an outline structure in the minds of students. This kind of lesson is designed to provide an initial structure on which students will attach particular elements until the structure is finally filled out in detail. The structural lesson is especially valuable when the material to be presented is not only crucially important but also new and complicated. It has three parts. In the first segment, the teacher directs the students to "listen and enjoy." They must not take notes and need not try consciously to remember anything in particular. "This is my day to perform," the teacher says, "You just relax and listen." The teacher then goes through a complete presentation. In mathematics, the Mean Value Theorem is an ideal subject for such treatment. In the first segment (one whole class period, usually), the teacher presents motivation, geometric interpretation, and a complete detailed proof with all sorts of helpful added comments. The presentation is rich, elaborate, and comprehensive. Its aim is to lay down an outline structure.

In the second segment (and, of course, the teacher informs students at the outset that there will be three segments), the teacher may say, for example, "Now, we need to write an equation for this secant line, using point-slope form. What shall we write?" This segment attempts to attach details to the outline structure. If the teacher finds that students cannot execute details even when prompted, then the lesson is aborted and appropriate drills are undertaken so that subroutines do not interfere with the understanding of the theorem.

Assuming successful conclusion of segment two, the teacher enters segment three by inviting the students to guide him or her through the proof. Now the students contribute the major moves, and the teacher (with collaboration of students) executes the subroutines. At the conclusion of segment three, students should have a firm grasp on the detailed structure.

Can we afford to spend so much time on one theorem? If it is an important and difficult theorem, we cannot afford to do otherwise. Similarly, in all subject matter, important topics may be introduced in a completely "receptive" fashion; nothing needs to be rushed. This is important, interesting, worthy of our time and attention. It is amazing how much we learn when we "just listen."

Another specific technique to increase receptivity is concatenation. We mentioned earlier that mathematical formulas can often be reproduced, when they have slipped from memory, by a process of concatenation or putting together rather than by a full, rigorous development. In what way is this process "receptive"? In contrast to our first technique, which involves receiving what is out-there (coming from the teacher), this technique involves receiving what is in-here, in the cognitive structures of the student. Recall, here, that the intuition operates on two domains; we now operate on the mind-scape.

Suppose our problem is one mentioned in the previous chapter. We need the "addition formulas" in trigonometry, but we have forgotten their precise form. What *is* the formula for $\sin (A + B)$? There are several ways of going at this, but here is one that is marvelously effective for many students. "Can you remember anything about it?" the teacher asks. Or the student learns to ask, "Can I remember anything about it?" Suppose the student remembers that the formula is one of four—$\sin (A + B)$; $\sin (A - B)$; $\cos (A + B)$; $\cos (A - B)$—

and that the text displays these formulas in a configuration that looks something like figure 6.1.

Figure 6.1

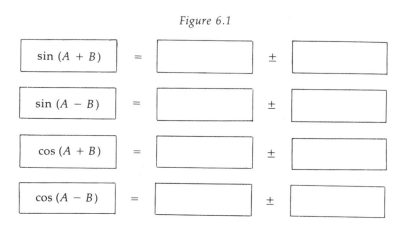

Now, what goes in the boxes, and which signs shall we choose? We have a visual display, but it contains mostly blanks. Suppose we know that the boxes are filled by combinations of sin's and cos's. Thus we might have sin A sin B in one box, sin A cos A in another, cos A cos B in another, cos B sin B in another, and so on. Suppose, drawing on a rhythmic sense, we guess sin A cos B, cos A sin B for the first boxes. (For purposes of shortening the exposition, we are deliberately seizing on the right combination but, in fact, a rhythmic sense often *does* choose this right combination.) Our first guess for filling in the blocks, then, is figure 6.2.

Figure 6.2

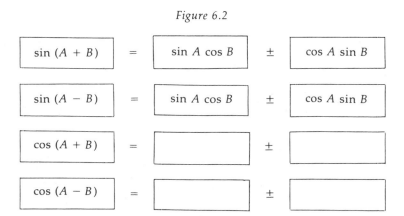

Now, how do I resolve the problem of signs? Perhaps my visual memory contributes an order: $+, -, -, +$. If it does not, I have to guess; and even if it does, I have to check my guess. How can I do this? A sensible thing to do is to try known cases. Suppose I know that $\sin 90° = 1$, $\sin 30° = 1/2$, and $\sin 60° = \sqrt{3/2}$; then I also know that $\cos 30° = \sqrt{3/2}$ and $\cos 60° = 1/2$.

Then $\sin 90° = \sin (30° + 60°) = 1$ and

$$
\begin{aligned}
1 &= (\sin 30° \times \cos 60°) + (\cos 30° \times \sin 60°) \\
&= (1/2 \times 1/2) + \sqrt{3/2} \times \sqrt{3/2} \\
&= 1/4 + 3/4
\end{aligned}
$$

Wonderful! So the appropriate sign is "$+$." The second must be "$-$," and I can check this easily. We can proceed in this fashion filling in the blocks until we have a complete set of formulas. It is obvious that familiarity with the domain is absolutely essential in using this technique, but it reduces brute memory work to a minimum. It calls upon the ability of intuition to see and hear what is stored within, and intuition scans the mindscape as readily as it does the external world.

We give far too little attention to this sort of visual relational thinking, and too often we allow students (and ourselves) to give up on problems that we could solve if we remained receptive to what is already stored within our minds.

ACQUIRING FAMILIARITY

Although intuition sometimes sparkles in new and strange realms, it more often achieves impressive results in familiar domains. We saw, in the last section, how familiarity with basic facts in trigonometry enabled us to reconstruct a set of formulas whose exact statement eluded us. We began by asking: What can I remember? What do I see when these formulas are mentioned? Bit by bit, retrieving visual schemes and scraps of information, experimenting and looking, we produced the formulas by concatenation.

In general, an emphasis on intuition as opposed to one on reason requires that we put understanding at the end—rather than at the beginning—of technical and manipulative procedures. The curriculum makers working on modern mathematics held understanding as their single, greatest goal. They wanted children to comprehend mathematics, to understand its basic structure, and they had faith that students who understood this fundamental structure would be able to carry out any calculations they needed with less (because thoroughly understood) practice. Both goal and faith are lovely but, from the point of view taken here, the faith is entirely misplaced.

Understanding cannot replace rote memory and manipulation entirely, because it is dependent upon them. Understanding is itself an act of intuition. When intuition looks at what reason has accomplished by way of analysis or calculation, it supplies the Will with a holistic and meaningful picture together with the message of certainty: Here is what you've been seeking. And the Will answers: Aha! This means, of course, that there must be objects and operations in the mindscape; there must be things happening. A list of principles, theorems, and proofs that represents explanation is not synonymous with understanding.

While the discussion in the last few paragraphs may be thought to give comfort to the people who are now chanting, "Back to basics," it really does not, at least not unequivocally. Basic skills must serve the purpose of understanding; they must not become ends in themselves. This means two things for curriculum makers and teachers. First, the Will must be engaged; students must participate in the construction of their learning objectives. Understanding, after all, is a response to the Will's quest for meaning. Second, skills, definitions, and simple concepts must be gathered together as precursors to main ideas—not strung endlessly together in a progression that is likely to appear "mindless" to students. Important results must act as organizers for sets of material. A detailed, global presentation induces outline structures; drill and practice produce facility with subroutines; attempts to reconstruct the structure induce further familiarity; and, finally, cooperative reproduction sets the stage for a series of applications. Whenever feasible we make it possible for students to take charge of what they are asked to do. At the first stage, listen and enjoy; at another, practice routines; at still another, look inside and fetch out material for reconstruction. We do *not* put students through exercises with detailed instructions and hope that the end result will be discovery. Students must be seeking something in order to discover, and they must have some responsibility for the connection of means and ends if either the quest or its outcome is to hold meaning.

It is appropriate, now, to discuss particular methods and techniques. One important method that may be used to increase familiarity is induction. Inductive methods were used, of course, in "discovery" lessons, but they were used for the purpose of getting students to "discover" a generalization. The students rarely knew why they were doing the things that texts directed them to do except that some pot of gold supposedly lay at the end of the experimental rainbow. This is *not* what we mean by "induction." Meaningful induction is always preceded by what C. S. Peirce called "abduction"; this is the mysterious process of coming up with a hypothesis that may be tested inductively. If it were not for such hypotheses, "induction" would have no meaning, for successive cases would have the same status as previous cases. A new case means something only if we see it as a case of the events hypothesized. It is not necessary that the students actually perform the abduction, although this may occur in "pure discovery," and for that reason the pure form of discovery has a proper place in curriculum making and teaching for intuitive engagement. But the students must be aware of the hypothesis; they must know what it is they are testing out when they undertake something called the inductive method.

Induction, thought of this way, as a method of trying and looking *is* intuitive in itself, and it tends to increase intuitive powers by increasing the intuiter's familiarity with the given domain. One finds out how things work by trying case after case. Jean Dieudonné remarks:

> I remember having been a student of Polya, who was himself a friend of Hardy. The former always used to say to me that Hardy would recommend to his students who wanted to demonstrate a theorem dependent on a parameter with n dimensions, to do the following: Begin by demonstrating the theorem for n = 1, then for n = 2, n = 3; at this point they would perhaps begin to grasp a little bit of what was going on and to have an idea of the demonstration of a general case. This method is not always successful, but there are some cases where it is valuable.[12] (author's translation)

He affirms, also, our point about familiarity:

> To begin with [I shall make] a statement which is general and completely banal. That is that intuition of a mathematical subject is obtained progressively and is above all a function of familiarity which one has with the subject.[13] (author's translation)

We would not, however, put the case so strongly. Certainly familiarity is not sufficient for intuitive insight nor, as we have seen, is it even necessary. What is necessary, if an intuition is to be communicated intelligibly, is familiarity with the language and notation of the domain. This fact, of course, re-emphasizes the need for carefully organized and patient practice and, more than that, for generous dialogue so that students may become accustomed to the new symbol system. Mathematics instruction is often stingy in this regard, hoarding its wealth to its present owners. By its nature, all of the definitions of mathematics are removable, taking their places in a strict line of convenience from primitive terms and axioms. No extraneous word or symbol can properly penetrate this chain, but the maker of the chain does not necessarily move link by link inexorably and infallibly from start to finish. The human thinker uses metaphorical domains and concrete objects to see what it is that is being constructed and moves to precision and rigor in the full light of *perceptive* reason. The learner especially needs the familiarity induced by metaphor.

This need for visual images, concrete objects, and metaphorical domains is revealed not only in mathematics but in all subjects. We highlighted the need in social studies, recommending the generous and judicious use of visual materials. The need exists in the study of literature, also, but the best literature does a good bit toward providing its own visual images conjured up by words, its own concrete objects, and its own lasting metaphors. Thus literature may be used effectively in all other subjects to enhance familiarity and invite engagement. *Alice in Wonderland, Flatland, Fantasia Mathematica* all have their place in the mathematics classroom.[14]

A consideration of literature in the curriculum suggests another dimension in the problem of acquiring domain familiarity. The literature that we love best we read again and again. We do not read it to say we have "had it" or "been through" it as we have "been through" school or "had" an education. We return to it periodically to gain new insights and unending delight. Lily Briscoe's cry, "Mrs. Ramsay, Mrs. Ramsay!" may stay with us for months after reading *To the Lighthouse,* and in moments of longing for a center of unity and security in our own lives its echo may send us back to read the work again.[15] Yet in school, we pass through everything once as if the point were somehow to get it all behind us and be rid of it. A curriculum that takes intuition seriously must build a considerable redundancy (or what appears on the surface as redundancy), for the inner eye—like the physical eye—delights in familiar scenes colored by the passage of time and the growth of perception.

Even in mathematics, where things are inevitably built one into the other, we fail to incorporate the appropriate amount of repetition in our instruction. We teach the usual multiplication algorithm, for example, in third or fourth grade. Everyone learns how to do the following:

$$\begin{array}{r} 43 \\ \times\ 52 \end{array}$$

Later we teach something called the "distributive property," but we rarely go back to our fourth grade problem and say, "Now let's try a different procedure on this. Instead of starting by saying '2 times 3 equals 6,' let's start at the upper left corner and say, '4 times 2 equals 8' or '4 times 5 equals 20.' Where shall we write the '8' or the '20'?" Then we invite our students to invent their own processes as in the following:

$$\begin{array}{r} 43 \\ \times\ 52 \\ \hline 2000 \\ 80 \\ 150 \\ 6 \\ \hline 2236 \end{array}$$

There are, thus, both backward-looking and forward-looking aspects in the acquisition of familiarity. On the one hand, we must make strange territory familiar in order to find our way about in it; on the other hand, we must occasionally make the familiar strange in order to look upon it with renewed interest and insight.

CREATING REPRESENTATIONS

Intuition is the mental capacity that receives and creates representations. We have seen that "receiving" always contains a central core of creativity inasmuch as the Will is active in its search for meaning; similarly, "creating" is never a pure act of the human creator, since what-is-there plays its substantial part in contributing to the creation. In this section, we shall concentrate on the creation of representations as that activity is undertaken in problem solving.

In the area of mathematical problem solving — solving those traditionally dread-filled things called "word problems" — mathematics educators once thought that the first and most crucial step was "translation." The problem solver, we thought, had to decode the verbal message and then encode it into mathematical language. By this mysterious process, translation, a set of English sentences was transformed into a set of mathematical sentences. Most of us now feel that this version of what goes on in mathematical problem solving is far wide of the mark.[16]

Instead of using a direct process of translation, the problem solver constructs a representation of the problem. When the initial problem is one that can be immediately "typed" by the problem solver, the "typing" is the major component of representation that mediates between words and mathematical symbols. Thus, if I read a problem and see immediately that it is a "time, rate, and distance" problem, I may write directly: $d = rt$. In this sort of limited problem solving, "translation" very nearly captures what I am doing. School word problems are designed to capitalize on this "typing" activity and, insofar as they are limited to this activity, they cannot be considered representative of the full range of problem solving.

If we are novices, or even if we are experts faced with a new and baffling problem, we cannot simply translate. We must ask what sort of objects we are dealing with, what sort of answer we require, what purposes are being served, how the objects are related to each other. In a very real sense, we create a mental space that represents the object space; we denote its boundaries and place objects within it and in relation to each other. We experiment mentally on this space and observe the results of our experimentation. Sometimes we have difficulty placing items in our mental space because we do not understand what the word-object in the word space refers to, and therefore we do not know what sort of object to use as its representation nor how to locate it in relation to other objects. Novice problem solvers are especially handicapped in this respect; they get bogged down in peripheral vocabulary. Expert problem solvers ignore the meanings of unknown nouns, for example, if the operation to be performed on them is perfectly clear. Where the novice will pause to ask, "What *is* a 'widget'?" the expert passes easily over "widgets," "gadgets," "gizmos," "thing-mes," and the like. But, in part, the reason for the expert's casual treatment of vocabulary is embedded in the artificiality of school problem solving. We know the "problem" will yield to a purely mathematical treatment and that we do not have to concern ourselves with empirical reality. In real-world problem solving, however, substitution of one real object for another may be a critically important matter. Hence children who want to know what a "papaya" is before they figure the price of fruit are not behaving unintelligently; they are simply reacting with real-world intelligence instead of the more directly appropriate (and time-saving) school-mathematical intelligence.

Since the creation of representations, both in this technical sense and in our broader intuitive sense, is a nonpublic process, we are in some difficulty *teaching* it. We often create public representations for our students and are appalled by the interpretation they put upon our carefully constructed pictures. But, from the viewpoint we have taken, this unhappy result is entirely predictable. No thing-out-there is in itself a representation for a person other than its creator. Another observer must create his or her own representation of the thing lying behind this "representation." Hence, if the picture we create is useful for the student observer's intuitive capacity, it may facilitate his or her own creation of a representation; if it is not, it merely adds to the hard work of creating an effective representation. Even concrete objects, that is, objects that can be picked up and handled, may add to the complexity of creating a problem space if their use is not self-directed. Used by recipe, they can be as abstract as any written symbols.

Clearly, then, teachers and curriculum makers who take intuition seriously will not suppose that presenting a structure insures that students see a structure; nor will they try too strenuously to reduce everything to bits and pieces so that the structure disappears entirely from view. Rather, they will present overviews from various perspectives, many opportunities to grapple with objects and incidents, and lots of opportunities to create pictures. Students must plan, organize, and argue if they are to participate in the construction of representations. This cannot be done for them. But what is it, you may ask, that we do for them when we present structural lessons of the sort recommended earlier? This is a central, very important point. We do not *present* a structure in such lessons. What we do is to make possible the tracing out of an outline structure by heightening receptivity. This initial presentation, with its complementary receptivity, gives what-is-there a chance to appear. After what-is-there has been received in rich detail, the student must struggle to attach the elements to the appropriate part of the skeleton structure. We still do not assume that the "student has the structure." Finally, in the last phase of the lesson, the student is challenged to bring the structure to the foreground while the details fade into the background.

When we begin units with precise statements of learning objectives, we not only deny the autonomy of students, we also deprive them of the necessary opportunity to create their own structures. We

are not arguing against *helping* students to do this; most of our recommendations are aimed at exactly this — helping to engage and
enhance the intuition. But we are arguing against doing this organizing for them. Whenever we make it possible for students to respond
without really looking at the material, we neglect the intuition and,
as a result, affective connections are not made, and the material is
quickly forgotten. So far, then, we have argued strongly against two
popular modes of curriculum arrangement: the presentation of formal structures (fundamental ideas disembodied from particular objects and events) and the precise behavioral prespecification of what
is to be learned.

Learning is at once easier and harder than those two methods
assume. It is easier in that human beings learn marvelously well
when they are totally engaged with the objects of knowledge. It is
harder in that no one arrangement provided by teacher or curriculum
maker can be guaranteed either to secure engagement or to facilitate
the creation of useful representations. What, then, might we do?

Z. P. Dienes' and E. W. Golding's idea of multiple embodiments
suggests one sound technique.[17] Curriculum makers, in this plan,
ask seriously in how many ways they can capture or "embody" a
given concept or skill. Is there a variety of concrete objects that are
likely to be handled in the way envisioned? Are there stories that will
whet the appetite and suggest things to try? Are there pictures that
illustrate particulars with special vividness? Is there more than one
way to demonstrate the theorem, develop the formula, calculate the
answer? Now, from this last question, we see that multiple embodiments do not necessarily require the use of "manipulables." The
method does require, however, placing before students an array of
possibilities. By teaching in this way we take intuition into account
in at least three ways. First, we appeal to the student's evaluative
sense, which involves looking, judging, expressing a preference;
second, by presenting several possibilities, we increase the likelihood that the student will be able to use some of the objects and
methods in creating his or her own representation; and, third, by
supplying more than one method, we encourage experimentation
and provide a means of checking on the experiments. Further, the
richness of the total presentation increases familiarity with the domain of study.

Another specific recommendation concerns the use of pictures,
schematics, maps, and the like. It is has been our custom in textbook
presentation to follow the usual publishing format and separate illustrations from textual material. This custom is revealed even in special

tables of contents for illustrations, charts, maps, and tables. It is an orderly and efficient procedure for the printer. But it may not be the best arrangement for learners. When illustrative and tabular materials are sharply separated from text, it is easy to skip over them, saying to one's self, "I'll come back later and look at this." Therefore, if the materials play a serious pedagogical role and are not included for mere window dressing, they probably should be incorporated in the text itself in a way that makes their scrutiny unavoidable. Rows and columns of tables might be examined individually and within sentences; pictures and parts of pictures might be presented off-center, again as part of the text; and bits of a larger map might appear on the right side of a page two-thirds of the way down. Such a suggestion may give nightmares to publishers, but curriculum researchers should begin to investigate the effects of such placement in trial materials. The basic idea, of course, is to embed the visual materials in the verbal materials in such a way that they—along with the words —contribute to the creation of representations.

We may also make a specific suggestion concerning instructional arrangements. Even though intuition puts the individual into immediate contact with the object of knowledge, our attention is often directed at objects or perspectives by other people. We can do things, even see things, in the company of supportive others that we cannot yet do or see by ourselves. The psychologist Vygotsky claims that mental operations arise in social relations — that children first do things in intercourse with each other and then internalize these "doings" in mental schemata.[18] If our interest were primarily in the development of logical thinking, we would dwell at some length on this thesis, but, even with an emphasis on intuition rather than reason, we can point out something valuable in Vygotsky's model. The presence of others, their contributions and challenges, tends to stretch existing domains and to add new ones. Hence the individual intuition comes to rove over larger fields. Further, challenges to one's positions force one to look again at the problem space and its objects. This is especially true if the challenge comes from peers. If the challenge comes from a receptive and sensitive teacher, the result may be the same, but often a challenge from the teacher causes the student simply to abandon his own construction of the problem space and do whatever the teacher suggests. Small-group settings in which peer interactions occur should, then, be highly useful instructional arrangements.[19]

We saw earlier that, in becoming familiar with a domain of study, we face two broad problems: We must learn something about the particular objects with which we must work, and we must find out about the domain itself—how things work in it, how objects are named, where they are situated, and so on. Realizing that these two great problems exist, teachers and curriculum makers should try to reduce the two problems to one whenever possible; we should, that is, introduce new objects in familiar structures or trace out new structures using familiar objects. It is surprising how often we fail to do this. Consider, illustratively, how we might teach the addition of fractions.[20] However we approach the general rule for finding common denominators, creating equivalent fractions, and calculating the sum, we should provide generous practice with known mathematical objects. Children are already familiar with the whole numbers as objects, and they also know how to operate on them—how to add, subtract, multiply, and divide them. It therefore makes sense, first, to show how these familiar objects may be renamed, for example:

$$2 = 4/2, 8/4, 14/7 \qquad 5 = 10/2, 20/4, 25/5$$

Second, we show how the new rule for addition of fractions can be applied to these essentially familiar objects. We know:

$$(1) \qquad 5 + 2 = 7$$

Suppose we are asked to add:

$$(2) \qquad 20/4 + 14/7$$

Applying the new rule, we obtain:

$$(3) \qquad \frac{(7 \times 20) + (4 \times 14)}{28} = \frac{140 + 56}{28} = \frac{196}{28} = 7$$

Since we know at the outset that the answer is "7," we have a way of discarding improper techniques if they tempt us and of reassuring ourselves when we have chosen the right rule.

When we use a presentation of the sort just illustrated, we embed familiar structures in new, extended structures, and we rely on our familiarity with well-known objects to help us gain knowledge of new objects. The important new point made here is that our choice of concrete objects can be made from structurally important objects in the domain of study that were themselves once "abstract." We do not always have to return to the ordinary world of tangible objects in order to activate the intuition. We are not arguing against applying what is learned in the real world. Rather, we are arguing against limiting the intuition to the ordinary objects of perception.

Intuitive arrangements must capitalize on the fact that the domains of intuition can be expanded; objects that were once abstract become familiar and can be used as concrete objects. Proceeding in this fashion, we organize subject matter at increasing levels of sophistication, always establishing firmly the structural bridges to known objects and operations. We nest structures successively in each other.

In literature, we need not always refer our discussion to actually known persons and situations; we can refer progressively to the known fictional persons and situations with which we have become familiar. In teaching foreign languages, we need not move always from English to the new language (or vice-versa), but we can start with simple known expressions in the new language and build on them. (In this practical sense, transformational grammar might still be very useful to build linguistic intuition.) In all of these ways, we *use* the structure that we as experts perceive in order to acquaint our students with it; we do not *present* the structure, but we make it easier and more natural for the student to construct it.

DEVELOPING UNDERSTANDING

Understanding is another favorite word among educators. While no one, we suppose, would argue against understanding as a goal of instruction, the term holds considerable difficulty for both theorists and practitioners. Theorists have usually associated understanding with a knowledge of the structure of the disciplines. In this view, someone "understands" the multiplication algorithm for, say, two-digit numbers, if he or she can relate the steps in the algorithm to a system of expanded notation and a sequence of one-digit multiplications. The notion that students should be able to use mathematical structures to show *why* their techniques work is so pervasive that we rarely question it. Yet, clearly, there are many useful levels of understanding that do not require this sort of structural knowledge.

I understand very well, for example, how to drive my car, but I do not know how to repair it, nor need I know this in order to drive safely and comfortably. Another person knows both how to drive and how to repair, but he does not know from a theoretical perspective why the car works or what physical principles are employed in its construction. Nor, again, does he need to know all this in order to understand that a given breakdown is caused by a faulty connection, clogged tube, or worn mechanical part. Similarly, one does not need to understand programming languages in order to use a computer in problem solving; indeed, one need not even understand how to do things with the computer if one has an understanding of the kinds of problems that will yield to computerized methods and access to resources that will employ these methods on one's behalf. Understanding, like explanation and measurement, properly varies in depth and precision with the uses for which we seek it.

We educators, following the ancient Greeks, have been notoriously snobbish in our insistence on theoretical understanding as *the* form of understanding worth pursuit. As a result, we turn students away from our beloved subjects in droves and pride ourselves on ever tighter measures of selectivity. From the perspective we have taken, it is very important to distinguish levels of understanding and to work patiently through stages of increasing familiarity toward fuller understanding at each chosen level.

We have already discussed the connection of understanding and intuition, but we need to analyze that connection closely now. We have insisted that intuition operates in the quest for understanding. In this claim, we are certainly not alone. Michael Polanyi, for example, says of the intuitive acquisition of the solution of a problem:

> Therefore, as it emerges in response to our search for something we believe to be there, discovery, or supposed discovery, will always come to us with the conviction of its being true. It arrives accredited in advance by the heuristic craving which evoked it.[21]

Thus, understanding is not the direct result of a way of teaching or presentation; it cannot be "built-in" to any arrangement of subject matter. It is firmly tied to the dynamic center of the learner; it must be sought after. The mathematician Henri Poincaré discussed the problem of mathematical understanding. In a famous essay, he asks the question that intrigues many of us:

> How does it happen there are people who do not understand mathematics? If mathematics invokes only the rules of logic, such as are accepted by all normal minds; if its evidence is based on principles common to all men, and that none could deny without being mad, how does it come about that so many persons are here refractory?[22]

His discussion leads us to confirm what we have already claimed —that what is learned and understood depends to a large degree on what one seeks, on the meaning that is attached to what is presented and encountered. As he continues his exploration, he locates the heart of mathematical activity and mathematical understanding in what we have been calling the Will—the center of interest, choice, and meaning:

> In fact, what is mathematical creation? It does not consist in making new combinations with mathematical entities already known. Any one could do that, but the combinations so made would be infinite in number and most of them absolutely without interest. To create consists precisely in not making useless combinations and in making those which are useful and which are only a small minority. Invention is discernment, choice.[23]

It is impossible to overemphasize this point in connection with curriculum making and teaching. At every level of possible understanding, it is essential to offer, even to demand, choice. By choosing, selecting, employing, students engage the intuitive functions that will work in their quest for meaning. So the very first level of structure that is involved in understanding is the structure of the student's own goals, purposes, and desires. The student, like the mathematician, must be sustained by periods, even if they are intermittent, of great excitement. Poincaré emphasizes this when he says:

> I shall make a last remark: when above I made certain personal observations, I spoke of a night of excitement when I worked in spite of myself. Such cases are frequent, and it is not necessary that the abnormal cerebral activity be caused by a physical excitant as in that I mentioned. [He had consumed too much coffee and could not sleep.] It seems, in such cases, that one is present at his own unconscious work.[24]

Now, we have been at pains to insist that intuitive activity is highly conscious, not "unconscious." It is unaware of its own workings; in that, we have agreed entirely with Poincaré. But we have spoken of it, primarily, as intense consciousness of the object of knowledge or feeling. What Poincaré discusses at such length is the operation of intuition through the period of "incubation," that period in which consciousness is directed at other things until, suddenly, the thing long sought and temporarily abandoned pops into mind with the conviction of its own rightness. To account for this apparently genuine phenomenon of unconscious intuitive activity, it is useful to return to the Epicurean notion of "anticipations."

At whatever level of understanding we may be working, there

seem to be two fundamental and essential points at which we are aware of our understanding. At the first, we anticipate a result; we see or hear with utter clarity that which we cannot fully explain. Indeed, the initial clarity may give way to vagueness, error, and difficulties of all sorts. But the initial anticipation or intuition serves like a torch in a dark cave to light our way. Efraim Fischbein identifies "intuitive thinking" with the anticipatory stage:

> Let us first refer to the distinction between *anticipatory intuitions* and *affirmatory intuitions*.
>   Anticipatory intuitions have been investigated and described by psychologists in relation to problem solving. . . . The fact to which they refer is that, while striving to solve a problem one suddenly has the feeling that one has grasped the solution even before one can offer any explicit, complete justification for that solution.[25]

With this point of intuitive activity we are already familiar. Our task as educators is to help students maintain the tension between the subjective certainty already felt and the objective uncertainty that must be recognized. The period of incubation that Poincaré describes often follows on the heels of long and frustrating attempts to verify the contents of our anticipatory intuitions. Indeed, we must consider this period as one in which the intuition is "on hold" so to speak, waiting for some automatic, internal scanning mechanism to place before it something of interest. The scanning itself cannot be regarded (at least not in the framework we have established) as intuitive, but it is set into motion by the intuition which sets the problem: Here is what I am looking for. When the thing is tentatively found, intuition looks again, and we find ourselves at the second intuitive point.

This second level of intuition, described by Fischbein as "affirmatory intuition," has received far less attention. Throughout this work, we have called attention to the need for intuition to play over the domain of cognitive constructions so that understanding may be achieved. Fischbein first describes affirmatory intuitions in the traditional sense as grounds for knowledge and calls for psychological research in this area:

> *The fact that there are representations, notions, interpretations, statements, which are accepted directly as intrinsically meaningful while others are not, has not been investigated by psychological research.*[26]
> (Italics in original)

Fischbein is not alone among mathematics educators in wanting to identify and build upon intuitions that are affirmatory in this sense. Morris Kline and Robert Davis have also recommended building upon and toward "educated intuition."[27] Two cautions are warranted here. First, if our description of intuition is accurate, what is intuitive to some thinkers will not be intuitively obvious to others. Second, there are surely times when we want students to challenge both our intuitions and their own. Indeed, some of our culture's greatest advances have come through challenging ideas that seemed intuitively beyond challenge, and some of the methods of mathematics are designed purposely to remove the clarity of intuition so that the foundations of mathematics can be rigorously examined and methodically rebuilt. Bertrand Russell went so far as to say (half humorously): "The fact is that symbolism is useful because it makes things difficult. . . . What we wish to know is, what can be deduced from what."[28]

In an important sense, then, we sometimes wish to make the familiar strange in order to investigate it from a new angle and to circle back on it with new insights. An important message for educators in all this is that we should be wary of building our new curricula and instructional methods in mere reaction to the unsound methods that already exist. When we attempted to discard rote methods in favor of understanding, we failed to examine the meaning of "understanding" with sufficient care. If now, in reaction to the errors of formalism found in the new math, we hastily embrace "intuitive" methods without carefully laying out what we mean by "intuitive," we run the risk of making new mistakes. As we have described it, the "intuitive" does not merely point to what is obvious to common sense nor does it establish by itself an infallible ground for knowledge.

Let us return briefly to Fischbein's discussion of affirmatory intuitions. He makes another point similar to one that we have underscored repeatedly:

> Consequently we submit that the essential function of (intellectual) intuition is to be the homologue of perception at the symbolic level, having the same task as perception: to prepare and to guide action (mental or external).[29]

Here we need to add that, in our view, intuition (both sensory and intellectual) operates both prior to and in conjunction with inner and outer perception to separate those sensory and intellectual details that matter in our program of action from those that do not. Intuition is not exactly like perception either in its ability to give global pictures or visceral evaluations. Rather, at least in its affirmatory or second stage, it culminates in a flash that results from considerable familiarity, long work, and prolonged contemplation. Intuition does not merely "see" by some magical process; it *looks*, and it is this process of looking and the climate in which it best takes place that educators must investigate and establish. Thus affirmatory intuitions are not, for us, collective intuitions but are, rather, marks of successful completion in the personal quest for meaning. With their arrival, we see that what we had anticipated can now be carried to rigorous, public completion and, even more satisfactorily, that what we have done or propose to do by way of public demonstration is fully understood. It is grasped by us with the full clarity of intuitive givenness.

It is clear from all this that we need to consider a much broader range of understanding than we have in the past. The understanding of the expert need not be reproduced nor even approximated in all students of a given subject. We do not all seek that level of understanding. Further, what is offered to students (not what is demanded of them) should be far richer in detail, so that the concrete, idiosyncratic, and complex can all make their impressions upon learners. We need to relearn ways of dwelling on things and in them. To slow down the pace is not necessarily to teach and learn less. Delight, humor, contemplation, and sharing are all properly parts of an education that takes intuition seriously.

This last discussion completes our exploration of intuitive arrangements and presentations so far as the intellect is concerned, but it foreshadows the exploration to be undertaken in the next chapter. The human being, an intuitive being, seeks both to understand and to be understood. To teach well, educators need to feel something for their students; they need at least to have some grasp of what it is their students seek by way of knowledge and understanding, how they (as individuals) best acquire what they need and, more specifically, how they go about creating their representations of reality. It is appropriate, then, that we should turn next to an examination of intuition and love in education.

SUMMARY

In this chapter we have offered a variety of specific suggestions for intuitive arrangements and presentations of subject matter together with rationales for their acceptance and implementation. We discussed ways in which to engage the Will by reducing anxiety, connecting to personal meaning, providing for choice in the construction of objectives and modes of performance. We looked at ways to increase or maintain receptivity through drama, delight, and dissonance. We described structural lessons in some detail, as well as examining various "inductive" methods and the importance of redundancy in gaining familiarity with various subject domains.

We discussed the creation of representations, and here we emphasized the importance of allowing students to plan, organize, and discuss their own programs of action. We also recommended the use of multiple embodiments, embedded pictures, metaphor, new levels of the concrete created from former abstractions, elaboration, and nested symbolic structures.

Finally, we looked at the role of educators in planning for understanding, and this discussion gave us an opportunity to circle back on some earlier arguments and to strengthen them. At the same time, we argued for a careful examination of what we mean by "understanding" and for an enlarged conception of it in our practices. We closed by foreshadowing the coming exploration of intuition and love.

Chapter 7

INTUITION, LOVE, AND EDUCATION

> Ethical friendship on the other hand is not formed on specific
> terms; a gift or any other good is bestowed as to a friend.
> Aristotle, *Nichomachean Ethics*

WHAT IS LOVE?

THIS CHAPTER DEALS with the interrelationship of intuition
and love, and with the importance of these two forces for education.
And just as we have tried to define *intuition*, we must offer a fairly
precise definition of what we mean by the word *love*. This is a far
more difficult task than it might at first appear, for virtually no word
in our language has been abused as much as *love*, and few words
make contemporary psychologists and philosophers as uneasy.
Nevertheless, human love is inextricably bound up in both the use of
intuition and the act of teaching, and, despite the frequent reluctance
of educators to appreciate its importance, plays a critical role in
bringing intuition and education together.[1]

What is love? A striptease marquee announces "Live Love Act
On Stage"; a middle-aged businessman asserts that he loves to go
fishing; lovers vow their love to one another; while religious leaders
call upon nations to cease fighting and love one another, or to fight to
the death because of the beliefs they love. The word *love* is called
upon in each case to signify something different, and the result is a
cacophony of confusing and contradictory meanings that often
stymies serious discussion of love. In large part, this confusion is due
to the vagueness of the English language, which provides only one
word for these widely varying experiences and feelings. This ambiguity is also found in other modern languages in which

philosophers have written on the subject of love. Not surprisingly, the language of the ancient Greeks made a number of important distinctions among the different types of love that can help us gain a clearer understanding of what we mean by the term. Three Greek words for love—*eros, agape,* and *philia*—provide particular insights into the types of love that interact with intuition.

The first word, *eros,* is familiar to readers today but is often imperfectly understood. To many individuals, *eros* specifically implies the sexual drive and nothing else. To the ancient Greeks, however, *eros* included a far wider range of concerns; in fact, interest in the entire physical, sensual, living world was embodied in the idea of *eros.* The closest expression existing in English is the somewhat trite phrase "love of life," which does not convey all the aesthetically rich and physically stimulating possibilities of *eros.* The Greeks did not characteristically separate sexual experiences and feelings from other physical ones as we do today, so that appreciation of a beautiful sunset, an athlete's body in motion, a sexual experience, or merely the sense of being glad to be alive all came within the scope of *eros.* Furthermore, the original notion of *eros* is an important part of the love that is present in the acts of teaching and learning.

As Rollo May noted, for Plato *eros* embraced all these concepts and more:

> Eros is the drive which impels man not only toward union with another person, in sexual or other forms of love but incites in man the yearning for knowledge and drives him passionately to seek union with the truth. Through eros, we not only become poets and inventors but also achieve ethical goodness. Love, in the form of eros, is the power which generates, and this generation is "a kind of eternity and immortality"—which is to say that such creativity is as close as men ever get to becoming immortal.[2]

Such claims are not poetic flights of fancy. They represent the fusion of some of humankind's most urgent concerns into a cohesive whole. This need to seek union with the truth or to have an intuitive encounter with knowledge is of utmost importance to the examination of motivations behind teaching and learning, and is a subject we shall return to later in the chapter.

Agape is well known as the form of love that Christians are commanded to feel for one another and is the term for the early love feasts of the primitive Church. It is the word translated in the King James Bible as *charity* in the beautiful thirteenth chapter of Paul's First Epistle to the Corinthians and elsewhere in the New Testament.[3] The *agape* described by Paul is a selfless brotherly love that is commanded by God, reflecting the love God feels for all humans and devoid of any physical, and most especially, sexual overtones. But, as in the case of *eros*, the popular conception of the word *agape* neither conveys all of its meaning, nor provides us with all the information we need to determine how intuition, love, and education connect. *Agape* existed as a word and as a concept before the advent of Christianity and before Christianity linked it to divine love and, most significantly, to the divine commandment to love one another. In its earlier form, *agape* meant simply an unselfish, caring feeling of one individual for another, irrespective of sex, age, or other differences. It is from this meaning of *agape* that we will draw to develop our definition of love in an educational setting.

The last of the three Greek concepts of love which we shall examine is *philia*, which is also the broadest of the three concepts. *Philia* is related to the word *philos*, meaning friend, and is closely tied to the ideas of friendship, brotherhood, and comradeship. *Philia* is also the suffix attached to many other roots to indicate a love for something or someone, as in *ailurophilia*, or love of cats. Here the key ideas for the educator are *philia* in the sense of comradeship, or even partnership, and *philia* in the sense of loving or being passionately interested in a subject or field of study. Another educationally significant interpretation for *philia* refers to a natural force uniting discordant elements and movements. Isocrates envisioned *philia* as the drawing together of seemingly incompatible substances to create a new entity.[4] This image provides an excellent metaphor for the contact and exchange between teacher and student that can occur when intuition and love are both openly acknowledged and valued. As we shall see, love of subject matter and love of student are important parts of the total experience of love in education and are foci for intuition on the part of both student and teacher.

EDUCATIONAL CARITAS

We have now presented three major Greek ideas that may be included in the exercise of love in education, yet we still need to be more precise about what we mean by love in education or, as we might call this experience, educational caritas.[5] Such specificity is important not only because of the need to draw together the distinct and diverse philosophical notions we are drawing on, but also because of the skepticism with which many educators and social scientists view any discussion of love. P. A. Sorokin has written:

> The sensate minds, our minds, disbelieve the power of love. It appears to us illusionary—we call it self-deception, the opiate of a people's mind, idealistic thoughts and unscientific illusion. We are biased against all theories that try to prove the power of love in other positive forces in determining human behavior and personality, in influencing the course of biological, social, moral, and mental evolution, in affecting the direction of historical events, in shaping social institutions and cultures.[6]

Our position is in distinct opposition to such a denial of love's existence, and we instead assert that love in education, or educational caritas, is something very real. It is a force that can be the most powerful agent in the classroom, leave the most lasting impressions, and touch lives most deeply.

It is now time that we stated clearly what we mean by educational caritas. First, it is a desire to come into direct, undiluted contact with the human partner of the educational enterprise, to go beyond superficialities and become involved with the other person. Notice that we emphasize "desire"; this desire may not be fulfilled as external circumstances intervene, yet the desire is the evidence of love, not elusive material results. Educational caritas may also involve a deep interest and even passionate commitment to the subject matter being taught. It is difficult to imagine a successful, mutually rewarding course in calculus, music, or American government being taught by a teacher who has little enthusiasm for or insight into the subject. Furthermore, without enthusiasm for the subject being studied, learning is clearly more difficult. Engagement with a subject brought on by love also can lead to the sort of intuitive insights and experiences we have already discussed. Of course, this enthusiasm for a subject, if it blinds the teacher to the students' capabilities, interests, and level of engagement, can be destructive. Subject and student must be linked inseparably in the act of teaching.

Linked to this passion for the material being taught, but probably more important, is love of the acts of teaching and learning. From this source comes much of the energy and excitement needed to sustain student and teacher through the stultifying routines found in so many schools. The love of teaching, furthermore, must be complemented by a love of learning and an awareness that it is not simply the teacher who teaches and the student who learns; sometimes the roles are reversed, and frequently learning and teaching occur simultaneously and mutually. Often this aspect of educational caritas is described as "learning for its own sake" or "teaching just for the pleasure of teaching," but this is only a partial explanation, for teaching and learning are in reality manifestations of the same drive to explore, discover, and share, a drive that is at the very center of the interaction of love and education. A little later on we shall say more about these aspects of love as they relate specifically to teaching today.

There is one other facet of educational caritas that deserves mention, although by nature it eludes easy definition. It is a sense of rightness and of appropriateness, what might even be called a sense of mission or a "calling" that teachers have often felt through the ages. Some individuals sense intuitively (and we use the word here deliberately in the way it was meant in the preceding chapters) that they can be effective, inspiring teachers; they have known that working with children or adults would be rewarding and meaningful, that teaching was "for them." Admittedly many teachers do not maintain this sense of *philia* for teaching throughout their entire careers, and for many the experience occurs only infrequently. In fact, it may be unrealistic to expect more than a small minority of teachers today to maintain *philia*. Yet this sense of being drawn to, and linking with, the role of teacher ("didascophilia," as the Greeks might have called it) is a significant part of the reason that it is so often more than simply a job, but is an exhilarating, if challenging, experience.

Many of the points made in this discussion are so well known to anyone who teaches that they may seem unnecessary or even trite. Nevertheless, both the facts of the affective aspect of education and their interrelatedness need to be made clear in order to set the stage for our discussion of intuition and love in education. These facts, once stated openly, also provide a basic frame of reference in which to place our investigation of several educational settings and philosophies that make use of both intuition and love.

Let us now look at several philosophical systems that have recognized the importance of love and intuition in education.

ZEN BUDDHISM

Zen is fundamentally intuitive and nonrational. That is, the knowledge one acquires does not derive from syllogistic reasoning, is frequently free of any symbolic interpretation, and indeed often cannot be expressed at all in words. This knowledge or enlightenment is arrived at spontaneously, although long periods of preparation may precede it. A sudden remark or action of a Zen master can reveal to the neophyte the truth he has been seeking. In Zen writings numerous short exchanges, called koans, exist that illustrate (or at least point toward) what happens when enlightenment takes place. Here is a characteristic koan:

> A master was asked the question, "What is the Way?" by a curious monk.
> "It is right before your eyes," said the master.
> "Why do I not see it for myself?"
> "Because you are thinking of yourself."
> "What about you: do you see it?"
> "So long as you see double, saying 'I don't,' and 'you do,' and so on, your eyes are clouded," said the master.
> "When there is neither 'I' nor 'You,' can one see it?"
> "When there is neither 'I' nor 'You,' who is the one who wants to see it?"[7]

In this koan are several important clues revealing the importance of intuition to Zen. First, notice that the metaphor for understanding the Way (Tao) is *seeing*, paralleling *intuition, Anschauung,* and many other terms relating to intuition. When the Way is finally comprehended, the Universe is seen clearly and without distortion or illusion. One of the key words in the teaching of Zen is the Chinese word *chien-hsing*, meaning "to look into the nature [of the mind]." The character *chien* consists of an eye alone on two outstretched legs and signifies the pure act of seeing.[8] Thus the idea of seeing clearly, without hindrance, is imbedded deeply in the teaching of Zen. This seeing goes beyond mere observing, as the koan implies, for it really means a fusion of seer, object seen, and observer (teacher), and, most importantly, master and student. The distinction between such frequently opposing entities as student and teacher, human beings and nature, and the positions of two arguing debaters dissolves in the realization of a greater truth, in much the same way as Plotinus conceived of intuitive insight. This fusing of seemingly incompatible entities, like the Greek meaning of *philia* mentioned above, is a concept Western educators should not dismiss lightly. Intuitive connections between experiences of teachers and students, between underlying concepts and principles of different disciplines, and the potential for a shared educational experience among teachers, students, and others are all of great importance, and are areas where the unique, penetrating perspective of Zen can provide clarification and inspiration.

Zen Buddhist training is also concerned with love in a number of the ways we have sought to define it, although this may not be readily apparent to someone approaching Zen for the first time. Zen masters described in koans appear brusque or even cruel to students. Hiju Yesho, a famed Zen master, was once asked by a student, "What is Buddha?"

> Yesho answered: "The cat is climbing up the post."
> The monk confessed his inability to understand the master.
> The latter said, "You ask the post."[9]

Leo Buscaglia, in *Living, Loving, and Learning,* relates another even more dramatic example of what might to the uninitiated seem like impatience or even hostility. While walking through a Japanese garden with a Zen master, Buscaglia had been talking rapidly about the many supposedly important things that he knew. Suddenly the Zen master turned and struck Buscaglia on the mouth. When Buscaglia asked why, the master replied, "Don't walk in my head with your dirty feet!"[10] What seems to us to be at once an obscure yet dramatic method of communicating is the way Zen masters reveal their commitment and concern for both their philosophy and for their disciples. The individual enlightenment of the student and the wisdom of the master are to be treasured and under no circumstances sullied by trivia. If they are, a normally gentle Zen master may suddenly become physical. Of course, we do not advocate striking students when they do not do what we want them to do, but the concern and decisiveness that Zen exhibits, albeit in a radically different cultural and pedagogical setting, provide a clue to how educational caritas can become an important part of teaching and learning.

Before we close this brief glimpse into Zen, let us look at other ways in which caring and love are woven into this philosophy. One of the most conspicuous examples occurs in Zen's relationship to nature. Unlike the Western tradition, which pits man against natural forces, Zen sees no conflict between the two, but instead emphasizes unity, harmony, and friendship (*philia*), and does not acknowledge a sharp distinction where an individual leaves off and the outside world begins. D. T. Suzuki has expressed this aspect of Zen clearly:

> While separating himself from Nature, Man is still a part of Nature,
> for the fact of separation itself shows that Man is dependent on

Nature. We can therefore say this: Nature produced Man out of itself; Man cannot be outside of Nature, he still has his being rooted in Nature. Therefore there cannot be any hostility between them. On the contrary, there must always be a friendly understanding between Man and Nature. Man came from Nature in order to see Nature in himself; that is, Nature came to itself in order to see itself in Man.[11]

Here is the harmony, reciprocity and unity in Zen's worldview presented in a way easily comprehensible to Westerners. Similarly, Zen attitudes toward creativity can be grasped without great difficulty, and two forms of expression directly influenced by Zen, the haiku and sumiye, are already familiar to many in this country. The haiku, a short poem with a limited number of syllables and the potential for powerful, evocative imagery, is so well known to teachers that we do not need to discuss its form here. The sumiye, however, deserves brief mention as a fine example of Zen's concern with aesthetics and communication. Sumiye painting or, more accurately, ink sketching, uses paper that is so light that no corrections, erasing, or even lingering with the brush are possible. The drawing must be executed rapidly, without rational deliberation about perspective, shading, and so on, and it must reflect the artist's spontaneous intuition. The viewer must, then, intuit the inner "spirit" of the drawing and seek to understand the artist's vision. Unlike much traditional Western art, which sought to reproduce a particular moment in the physical world, sumiye conveys the artist's own imagined landscape, tree, or bird to the viewer, and thereby introduces the viewer to something never seen before, but something filled with meaning and affective content. Sumiye painting is in fact a fine metaphor for Zen Buddhism's approach to life and learning itself: recognizing individuals, yet holistic; seemingly obscure or eccentric, yet conveying profound messages about enlightenment and life.

PESTALOZZI'S PEDAGOGY OF LOVE

In chapter 1 we saw that Johann Pestalozzi's educational ideas put considerable emphasis on intuition in the derivation of meaning from observation. Pestalozzi also recognized love as an important force in the education and development of the child, not as an added frill or sentimental triviality, but as a central concern of educators. In 1805 he wrote:

Amongst human emotions it is the feeling of love in the child which clearly expresses this ideal [of man's inner sanctity]. Love therefore is the central force to which all other emotions must be in due subordination if harmony with the ideal is to be preserved. Again, in the same way, intellectual activity, inasmuch as it springs up side by side with love, is the central force which clearly expresses the ideal in human action.[12]

Pestalozzi, then, saw love as the motivating force behind what he considered the best human actions. The child's discovery of and respect for his own potential to love forms a major part of his maturing, and teachers must see to it that education does not hamper this development. Indeed, for Pestalozzi they must do more than this: They must provide a program of moral and religious education that will encourage the development of the child's better self. He believed that parents, particularly the child's mother, play an important role in developing the child's faith in God and his desire to act fairly. The end result of such experiences will be an adult who respects himself and others, believes in God, and is a content and happy human being.[13]

There are several differences between the role of love in education as Pestalozzi conceived of it and the way Zen approaches the same subject. First, Pestalozzi wrote in an extremely straightforward, even blunt fashion about love, whereas the importance of love to Zen, like so many issues in that philosophy, is only hinted at indirectly. Again, Pestalozzi built his argument for love on a belief in a Christian God, while Zen does not claim the existence of an anthropomorphic deity.[14] The similarities between Pestalozzi's position and that of Zen with regard to education, however, are significant and worth emphasizing. Both systems stress the importance of personal discovery and growth and the need to be in harmony with a greater whole. Both recognize that these goals cannot be accomplished merely through logical thought processes but require the interaction of human beings and introspection, sometimes over long periods of time. We should also notice that both approaches to learning take a basically positive attitude toward human potential and change, and neither one advocates intolerance or a hierarchical view of humanity.

Pestalozzi was not simply an educational theorist; he practiced what he preached. His school at Yverdon stood in dramatic contrast to other schools in early nineteenth-century Europe, where beatings, endless recitations, and harsh teachers were common. At Pestalozzi's school, children were treated with respect and kindness, given tasks equal to their abilities, and above all taught by word and by example that love in its most generous, altruistic form is important. So pervasive and so genuine was the emphasis on love as an educating force that when a peasant came to visit the school at Yverdon, he exclaimed, "This is not a school, it is a household." Although Pestalozzi's school fell into decline and eventually closed during his own lifetime, his message to educators to fill their teaching and living with love was not forgotten and remains one of his most important legacies.

Pestalozzi tried to combine the roles of benevolent parent, gentle schoolmaster, and perhaps even that of village pastor, a task few modern teachers would be willing or able to undertake.[15] His success in creating an environment fostering both intuition and love must therefore be credited in part to his ability to exercise such a wide-ranging influence on his students in much the same way A. S. Neill did at Summerhill. By contrast, teachers today must operate under significant time constraints that reduce markedly their influence on students. Later in this chapter we shall take another look at this major obstacle in the fostering of intuition and love.

MARTIN BUBER AND *I AND THOU*

Among the many philosophers and theologians of the twentieth century who have been concerned with caring and love, Martin Buber is perhaps the most influential. His essay *I and Thou*, which has had a great impact on both the general public and on Christian theologians, is now regarded as one of the most important statements on interpersonal relations of our time. Buber characterizes the evolution of interpersonal relations as a progression from the *I–It* relation, in which an individual does not really experience the existence of the other, to the *I–Thou* relation, which is filled with richer and deeper significance. In explaining the nature of the *I–Thou* relation, Buber writes:

> Relation is mutual. My *Thou* affects me, as I affect it. We are molded by our pupils and built up by our works. The "bad" man, lightly touched by the holy primary word, becomes one who reveals. How we are educated by children and animals! We live our lives inscrutably within the streaming mutual life of the universal.[16]

In the *I–Thou* relation, Buber believes, we are drawn into a new sort of existence, one filled with infinite possibilities for wonder, mystery, and closeness to God. The precise terminology, liturgy, or symbolism through which a person comes to recognize and participate in this relation are far less important than the act of participation itself.

> Spirit in its human manifestation is a response of man to his *Thou*. Man speaks with many tongues, tongues of language, of art, of action; but the spirit is one, the response to the *Thou* which appears and addresses him, out of the mystery.[17]

In an approach that is markedly different from that of Zen, Buber seeks to show the possibility of two individuals drawing close and sharing without words or symbols, in fact sharing in silence. This type of experience is not unlike the sense of wholeness and unity sought after by followers of Zen, and reminds us of the writings of Plotinus discussed in chapter 1.

Buber's vision of the *I–Thou* relation is of an intuitive experience. It is also inseparably linked to notions of caring and love, and complements many of Pestalozzi's views on education. While not condemning the use of reason to solve problems, Buber places great value on feelings, telling us that they bring us messages we cannot receive in any other fashion. "Feelings are 'within'," he says, "where life is lived and man recovers from institutions. Here the spectrum of the emotions dances before the interested glance."[18] This "inner" set of messages contains many of the revelations about ourselves and our relations to others that guide us in making important choices. Ultimately, the foundation of Buber's *I–Thou* relation, like the educational values of Pestalozzi that stressed caring, rests on a belief in God. This God is not specifically described as either the God of Judaic mysticism or the God of Christianity, but in more general terms as the real entity behind each *Thou* that we address. In Buber's words, "Every particular *Thou* is a glimpse through to the eternal Thou."[19] Our search to experience other human beings is really the same as our search for God, although God is not to be confused with other, collective, *Thous*. Furthermore, God's presence is everywhere, thus making true the Delphic response, *Vocatus atque non vocatus deus aderit*—" called or uncalled, God will still be present." By fusing the quest for human contact with the search for God, Buber brought together two of the major issues of modern man in a manner that was highly intuitive and at the same time emphasized the growing, evolving aspect of humanity that is so crucial to education.

Buber's concerns are more all-embracing than those of others who have written about intuition and love in an educational setting, but, however, contain religious emphases that may be inappropriate for the public-school classroom. Nevertheless, the basic message of Buber's book is still of great value to all concerned with the development and interplay of love and intuition; that is, the individual with whom we interact, whom we teach, or whom we care about, must be viewed and experienced directly, without the mediating and diluting influence of words or symbols that turn the *Thou* into an *It*. In the frequently overcrowded and occasionally impersonal setting of the modern school, the distinction between an *I–It* and an *I–Thou* relation is worth remembering, and an *I–Thou* relationship is worth cherishing.

INTUITION AND LOVE INTERACTING

Intuition and love interact in three specific ways in a learning setting: the sense of caring and intuitive sensitivity between teacher and student, the love and intuitive "feel" for a subject area that may be felt by both teacher and students, and love for the act of learning or teaching. We shall take a look at each of these in turn, seeing how they relate to the ideas concerning intuition which we have already explored.

LOVE BETWEEN STUDENT AND TEACHER

Love between student and teacher has been commented upon and praised by many commentators concerned with education, beginning with the ancient Greeks.[20] This sense of love seems to have been forgotten during some historical periods, such as during the seventeenth and eighteenth centuries when canings and other forms of brutality were the norm. In the twentieth century, first the exponents of the Progressive movement and then other educators began to emphasize more humane, sensitive treatment of children, and today the ideal teacher is a caring, involved instructor, prepared to become personally involved with students. Of course, the reality often falls short of the avowed ideal, energy flags, and the entire teaching/learning experience lapses into simply a repetitive exercise. There is no easy solution to this difficulty, and indeed it is not one problem but a multitude of issues varying in importance and configuration depending upon the individual case. However, we shall make some general observations about the sustaining of educational caritas in the midst of the stressful job of teaching and about the relation of caritas to intuition in the hope that they will shed some light on an area that thus far has been little explored.

When either teacher or student "opens up" to the possibility of engaging the other as a *Thou*, while at the same time recognizing and respecting the intuitive impressions he or she is receiving from people and the surrounding environment, teaching or learning can become easier. Selecting the best response, assessing what the other person really needs or wants, recognizing appropriate limits of conduct—all these processes draw upon intuition as well as analytical reasoning, an intuition of which the educator is aware and that he or she values. In particular, the teacher should strive to discover what it is that the student in fact wishes to learn. The student's interests may coincide with the program that the teacher has in mind, they may seem to lie utterly outside what the curriculum has to offer, or they can touch the themes of the course only peripherally. The teacher's intuitive regrouping of concepts and facts can often bring a union of the student's concerns and the themes of the course that will enhance both. Beyond this always lies the potential for the student's interests and concerns to enlarge the teacher's conception of the subject being taught and even of the mission of teaching itself. This enlightenment is itself a kind of intuitive breakthrough, one which can enrich the experience of teaching and give the teacher strength and motivation to continue participating in the lives of students. We must stress that we are not advocating merely a child-centered curriculum, although aspects of such a curriculum may apply. The teacher does not have to sacrifice all leadership or dismantle preestablished curricula. Students' interests and concerns can be introduced as a factor in the curriculum equation without doing violence to ordained subjects and procedures.

LOVE OF SUBJECT

With this introduction, let us now turn specifically to love of subject, something that either students or teachers can feel. An interest in or even a love for a particular subject, such as geography or mathematics, should not be equated with ability in the subject, although these characteristics may often occur together. Indeed, on occasion a child may remain voluntarily preoccupied with a task or concept that he or she has great difficulty mastering. This type of preoccupation, however, may not reflect an interest in a particular subject as much as it may be a token of another conflict or concern in the child's life. In this situation, as in many others, the teacher's sensitivity and concern can combine with intuitive impressions of the child's needs to help the teacher devise a strategy to aid the child in getting more satisfaction for the efforts made. This type of preoccupation, however, is by no means the only area where intuition and love of subject matter are both active. Consider the case of a student who exhibits a fascination for old coins. The reasons for the development of such an interest are possibly complex and obscure. Perhaps her parents or older siblings are amateur numismatists, or by chance she found an old coin in her grandparents' attic. However triggered, her curiosity is now awakened, and she comes to her fifth grade teacher full of questions about Indian-head pennies and buffalo nickels. Here is a case where the student's interest would not necessarily have to be channeled into the mainstream subjects the class was studying; the interest in coins (or dinosaurs, or flying, or whatever) should be left to develop as much as time and other classroom constraints allow, since the girl will undoubtedly gain from the learning experience. Naturally, there are many possible complicating factors: the teacher may not be able to answer any of the girl's questions, or the school's library may not have enough material to carry this student's inquiry forward. Whether a particular teacher chooses to invest time and effort in order to learn more about a particular subject is less important than the message the teacher sends to the student about the subject's interest. One hopes this message will be supportive and encouraging, telling the youngster that it is good to want to learn more about a topic, that a deep interest in an area, whether it is taught as a school subject or pursued outside of class, is a worthy form of engagement. Emotionally healthy children are by nature inquisitive, imaginative, and creative; and left to their own devices, they will experiment and explore on their own. George Leonard put it well:

> What we fail to acknowledge is that every child starts out as an Archimedes, a Handel, a Nietzsche. The eight-month-old who succeeds in balancing one block on another has made a connection no less momentous than Nietzsche's. He cannot verbalize it so eloquently and probably would not bother to if he could, for such moments are not so rare for him as they are for Nietzsche.[21]

In acknowledging the creative potential of a child, we are also recognizing the ability of the youngster to *intuit* concepts, relationships and solutions. This endorsement of a child's nonrational potential to explore and discover also offers an alternative to the stultifying ritual of classes and sends a message to students that their own discoveries and thoughts are important. Too often children receive instead other messages suggesting that school subjects are boring and not worth taking an interest in, while extracurricular interests are "fun" but likely to meet with little endorsement from parents or teachers.[22]

The communication of love of subject matter moves in another direction as well: from the teacher who is passionately drawn to a field to his or her students. In order for this communication to happen, several things must be present: a fascination with the particular subject, an intuitive sense of some (but not necessarily all) of its relationships and concepts, a desire to give this knowledge to others, and the ability to communicate effectively and engagingly. Intuition figures importantly in each of these factors, for the teacher needs to draw upon instantaneous impressions of students' interests and aptitudes, the atmosphere of the classroom on any given day, and many other factors that cannot be analyzed rationally in the fluid, dynamic setting of the schoolroom. Intuition needs to be cultivated and trusted as the teacher decides how, when, and in what amount information about the subject should be communicated. But we must keep in mind that not only factual information but *love* of the subject area can be communicated, and for the latter we have no simple procedures, no foolproof strategies. The most specific statement we can make is that a caring teacher who is genuinely excited about a subject or approach will convey this excitement to some of the students—possibly only one or two. A little later we shall discuss problems centered on this seeming lack of success in communication.

LOVE OF TEACHING AND LEARNING

Finally, there is the love of the acts of teaching and learning, a love that is at the center of the entire educational enterprise. Without a love of teaching in the broadest sense, teachers can do little that is useful, and students who have lost the desire to learn will gain few benefits from any form of instruction. Yet conventional instruction all too often blunts the desire to learn and drains enthusiasm from the instructor. Learning and discovering, despite the best intentions of the architects of many educational systems, have been made difficult, almost impossible. As Albert Einstein, a noted failure of public schools, remarked: "It is in fact nothing short of a miracle that the modern methods of instruction have not entirely strangled the holy curiosity of inquiry."[23]

Children begin their lives curious, full of a delight in finding out, in reorganizing, in taking apart, and, significantly, in showing others what they have found and learned. In these characteristics lie the seeds of a sustained passion for inquiry and a desire to share and communicate what is learned. Neither trait needs to be "created" or "kindled" in the classroom so much as it needs to be kept alive and encouraged. Teachers know this is not easy. By the time the students reach their classes, the youngsters' initiative, curiosity, and love of learning may already be suffering from the disparagement and discouragement offered them by insensitive parents and educators and by unresponsive institutions. Teachers demanding the correct answer the first time and "learning" situations stressing speed and precision repress the natural tendency of children to use their intuition. As Jerome Bruner has noted, guessing is frequently penalized and associated with laziness.[24]

The enlightened teacher must struggle against such obstacles, drawing upon a love of teaching broad and tolerant enough to revel in even the naive mistakes and enthusiastic, if hasty, conclusions of students. The teaching that is the object of this love and identification is a most demanding sort of exercise, not always attainable, not always successful, and certainly exhausting at times. More properly, this act should be called teaching/learning, for the two activities are inseparable. No one truly committed to helping others discover the universe can help but learn about the subject, about himself, and about how other people organize their reality. As all primary teachers know, new perspectives and ways of looking at the world are the constant bonuses that come from working with young children. With toleration, patience, a sense of humor, and transparent enthusiasm for the process of discovery and learning, teachers can find sparks of curiosity and courage among older students, and even among adults. For many teachers, such encounters with intuitive students provide the motivation to remain in teaching and the inspiration to continue to feel such enthusiasm for the act of teaching/learning.

OBSTACLES TO LOVE

Being a caring teacher is a difficult job. The suggestions we have made are to teachers working in a real world filled with unsympathetic bureaucracies and administrators, huge social problems in surrounding communities, apathetic youngsters, and a host of other obstacles that make the fostering of intuition a task that often seems impossible. Lest we seem to be writing to educators of a never-never land where such issues do not exist, we must try to address the concerns of real teachers facing great difficulties in an underpaid and underrecognized profession. We do not pretend to have all, or even most, of the answers, but we will try at least to identify and shed light on the problems inherent in openly introducing the notions of intuition and love into the curriculum.

By nature the administration of large organizations is oriented toward stability, continuity, and predictability. Larry Cuban, among others, has shown that despite the efforts of many reformers and pressure groups over a hundred-year period, the curriculum of American public schools shows an amazing degree of continuity.[25] Educational bureaucracies, then, are unlikely to be excited about a new curricular and instructional emphasis on such elusive, nonquantifiable entities as love and intuition. Teachers may receive subtle (or not so subtle) messages from superiors advising them to concentrate on materials and procedures that are included on the state's minimum competency tests. More conservative colleagues, threatened by nontraditional approaches to learning and the values these approaches imply, are likely to apply pressure to the novice who treats students in a different way. Taken together, these forces constitute the powerful pull of inertia, a centripetal trend toward uniformity that is the hallmark of our educational system. They are also great inhibitors of love and intuition in the classroom.

A teacher must decide how to deal with these pressures, beginning with the decision of just how committed he or she is to intuition and to love. If the commitment and belief are not there, then the teacher will probably do better to keep to more traditional practices than to embark on a halfhearted crusade. If, however, a teacher feels that intuition is something children deserve to discover and that love is an important part of the process by which this discovery is made, then careful planning is in order. Fortunately, the classroom teacher still retains considerable autonomy "after the classroom door closes," and, despite the encroachment of competency-based tests, teacher-proof materials, and other factors, he or she can control to a large extent what happens each day in the classroom. If administrators or colleagues are hostile or skeptical, the intuition-enhanced curriculum can be introduced quietly. Be honest with your students; let them know that you are advocating ways of approaching and feeling about learning that are different from what they have probably encountered before. If they seem doubtful, explain how so many of the most important and exciting developments in virtually every field have been the result, not of by-the-book approaches, but of intuitive interpretations, "guesses," imaginative regroupings of ideas or data, and spontaneous insights into function and meaning. Energy and sincerity are essential, for if the teacher has not won over at least a portion of the classroom before the intuitive approaches to subject matter discussed in chapter 6 are introduced, he or she will find most students unwilling to leave behind their familiar ways of dealing with schoolwork.

This brings us back to the subject of love, the tricky but extremely important element of the equation that is the theme of this chapter. Love of teaching, what we might call "pedagogical *eros*" is not a giddy, overly optimistic, Pollyanna attitude toward the task of teaching that breaks down when the first real pressure is applied. It is not an emotion founded on the expectation that major positive changes will come quickly or easily, that problem students will suddenly change character, that the tedious or demanding aspects of a teacher's life will be miraculously transformed. Love of students, subject, and teaching/learning does invoke belief, but it is belief in one's own ability to find solutions to new problems, belief that one will encounter students whose lives will be touched and whose lives will affect ours. All the forms of love mentioned here, but most especially pedagogical *eros*, contain this kind of inner reserve of hope that makes satisfying teaching possible. If calling this commitment and involvement "love" seems overdramatic, consider the definition of love offered at the beginning of this chapter: a desire to draw close, a deep concern akin to what Paul Tillich called an "ultimate concern," [26] comradeship, and a strong sense of caring. Love in the classroom is neither naive expectation nor stoic resignation, but a commitment to the whole experience of learning and teaching. It is also an eagerness to use intuitive feelings to guide students and ourselves, and a strength to endure inevitable setbacks and disappointments.

WHEN LOVE SEEMS TO FAIL

Teaching may be fraught with disappointments — real setbacks that no amount of energy, emotional involvement, or reliance on intuition may seem to help. These disappointments cause many teachers to re-examine their careers, and indeed influence some teachers to leave the profession. As teaching becomes an increasingly demanding occupation, and greater numbers of teachers come to feel discouraged, more and more attention has been devoted to the phenomenon of "teacher burnout," the sensation of being unable to draw upon the emotion and energy needed to continue teaching. This section will focus on a particular issue within the category of burnout: how to retain the composure and balance needed to be a loving, intuitively oriented teacher when the effort seems to fall short of success.

Some children do not seem to respond to the attention and concern that teachers give them. No matter what we do, these children remain aloof and inaccessible at best, hostile and violent at worst. Some of them may ultimately be transferred to special resource classes or other programs, but many will remain in our classes, seemingly unreachable, absorbed with their own private fantasies or distracted by family or social problems. Teachers who encounter such children react in several ways. They may decide the social forces influencing the children are too huge to be affected by what goes on in their classroom. These teachers may in a limited sense be right. Others may blame themselves for the apparent failure of the students, and in doing so come to doubt their own ability to teach, their commitment to the educational enterprise, and even their sense of love in teaching. It is to these teachers that this section is addressed.

First, we should not automatically blame ourselves for what seem to be failures in the classroom. While love is by definition an absolute, its immediate perceiveable effects are infrequently absolute. Likewise, if our intuitions about students and subject matter have proved to be, at least on the surface, incorrect, we should not abandon intuitive approaches. Remember that intuitive skills, like other abilities, are improved with practice, and since such skills are human skills, errors are inevitable. But suppose things consistently go wrong? Lesson plans designed to encourage intuitive processes go flat, attempts to communicate care and love to students are rebuffed, and what was supposed to be an innovative classroom looks merely chaotic.

If this happens it is time to go back and re-examine the intuitive impressions that led us to make decisions about curriculum, seating arrangments, and so on. What were the circumstances surrounding our decisions? Did biases or prejudices influence our decisions? In short, were we striving for an intuitive mode when we made our plans and set our goals? This set of admittedly obvious questions is linked by the common emotion of educational caritas, in all the forms we have mentioned. This is the most profound connection between the intuitive experience and the emotion and involvement of love. More than mere professional commitment, but yet related to such a commitment, this love should be the motivation to evaluate critically cherished intuitive feelings and to strive to adjust classroom situations that are not working out. Equally important, educational caritas can be a source of strength to endure difficult times that even intuitive approaches cannot seem to improve. In this sense, love has not in fact failed at all, but is providing possibilities for future efforts, decisions, and intuitive insights. Love provides this strength best when the teacher can reflect in an undistracted way on events and draw conclusions that show respect for, but not blind dependence on, intuitive responses and approaches.

Love should also cause a teacher to recognize the time constraints encountered in a typical school day. Love can illuminate the importance of doing what is possible during the time allotted, while accepting one's own time and energy limits without rancor. Love can maintain a sense of urgency; but grim determination, resentment, or frantic activity are not love's best companions. In some cases the greatest gift love can give intuition is a sense of when to wait, or quit altogether. Indeed, the best thing to do in many difficult and stressful situations is simply to seek a setting where a revitalizing intuitive mode can be cultivated.

In the end this process brings the teacher back to a contemplation of *eros*, which calls for a rejuvenation of the spirit through attention to the beauty of the physical world. Pausing to look at autumn colors, to enjoy a meal with friends, or to listen to a favorite tune on the radio are all ways to recover contact with the force of *eros* that can supply energy, enthusiasm, and love. Such diversions can keep the act of teaching from becoming merely a job and help make it a special profession, one that is intuitively enhanced.

SUMMARY

As we have suggested, this chapter is not intended to be the blueprint for an educational cure-all. Clearly, many situations exist in which it may be impossible to offer students love, or to use intuition and love together to improve instruction or relations between teacher and student. There are, too, some children who will rebuff every attempt made to give them love or to foster their intuitive potential. The existence of such situations and such children means neither that intuition and love in education are failed panaceas, nor that the teacher, parent, or friend who encounters frustrating situations has indeed failed. While this may seem obvious, it is nevertheless a point worth emphasizing, since books on how to improve teaching too often emphasize easy solutions. No one technique or educational philosophy can overcome all of the possible difficulties it can encounter, whatever the ability or energy of the teacher, and the use of love and intuition is by no means exempt from this fact. Teachers can expect to find their students frequently confused or uneasy with the changes that a curriculum and teaching technique making overt reference to intuitive and caring values may make in their education and their lives. When added to the difficulties mentioned earlier, such as lack of time and administrators and parents who do not understand, the challenge of introducing students to an education including love and nonrational thought may seem too great. Yet the effort is not in vain if one realizes the tremendous significance of helping a few students — or even one student — to recognize their potential for using intuitive thinking and feeling to deal with problems of everyday life. Once again, this assertion seems obvious, but in reality it needs emphasis because the directions that caring take very often lead to the solitary individual. Teaching that emphasizes intuition and love therefore reaffirms the importance of the individual child and strengthens the personal bond between student and teacher that is one of the foundations of education itself.

The other argument for bringing a sense of educational caritas together with an appreciation for intuitive approaches to problem solving comes from the philosophical legitimacy of the concepts on which our definitions are based. As we have noted, intuition, although an important part of the philosophical and religious heritage of both East and West, has been neglected in the classroom. In much the same way, what we have called educational caritas has a place in educational theory (and indeed is practiced by many teachers) yet is seldom identified or openly articulated as an important part of a child's school experience. Both intuition and an openly recognized and endorsed attitude of caring need to be included in the theoretical and practical aspects of education so that they will receive the legitimacy they deserve.

This chapter has included brief glimpses of four major approaches to the issues of intuition and love in education. There are many others as well, and although they differ on specifics, each one recognizes that the educational experience should be more than simply a series of cognitive exercises. If education is to assist the development of the whole individual, as Dewey suggested, it must address different ways of knowing and feeling, ways that all of us use in our daily lives. It must also recognize the importance of adaptability and combinations of different techniques utilizing love and intuition, for not all situations require the same approach.

Finally, the ideas of love and caring have been introduced into this book on intuition and education because in education the two become truly inseparable. A caring, concerned teacher should be aware of the intuitive factors influencing impressions she or he has of students, and of the intuitive factors shaping student perceptions of subject matter. Likewise, as educators become more aware of the role of intuition in interpersonal relations, they will come to value caring and educational caritas even more than before. If we remain open to the possibility of expanding and strengthening the use of intuition and the expression of caring, then education can be a more meaningful experience for both student and teacher. Beyond this, the legitimization by schools of such generally deemphasized topics as love and intuition will aid their more widespread acceptance by the public and will earn these human capabilities a greater place in our conception of the functioning, thinking, feeling human being.

Chapter 8

RECENT INTEREST IN INTUITION

> The moment of truth, the sudden emergence of a new insight, is
> an act of intuition.
>
> Arthur Koestler, *The Act of Creation*

IN CHAPTER 2 we saw that the topic of intuition has been of
increasing interest to the general public and that many new books
and organizations concerned with intuition have recently appeared.
These books and organizations, aimed at scholars and laypersons
alike, have done much to shape popular understanding of intuition. This chapter will take a look at a representative sampling of the
writings and organizations concerned with intuition and will emphasize the perspective of the educator seeking to use intuition in
teaching. We will also try to determine which books and studies have
put forward clearly defined notions of intuition and how these notions compare with our own definition of intuition and its uses.

IMPORTANT SURVEYS OF INTUITION

Among the books written about intuition during the past decade, probably the one most directly concerned with the development
of each individual's intuitive potential is Frances E. Vaughan's *Awakening Intuition*.[1] Vaughan holds that every person has the ability to
think intuitively and that intuition invariably yields truth. Problem
solving and personal growth are the central issues of this book, and
Vaughan devotes chapters to imagery and dreams and their relation
to intuition. The exercises Vaughan prescribes for helping to "tune

in" to intuition may be helpful for the teacher wishing to cultivate intuitive awareness.

Among the many exercises described are relaxing and "open focus" procedures that develop awareness of one's body and the space around it without resorting to rational analysis of stimuli. Vaughan also stresses receptivity to all forms of subjective experience, such as images, emotions, hunches, or other experiences. Recognizing, accepting, and observing subjective experiences through introspection and relaxation are crucial to developing one's intuition, Vaughan asserts, as is "quieting your mind" by eliminating distractions and extraneous thoughts. The most interesting of the book's exercises involves reflecting on the word *intuition* itself and its meaning to the individual. By treating the word as one would a mantra, repeating it or concentrating on an image of the word, one can gain insights and find conflict resolution less difficult. Finally, Vaughan provides "Guidelines for Awakening Intuition," listed at the end of the book and forming a succinct review of the book's most useful ideas. Vaughan's style is readable and informal without being excessively vague or overloaded with popular psychological jargon. The relationship between intuition and mysticism, particularly in Far Eastern thought, is acknowledged, but Vaughan does not push any particular religious interpretation of the intuitive experience. Readers are left free to relate intuition to whatever belief system they find compatible and are encouraged to recognize a variety of nonrational experiences as intuitive.

Despite these strong points, *Awakening Intuition* suffers from a major defect from the point of view we have taken in that it does not offer a clear definition of intuition. By insisting that intuition must yield truth, Vaughan further complicates the situation by separating her conception of intuition from those of the major post-Kantian philosophers we have mentioned in chapters 1 and 2. While many readers will not be troubled by the omission of a definition, philosophers of education will not find Vaughan's book a useful foundation upon which to develop a rigorous notion of intuition in education. Such a nonrigorous approach to the tricky problem of definition may also turn off skeptics who are reluctant to take intuition seriously.

Vaughan recognizes that intuition is involved in the quest for meaning, but in her nonrigorous description of the intuitive experience or process she does not emphasize the importance of the Will. We have argued that the driving momentum of the Will is essential to the intuitive experience. Vaughan appears to avoid the entire question of why we can and want to think intuitively, and, again, those concerned with the philosophical justification or affective motivation for intuition will likely be disappointed.

Nevertheless, Vaughan's book must be considered head and shoulders above virtually all the other popular material produced on intuition over the past decade. Vaughan is familiar with much of the recent psychological work on intuition, as well as some of the contributions of Eastern philosophers. Her style is poetic, but her book is filled with practical examples of fostering and using intuition. *Awakening Intuition* has already reached a sizable audience, and represents a serious attempt to bring some of the less accessible material on intuition to that audience. Clearly, no review of recent writing on the topic can afford to overlook this book.

In a far more scholarly vein, *The Nature of Human Consciousness* explores many of the same issues touched upon by Vaughan.[2] This collection of articles, edited by Robert E. Ornstein, ranges over philosophy, psychology, religion, and combinations thereof. Both modern scientific observation and traditional Eastern philosophy examine what human consciousness is and how we can understand more about it. Among the highlights of the book are the following:

- Arthur Deikman discusses "bimodal consciousness"—a receptive mode in which we simply let information "come to us" without conscious rationalization. Deikman's concept, which builds upon contributions of Buber and Zen Buddhism, clearly parallels many of the claims we have made for intuition. Deikman is also interested in mind-altering drug experiences and "mystic psychosis" experienced by practitioners of some religions, a subject we have not addressed but one of interest to many people exploring intuition.
- Idries Shah presents the basic ideas of Sufism in a way suggestive of intuitive processes, although some of the concepts remain elusive owing to the nonverbal nature of Sufi philosophy itself. As Shah notes, Sufism must be lived, not read about, in order to be understood. Shah's essay reminds us that in many non-Western cultures the intuitive part of one's nature is accepted and integrated into models of human behavior and thought. Later in this chapter we shall say more about non-Western systems that draw upon intuition.
- Ulric Neisser explains the process of vision in an intriguing and lucid article. Our reaction to stimulation by light is not

entirely passive, he says, since we extract patterns from optical input and then "make sense" of them. These ideas complement nicely Wertheimer's notions of the human tendency to complete broken or "disturbing" figures. Although Neisser does not use the word *intuition* to describe the process he discusses, the act of "making sense" of a figure that he describes cannot always be explained in terms of rational analysis. Reorganization of sense impressions as he explains it seems to involve another component, one we have called intuition.

Taken as a whole, *The Nature of Human Consciousness* is a rich collection of readable materials to stimulate the serious investigator of intuition. Although no concrete examples of ways to enhance intuition are offered and none of the articles spells out a clear definition of intuition, this collection is useful because of the uniformly high quality of the articles and the broad range of disciplines included. Ornstein's collection thus opens the door to the greater understanding of many other movements concerned with the fostering of nonrational thought processes.

Ornstein himself has written extensively on new views of the human mind and on intuitive knowing. His ideas are clearly set forth in *The Psychology of Consciousness*.[3] Ornstein explains contemporary theories of consciousness, stressing its subjective quality, and then explains the notion of the "split brain" in terms of both modern science and Eastern philosophy. There is a fascinating chapter on how we experience time that investigates "nonlineal" time experiences and the effects of drugs on time experience, as well as issues of duration, simultaneity, and causality. Ornstein takes on problems that have eternally plagued philosophers and psychologists, providing insightful observations (if not always solutions) to questions on how we perceive space and time.

Ornstein's book devotes an entire chapter to the development of intuition. Using an expression we, too, have employed—"the intuitive mode"—Ornstein explains that one's intuitive abilities can be sharpened, that is, the intuitive mode can be educated. Yoga, Zen, and the traditional beliefs of the Sufis all value and cultivate the intuitive mode, Ornstein says, and they maintain that humankind is part of a "larger organism" that influences and in turn is influenced by human beings. Interestingly, Ornstein never says whether this "organism" has a collective Will or intuitive consciousness. However, the reader receives no sermon on how all Eastern philosophies are invariably superior in their understanding of the human mind.

Ornstein examines the problems and contradictions of ascetic movements stressing humility, ritual behavior, or self-denial to the point where the original goal of higher consciousness or greater awareness is lost. He writes:

> If we can keep a wary eye on the excesses of both types of psychology [Western and Eastern] we may be able to rid each of imbalance, and achieve a synthesis of the highest elements in both types, rather than their excesses.[4]

The balance Ornstein advocates may be particularly appealing to educators trying to pick their way through the thicket of Eastern mysticism and Western psychology.

Ornstein goes on to enumerate other important aspects of the education of the intuitive mode:

1. Psychological self-mastery. In this state, highly trained individuals can regulate heartbeat, body temperature, and other vital signs.
2. The influence of body states on consciousness. Breathing exercises and special postures are, for example, used in Yoga to upset the balance of ordinary awareness so that another mode of consciousness can develop.
3. The esoteric concept of subtle body energies. Ornstein links in a general way Bergson's "élan vitale," the "vital principle" of Hans Driesch, the Japanese discipline of Aikido, and Chinese Tai-Chi Ch'uan, claiming all are expressions of the idea that living things contain a force that can alter physical objects or circumstances. Ornstein recognizes that Bergson's and Driesch's ideas have been largely discredited, but he retains the notion that "something beyond our usual concepts of energy" is operating in certain cases where mental concentration produces remarkable physical results.
4. The ignoring of thought. As we have seen in Zen and other disciplines, followers strive to rid their minds of extraneous thoughts and, in particular, to move away from the customary verbal mode of receiving and relating to the world. This component of education of the intuitive mode parallels some of the exercises discussed in chapter 5 and also is clearly related to Vaughan's recommendation to "quiet your mind."

The Psychology of Consciousness provides suggestions for developing the intuitive side of the mind and closes with a proposal for an "extended concept of man," one that would take into account a broad spectrum of factors influencing human consciousness. Among these are the contributions of Gestalt psychology, research on "paranormal" phenomena, and the ideas of Sufism.

Ornstein leaves us with the hope that human consciousness will be better understood in the near future, with significant benefits to all. His book is accessible to a wide range of readers, thoroughly documented, and provided with an excellent set of bibliographies. Intuition is not given a clear definition, but readers will find ample material for helping clarify their own understanding of the term. *The Psychology of Consciousness* is thus one of the most valuable books available today on the subject of intuition.

ORGANIZATIONS CONCERNED WITH INTUITION

One organization dedicated to the investigation of issues related to intuition and alternative ways of knowing is the Institute of Noetic Sciences. Founded in 1973 by former Apollo 14 astronaut Edgar Mitchell, the institute's purpose is "to support research and educational programs that expand humankind's understanding of the nature of consciousness and the mind-body link."[5] During the past ten years the institute has attracted a number of distinguished scientists as well as a large group of interested laypersons. Although the institute's goals are so extremely broad as to arouse skepticism among some, it has sponsored conferences on focused topics (e.g., "Conscious and Unconscious Mental Processes: Implications for Learning"), and it publishes a newsletter containing well-written articles and reviews of books relating to the study of mind and body. Most teachers would find this material accessible and stimulating, as would many high-school students.

Like Frances Vaughan's book, the Institute of Noetic Sciences is not wed to any particular philosophical or religious conception of the mind. Its literature implies that it is committed to re-educating and thereby changing society, but it does not spell out any political agenda. If there is a doctrine to which the institute adheres, it seems to be simply that the human mind has great potential, which, though not at present fully developed, can be investigated and developed in the future. Thus intuition is a topic of considerable interest to the institute, although at present it has not published any major work on the subject or provided a clear definition of the term.

The Institute of Noetic Sciences is an important potential resource for the educator interested in intuition. It is clearly not engaged in any sort of educational fraud or pseudomystical hoax, but is instead a group of sincere and largely competent individuals interested in a variety of exciting topics related to the human mind. From the standpoint of intuition the institute's major drawbacks are the breadth of its avowed sector of investigation, which could prevent thorough investigation of a topic such as intuition, and the absence so far of concrete contributions to educational practice. However, the prospects for the institute's overcoming these drawbacks are as bright as they are for any organization engaged in such investigations.

Another organization concerned with alternative conceptions of the mind, and particularly with intuition, is the Center for Applied Intuition of the Institute for Conscious Evolution. The center, headed by William H. Kautz, focuses on problem solving in scientific and business settings and seeks to bring intuition more directly into both creative and problem-solving processes. Although schooling and public education are not explicitly discussed in the center's promotional material, its techniques and goals have obvious implications for pedagogy. Most significantly, the center offers a definition of intuition that is succinct and comprehensible:

Intuition is that remarkable human ability of "direct knowing," or acquiring knowledge without rational thought. When intuition operates, information flows *not* from the conscious mind we are so used to dealing with but from somewhere beyond that mind, from a place we normally have no control over.[6]

This notion of intuition differs from the one set forth in this book by totally separating the functions of the conscious mind from those of intuition. No mention is made of the interplay of reason and intuition experienced by many individuals in the course of everyday life, and once again the Will as we have defined it is not seen as an important part of the intuitive process.

An unusual feature of the center's approach to intuitive problem solving is its use of "intuition experts," individuals who, according to the center's claims, "have developed their intuitive skills to the point where they can, at will, act as a clear channel of information on any topic, over and above their past education and experience." These skilled intuitives respond individually to questions posed them; then their collected responses are analyzed and compared to form a consensus that then forms the basis of action. The Center for

Applied Intuition thus seems to take the position that a few, rather than most or all, individuals are especially intuitively gifted. It then concentrates on utilizing the talents of the gifted instead of developing the intuitive abilities of all people. Some of the center's other programs do focus more on the development of intuition in formerly nonintuitive thinkers, but the general philosophy of the center appears to emphasize the abilities of the unusually gifted. Teachers will not find this approach especially helpful, although the notion of intuitive consensus is one that teachers may want to explore in classroom settings.

The center's claims for the value of intuition in discovering truth do not go as far as those of Vaughan, although the Center does claim a high degree of accuracy in the predictions of its skilled intuiters. Material collected by Kautz and his associates includes scientific evidence, legendary accounts of intuitive creativity, and more popular literature on intuition and parapsychology; all are presented as evidence of the power of intuition and the potential for success through the use of "intuitive consensus."

The evidence and arguments marshalled by the Center for Applied Intuition are intriguing. They offer interesting support for the notion of intuitive problem solving, even if the center itself offers little directly related to education. Whether intuitive approaches to problem solving and creativity will gain acceptance in business circles also remains to be seen. We hope that proper approaches will, since such an acceptance would make the introduction of intuition into the classroom much less difficult and controversial.

Turning now from books and organizations whose primary focus is on intuition, we shall look at a few of the books written recently that deal with intuition in a somewhat less explicit fashion. The number of recent books that may be regarded as having at least some connection with intuition is very large, and it was only with considerable difficulty that we were able to select the works that were at once most representative and most important in terms of influence from the list of possible candidates. What follows is a sampling of significant works that handle the issues of intuition in a variety of ways, some with major implications for education and others less so. All these books, however, are linked by a concern for nonrational ways of knowing and for issues of creativity, whether in the artistic, social, or political spheres. Also all have been eagerly read by those seeking a broader, fuller existence—one enhanced by awareness of intuition.

INTUITION AND SOCIETY

Some of the strongest appeals and greatest drawbacks characteristic of much of the literature concerned with intuition can be found
in two immensely popular books, Charles A. Reich's *The Greening of
America*,[7] and Marilyn Ferguson's *The Aquarian Conspiracy*.[8] Neither
book has intuition as its explicitly central theme, but both use notions of new types of consciousness that will help build the utopian
societies the authors envision. Reich's book, which enjoyed enormous popularity on college campuses and elsewhere in the early
1970s, is a complex collection of criticisms of contemporary American
society, arguments for the revitalization of that society, and observations on the influences of the youth culture of the late 1960s on such a
revitalization. Without attempting to analyze all the aspects of this
controversial work, we shall examine the way Reich uses ideas akin
to intuition in formulating his arguments and the problems such a
use of intuition presents.

Reich insists, along with many other writers of the time, that
Americans of the 1960s and 1970s suffered from alienation and fragmentation and that the country was trapped in a destructive romance
with materialism. According to Reich's model, this country could
escape from this dilemma by rising from Consciousness I (the negative situation now existing, according to Reich) through Consciousness II (the heightened awareness of others' needs and desire to
bring about reforms that has existed in America periodically) to Consciousness III. Consciousness III has a distinctly intuitive quality to
it: Reich cites as its sources Thoreau, James Joyce, Wallace Stevens,
and J. D. Salinger's hero, Holden Caulfield. All these figures rejected
the conventional wisdom of society and sought meaning in their
lives through an inner sense of "rightness." Reich argues that in the
youth culture of the 1960s large numbers of people "converted" to a
new consciousness inspired by the above-mentioned nonconfor-
mists and rejected the debased rationality of their elders.

This new consciousness, Consciousness III, "declares that the
individual self is the only true reality."[9] This subjective reality,
which at the same time involves a deep personal commitment to the
welfare of the community, is not unlike the "human nature" that
Rousseau predicted would emerge if children were allowed to develop "naturally." The notion of Consciousness III thus depends on
two assumptions. The first is that people are intuitively drawn,
without formal training or indoctrination, to the good for both themselves and their society. The second is that society is approaching the

point where a large number of people, perhaps the majority, will be raised to this higher level of awareness.

This brings us to the major difficulties with *The Greening of America* from the perspective of the educator looking for models of intuition to implement in education or in society in general. First, Reich's assessment of the power and depth of the youth revolution of the 1960s, viewed several years later, looks naive and ill judged. The Rolling Stones have not managed to make Beethoven's Ninth sound dated or irrelevant, and Madison Avenue has not succumbed to the generation of love. More importantly, the revolution in consciousness Reich hoped for has not materialized, and, in fact, many societal trends that Reich noted among young people seem now to be moving in the opposite direction. The rise of an intuitive approach to life along the lines Reich envisioned has been, at least for the time being, smothered by a return to the materialist, alienating culture that Reich deplores. The failure of Consciousness III to emerge in American society raises serious questions about the accuracy of Reich's assessment of the power of the inner sense of rightness that is supposed to guide the individual to a better life. Reich is vitally concerned with the individual's quest for meaning, but he does not develop the idea adequately enough to make clear the philosophical basis for the intuition-aided quest; and he failed to predict correctly where this quest would lead.

The other disturbing issue in *The Greening of America* is one common to many other works utilizing the concept of a personal intuitive guide. Like Vaughan and other writers, Reich is frustratingly vague as to what exactly this inner guide is. Influenced heavily by the dramatic events of the time in which he wrote, Reich calls Consciousness III "liberating," tells us that it "accepts no imposed system," and that all aspects of it are unified by energy. These platitudes are simply not adequate to identify the concept that is so central to the book. In short, Reich's view of intuition as a force for change in society is fundamentally a nonrigorous one, and he offers practically no constructive suggestions for fostering this intuition.

In contrasting Reich's scenario with the ideas and goals we have set forth, it becomes clear that Reich has given much less attention and emphasis to Consciousness II than we have. In fact, it seems that Reich does not view Consciousness II as a lasting or overly desirable stage of social and human development. Yet many of the characteristics of modern society (e.g., poverty, violence, competitiveness) suggest that real effort ought to be made to assure that Consciousness II at least takes hold. Reich seems to want to go to Consciousness III directly, while our suggestions and those of most of the other writers discussed in this chapter are aimed more at moving society successfully out of Consciousness I. Reich's refusal to recognize the uses of intuition in a far from utopian setting further limits *The Greening of America*'s usefulness to classroom teachers or anyone else working in the real world.

Ten years after *The Greening of America* appeared, Marilyn Ferguson published *The Aquarian Conspiracy*. Like *The Greening of America, The Aquarian Conspiracy* immediately attained wide popularity among those who wished to see American society move in a new direction, away from the rigid rationality that has always dominated intellectual life in the West. Also, like Reich's book, Ferguson's work predicts that such a change or revolution is possible in the not-too-distant future and that individuals could lead far happier lives in this new society.

There are, however, important differences between the two books. For educators, Ferguson's book is far more articulate and explicit in the development of its core ideas, including intuition. Ferguson calls intuition "tacit knowing," and claims that "it has been the silent partner to all our progress. The left brain can organize new information into the existing scheme of things, but *it cannot generate new ideas*. Without intuition, we would still be in the cave." [10]

Ferguson recognizes that traditional educational approaches have given little emphasis to intuition and that students have suffered as a result, but she also maintains that intuition is becoming recognized and will begin to have an increasingly important role in education in the future. When "whole-brain knowing," as Ferguson calls it, becomes more widely accepted, not only will students perform academic tasks with greater skill, but they will also gain greater access to unconscious anxieties that are blocking their progress. The net result is that when the Aquarian Revolution has taken place, schools or wherever children and adults are learning will be more wholesome, dynamic, and exciting places.

All of this is encouraging and not inconceivable, unlike the utopian society envisaged by Charles Reich, which may not soon come to pass. Ferguson goes even further, however, in making claims for a "collective intuition" that can guide individuals to important truths or help the decision-making process. She is not clear about whether this "collective intuition" needs to be linked to any philosophical or religious system or whether it is simply the product of the intuitive consensus of a group of individuals. Ferguson seems to have intentionally avoided making a commitment on this point because of her firm stand on the value of a plurality of philosophies and beliefs. Nevertheless, her lack of elaboration on the nature of any evidence for collective intuition is disappointing.

The Aquarian Conspiracy also addresses itself to questions of the relationship between mind and illness and to the influence of the mind on the body generally. This is a topic that we have intentionally avoided in our discussion of intuition but one that many who use the term *intuition* include in their definition of the word. Ferguson believes that all diseases can be tied at some level to emotional stress and mental state. She notes that the use of biofeedback, *Tai-Chi*, and other procedures for "getting in contact" with one's physical self have produced remarkable results. Hypnosis, biofeedback, meditation, and other exercises all obviously draw upon nonrational functions and can therefore be considered related to the domain of intuition. While Ferguson does not go into detail about the processes themselves, she does provide ample references for the reader who wants to investigate further.

Considerable space in *The Aquarian Conspiracy* is devoted to spirituality and to the role spirituality can play in the quest for meaning. As with many other books concerned with an intuitive understanding of life, Ferguson's book asserts that the Universe is whole rather than fragmented or dualistic. Understanding this oneness at a profound level is not possible if one uses only the rational side of the mind. Organized religion cannot provide this contact, either, since it has become, for the most part, bland and unengaging. Instead of rationality or traditional religious expression, "Aquarian Conspirators," we learn, are opting for direct contact with the spiritual through mystical experience. Ferguson is careful not to advocate one particular form of mysticism over another; instead she provides arguments and some documentation for the claims of mystics. The basic message is that there is a higher reality beyond the world we deal with empirically and that contact with this reality can give meaning to events we encounter in our everyday lives.

Even if one does not accept Ferguson's ideas about the mystical nature of intuitive contact, one can still find in *The Aquarian Conspiracy* a good deal of useful information and interesting speculation about the role intuition could play in a future society. Unlike Reich's sense of separation and alienation from the society in which he lives, the tone of *The Aquarian Conspiracy* is hopeful even within the context of existing American life. Ferguson believes that the revolution is already under way, and so she lists resources and organizations that can help the newcomer get involved in the "conspiracy." This list may be the most important concrete contribution of her book, although some of the information provided will grow obsolete with time. In summary, *The Aquarian Conspiracy* contains many intriguing ideas about intuition and at least some clues about how to follow up on these suggestions.

The Aquarian Conspiracy emphasizes the contributions of intuition to personal development and social change in a very broad sense. Other writers have been more concerned with putting intuitive skills to work in specific areas and with achieving material success or improving social skills. Many of the books written in these areas make extravagant claims for what nonrational knowledge can accomplish; some argue positions for which they provide little or no documentation or hedge the issues with vague, noncommittal language. A few attempt to give a responsible, if conceptually limited, view of intuition in a social setting. *Inside Intuition* by Flora Davis falls into this latter category.[11] Davis is interested in the nonverbal communication we send and receive and offers interpretations of what the signals mean. Each major area of communication is treated in turn: eyes, face, hands, postures, scents, and touching. Much of the information Davis provides will be useful to teachers trying to sort out the complex behaviors of students, but the emphasis of the book is not on these matters. Rather, Davis pays considerable attention to signals of courtship, sexual availability, and similar topics quite different from the large issues treated in Reich's and Ferguson's books.

Inside Intuition may be the only book currently available in this country that takes a totally social and communication oriented approach to intuition, and for this reason Davis's work forms a significant addition to the literature on intuition. The bibliography is both extensive and multidisciplinary, providing an excellent starting point for anyone investigating this subject. A major weakness of the book is similar to those of other popular books on intuition. One has an idea what Davis means by intuition by the end of the book, but an actual definition of the term is never spelled out. Davis also leaves unanswered several important questions about body language and cultural differences. Specifically, to what degree can we expect members of minority groups to exhibit the body language described in *Inside Intuition*? Davis offers examples of variations in body language in different cultures: the Israeli custom of staring at strangers, the Latin American custom of standing very close to the person one is addressing. These bits of information are, however, presented almost anecdotally, and Davis gives us no systematic analysis of these important differences. More work clearly needs to be done on intuitive communication through body language and the difficulties of conducting this communication across cultures.

Inside Intuition is more fully elaborated than the other popular book on this subject, *Body Language*, by Julius Fast. While the evidence for many of Davis's claims is lacking, she has nevertheless written a largely creditable work on an elusive yet important topic. The most significant drawback to *Inside Intuition* is its attempt to make intuitive perception into a rational process that can be monitored and manipulated like other rational processes. Since intuition is *not* the same as analytical reasoning, it should not be developed or manipulated in the same fashion. If *Inside Intuition* provides a less than adequate amount of information or theoretical base for teachers wishing to use their social intuition in the classroom, it will at least heighten their awareness of the importance of the unconscious sending, receiving, and interpreting of messages that are transmitted through body language and other physical, nonverbal means.

INTUITION AND SPIRITUALITY

Another major category of interest in intuition focuses on the spiritual or religious aspect of the concept—a topic that has attracted considerable attention in recent years. A complete survey, however, of all religious or spiritual movements of modern times that have concerned themselves with intuition would necessarily be a review of virtually the entire spectrum of recent religious thought. Rather than attempt such a survey, we shall take a look at some of the most significant work in this area in order to provide a better understanding of what is meant by an intuitive religious experience.

Spiritual and religious interest in intuition divides generally into two categories: philosophies and religions with a primarily Eastern focus and those which reflect a more Western, or Judeo-Christian, influence. As we noted earlier, the Judeo-Christian tradition has typically not been as intuitively oriented as the philosophies and religions of the East. Although its roots are in revelation and ecstatic nonrational experience, institutional Christianity, with the possible exception of some of the pentecostal and charismatic movements, has been notably devoid of an intuitive component. When intuitive experiences have been recognized and sanctioned by Christian churches, they have usually taken the more passive form of

revelation, in which the knower merely receives the knowledge —
sometimes even unwillingly. The Christian intuiter may feel at one
with God or the cosmos, but in a subordinate way that differs
dramatically from the Zen or Hindu intuitive experience. In recent
years some Christian writers have recognized these limitations on
the Christian notion of intuition and have attempted to integrate
more intuitive ways of knowing with Christian beliefs. One of the
most articulate and widely read of these religious thinkers is Alan
Watts.

Representative of Watts's writing on the subjects of spirituality
and consciousness is *The Joyous Cosmology: Adventures in the Chemistry of Consciousness*.[12] Watts's intentional eclecticism draws upon
twentieth-century novelists such as Hermann Hesse, the Far Eastern
systems of Zen and Taoism, and elements of psychoanalytical theory.
He blends together these varied elements into a poetic narrative relating "the reciprocity of Will and world, active and passive, inside
and outside, self and not-self."[13] Watts wants to move beyond the
separation of God and man that has existed since the beginning of
the Judeo-Christian tradition and bring human beings into closer
relation with the entire universe. This immediate contact with both
the physical and spiritual world is clearly an intuitive contact, for it
does not depend on analyzing, categorizing, and assessing. Taken at
a superficial level, Watts's observations may at first seem merely
restatements of the obvious: Of course the world is a totality that
shares many characteristics and whose relationships are so subtle
and profound that our current rational knowledge cannot adequately
explain them. But Watts is driving at something deeper than this. He
is trying to make clear his understanding of a world where opposites
are reconciled and where "instead of knowers and knowns there are
simply knowings, and instead of doers and deeds simply doings."[14]
Such a vision can only be reached through an intuitive view of life,
whether it is in a Zen, Taoist, reformed Christian, or essentially
nonreligious frame of reference. In this book Watts is not interested
in building sophisticated philosophical or theological arguments for
his position, but he remains persuasive because of his graceful style
and penetrating observations about Western culture. In a sense, the
reader must already be aware of an intuitive approach to spiritual
questions to appreciate what Watts is saying. Thus it may be that *The
Joyous Cosmology* and other of Watts's writings may not persuade
many individuals to accept the idea of an intuitive view of life, but
these books will offer support to those who already embrace the
notion.

For educators *The Joyous Cosmology* and other works by Watts are most useful as a secondary support to other books dealing more concretely with intuitive approaches to learning and social interaction. Skillful teachers may also find ways to use Watts's writings in the classroom to stimulate student writing or discussion. While Watts offers little in the way of practical application, his books can open doors to students and teachers alike who want to broaden their own understanding of consciousness. Watts also provides a useful introduction for Westerners to the intuitive models in Eastern philosophy.

Most of the major Eastern religions concern themselves in some way with intuitive ways of knowing. Two Eastern philosophies or religions that have especially captured the public's imagination in recent years are Zen Buddhism and Taoism, both of which were largely unknown in this country a few decades ago. In chapter 6 we took a brief look at some of the notions of Zen, and we shall now say a few words about Taoism and its popular manifestations in the United States today.

Books on Taoism are numerous; many are not clearly written or seem to distort the ideas of this ancient Chinese system of viewing the world. A few books are articulate about Taoism's approach to the intuitive experience and are written in language that will make sense to Westerners coming to the subject with a psychological view of mind. One of these books is *The Tao of Psychology: Synchronicity and the Self* by Jean Shinoda Bolen.[15] Bolen builds on Jung's notion of synchronicity, the idea that seemingly "coincidental" events that we cannot explain rationally can operate as messages to our conscious mind. Taoist methods of prediction such as the *I Ching* fall into this same category; the symbolic language or form of a horoscope or *I Ching* text awakens us to an intuitive awareness of relationships hitherto unrecognized. All of our intuitive impressions are important, Bolen maintains:

> To know how to choose a path with heart is to learn how to follow the inner beat of *intuitive feeling.* Logic can tell you superficially where a path might lead to, but it cannot judge whether your heart will be in it.[16]

Bolen recognizes the important role of affect in the intuitive experience, the sense of rightness and immediacy that urges the intuitive thinker onward. While such feelings are not always correct, as we have argued, they add a great deal to the excitement, intensity, and sense of purpose of the intuitive experience.

Educators will understand more about the Chinese notion of

Taoism after reading Bolen's short book, but they will also be re-
minded of some of the characteristics of Western culture as well: the
"masculine" emphasis on logical, linear, right-brain functioning;
the denigration of intuition throughout our society; our insistence
on the limited, scientific approach to knowing. While a rigorous
definition of intuition is once again missing from the discussion of
intuition's uses, Bolen's book, like Ornstein's, is a gateway to different perspectives on nonrational ways of knowing.

Finally, we should recognize the contribution of Asian writers to
the literature on religion and intuition. In the area of Zen studies,
one writer in particular stands out as an exceptionally clear and persuasive proponent of the Zen approach to understanding the mind.
This is Diasetz Teitaro Suzuki, who for over half a century produced
writings in Japanese and English that continue to be widely read in
Asia and elsewhere. Recently a collection of Suzuki's writings appeared under the title *The Awakening of Zen*.[17] Here Suzuki discusses the intuitive transcendental knowledge that is so basic to Zen.
This knowledge is called *Prajna,* and as Suzuki describes the experience it corresponds in many ways to intuitive ways of knowing proposed by Western writers we have quoted. Suzuki writes:

> When people talk about intuition it is connected with individual
> objects. There is someone who has an intuition and something in
> regard to which he has it. There is nothing between subject and
> object. These intuitions may take place immediately, i.e., without
> any intermediary; nevertheless, there are subject and object, though
> their relationship is immediate instead of being through an inter-
> mediate agent.[18]

Suzuki goes on to emphasize not only the immediacy of intuition but also an apparent union of perceiver and perceived; both
these characteristics are important parts of our own definition of
intuition, although we have not talked of "union" but, rather, of a
feeling of reduced "subjectness." Suzuki makes the unfamiliar notions of Zen accessible to the West and has enabled us to understand
the parallels between our own philosophers' ideas and the wisdom of
the East.

Suzuki is also concerned with the connection between intuition
and the human emotions, particularly love. He recognizes that love is
not a command given to us from something outside ourselves and
that if it is based in arrogant egocentrism it is false and destructive.
True love is never destructive, because, as Suzuki puts it, "Love

enters into its object and becomes one with it, while power, being characteristically dualistic and discriminative, crushes any object standing against it or otherwise conquers it and turns it into a slavish dependent."[19]

The Zen perspective thus has a message for the teacher or parent. Loving one's students truly requires going beyond merely directing or manipulating them; the teacher must try to turn the teaching/learning process into a more holistic experience focused not on power, but on direct contact among teacher, learner, subject matter, and the act of teaching/learning. This is the relationship we argued for in chapter 7, one that could make a significant difference in the experience of untold numbers of students. Suzuki does not provide concrete descriptions of how this intuition-enlightened love operates in social situations, but he had not promised to give this type of information. He was interested in presenting a broad view of the principles of Zen and left the reader to apply these ideas.

As a book of ideas and not applications, *The Awakening of Zen* offers a lucid introduction to one of the world's most important philosophical or religious systems concerned with intuitive knowing. The absence of applied information and concrete examples of life lived according to Zen precepts does not materially detract from the book's significance as a solid introduction to a point of view that is thoroughly intuitive. Suzuki also holds out the possibility that sameness need not mean boredom or mediocrity (we, too, celebrated appropriate redundancy), and that a truly intuitive experience need be neither passive nor aggressive, but is rather a willed and accepted elimination of barriers and a recognition (but not on the verbal level) of a higher unity.

One final word about *The Awakening of Zen*: Suzuki, like other writers on Zen, alluded to a collective or total intuition that supersedes the individual experiences of the solitary intuiter. This collective intuition seems to be not only the collective impressions of human beings or even of all living things, but of the entire Universe. Although such assertions cannot be proven rationally, the educator should not dismiss them lightly, for they can have profound implications for teaching. If it is possible to gain an intuition of a stratum of rock, a poem, a political system, or a microbe, then the reality and urgency of all forms of inquiry will be increased. How is this to be done? Serious readers of Suzuki must grapple with this question, keeping in mind the institutional and other restrictions we have discussed in chapters 5 and 7.

The Far East is not the only place where mystical or religious

ideas about intuition have developed uninfluenced by the Judeo-
Christian tradition. While a graduate student engaged in field research in the American Southwest, anthropologist Carlos Castaneda
encountered a Yaqui Indian shaman who introduced him to a "non-
ordinary reality" that could be achieved through use of hallucinogenic drugs. Castaneda's account of his partial initiation was
published in 1968 with the title *The Teachings of Don Juan: A Yaqui
Way of Knowledge.* [20] This book, and several others by Castaneda that
followed it, developing further the ideas set forth in *The Teachings of
Don Juan,* quickly became popular with recreational drug users, college students, and members of the contemporary counterculture.
Appearing, as it did, at a time when use of such mind-altering drugs
as peyote, L.S.D., and mescaline were enjoying wide use, *The Teachings of Don Juan* was hailed as a philosophical justification for the use
of hallucinogens. At the same time the book was also condemned by
many who felt that it encouraged irresponsible experimentation with
dangerous drugs.

Our concern with Castaneda's work is centered on the account it
provides of a nonrational experience that leads to enlightenment and
of the value of such an experience to anyone trying to understand the
intuitive mode. Castaneda's account is engaging and poetic, and it
conveys his growing appreciation for a different way of knowing.
But the description of Castaneda's gradual entry into the mystical
world of Yaqui sorcery is of little use to individuals concerned with
education in traditional settings such as the classroom. Aside from
the obvious legal and ethical difficulties surrounding hallucinogenic
drug use, the type of enlightenment that participation in Don Juan's
rituals leads to is limited in its value to educators or philosophers.
This is because the experiences Castaneda describes cannot be validated or corroborated in any context except the drug-induced one
that produced the initial experience.

This is a serious drawback, not only from a philosophical position, but from a practical one as well. Of course many other mystical
intuitive experiences also cannot be validated (and that is why we
have not treated them), but the presence of peyote calls particular
attention to the problems inherent in ascribing absolute truth or
reality to an intuitive experience. Rationally, we cannot prove
Suzuki's union with the flower he sees and touches any more than
we can prove that Castaneda became a crow after taking a mind-
altering drug. The latter, though—perhaps because we know drugs
were used and because of the specific and dramatic image that Castaneda's narrative calls to mind — seems harder to accept. In both

cases, however, we are dealing with experiences that lie beyond any sort of rational validation. It is important to remember that the intuition we have emphasized can be tested or at least made public and shared: Mathematical intuitions can be subjected to proof, intuitions about distant cultures can be verified by visiting the cultures, and kinesthetic intuitions can be enacted and observed on the spot. The universal occurrence of mystic intuitions, as illustrated by the striking tales told in *The Teachings of Don Juan*, serves as a reminder that some forms of intuitive experience must be regarded as important areas of investigation even though they cannot be responsibly used in education.

We have now seen samples of recent writing and research relating to intuition and social change, theories of consciousness, personal development, development of social skills, and several forms of spirituality. These books vary in quality and usefulness to the student of intuition, although many have been widely read. We conclude this selection with two very different books that take a decidedly serious view of intuition and of its importance in human thought and creativity. Both of these books hold out the hope that original, useful books discussing intuition can be written, and that such books can attain considerable popularity without becoming reckless or sensationalistic on the one hand or vague and noncommittal on the other.

INTUITION IN TWO IMPORTANT WORKS

Gödel, Escher, Bach—An Eternal Golden Braid by Douglas R. Hofstadter is an unusual book that does not fit into any category that we have yet identified.[21] It is a complex and highly original work that attempts to draw together ideas from the fields of visual art, music, and modern mathematics and computer science. Hofstadter, a professor of computer science, is concerned with, among other things, how we create models that organize bodies of knowledge and theories that explain physical events; in pursuit of this concern, he discusses nonrational knowledge. The full development of Hofstadter's ideas would require considerable space, and we shall confine ourselves instead to some of his observations on intuition. Like many of the other writers mentioned in this chapter, Hofstadter calls attention to the importance of Zen as a way of understanding what intuition is and how it operates. He devotes space to recounting several Zen koans and argues for an intuitive factor in the understanding of the physical sciences. In fact, virtually all of *Gödel, Escher, Bach* reflects a perspective on intelligence that requires the inclusion of an intuitive component.

How can Hofstadter's sprawling and complex book be of use to teachers and others concerned with fostering intuition? Only in indirect ways. Much of the book concentrates on issues relating to computers and artificial intelligence. Other sections deal with music and the intriguing symmetrical drawings of the Dutch artist M. C. Escher in ways that hint at some of the work of the Gestalt psychologists but address the issue of intuition only obliquely. Hofstadter confronts intuition directly in only a few places, for example, the passage on Ramanujan that we have mentioned in chapter 6. Nowhere does he fully explain what he means by the term, and indeed he does not indicate that a clear definition of the term is useful or even appropriate. However, Hofstadter should not be faulted for this omission, since defining intuition is not his avowed task.

Readers looking for clues on how to cultivate or encourage intuition will find more useful material than will philosophers seeking Hofstadter's underlying concept of intuition. Scattered through the book are pseudo-Socratic dialogues that shed light on Hofstadter's conception of nonlogical or nonrational thought processes, the limits of human logic, and approaches to intuitive conceptions of reality or mathematics.

Hofstadter's chapter on "The Location of Meaning" distinguishes between "information-bearers" and "information-revealers," the latter being messages that trigger a complicated interpretive process that can involve intuitive understanding. And his chapter on "Minds and Thoughts" addresses the way that the sounds of language influence our understanding—an obvious link to some of the characteristics of intuition that we have discussed earlier in the book. Buried elsewhere in Hofstadter's book are discussions of mathematical operations that hint at intuition (in the sense that we have used the term) but do not provide enough discussion of intuition's wider applications or importance in teaching mathematics.

Gödel, Escher, Bach thus makes only a modest direct contribution to our understanding of intuition and its educational applications, although its indirect message about intuition is important. Perhaps one of Hofstadter's greatest contributions is his ingenious fusion of disciplines and ideas in a fashion that is obviously intuitive, thus making *Gödel, Escher, Bach* a beautiful example of a successfully executed intuitive enterprise. By trying to grapple with the basic problem of how any finite system can ever really examine or understand itself, Hofstadter also shows that an intuitive knowledge of relationships may be essential to enrich understanding when limited logic can go no further. For the most able and ambitious readers, *Gödel, Escher, Bach* will trigger insights into our need for the broadest possible conception of the Universe, one in which intuitive knowledge plays a meaningful role.

The late Arthur Koestler produced several books on philosophical and psychological themes, and one, *The Act of Creation*, pays special attention to intuition.[22] Koestler sought to articulate a theory of creativity that encompassed both the conscious and unconscious processes producing scientific discovery, artistic originality, and comic inspiration. He also attempted to link human creativity to more general principles operating on all living things. While his search for broad commonalities in the experience of all organisms goes beyond the immediate issues of intuition in human learning, Koestler's ideas on the sources of human creativity and its relation to intuition should be of great interest to all educators.

Koestler saw analogy as an expression of intuitive insight, an experience that could not be attributed to linear thought. Citing Kepler, Lord Kelvin, Newton, and others, Koestler argued that scientific discoveries often occur when intuitive thinkers hit upon an analogy that connects some known relationship or event with some hitherto unknown one. Writers use analogies, metaphors, and similes to give power and life to their work, and the reader then is awakened by the analogy and gains insights or aesthetic experiences. Koestler explained the special quality of this kind of learning:

> Thus the real achievement in discoveries of the type mentioned in this section is "seeing an analogy where no one saw it before." . . . To put it another way: solving a problem means bridging a gap, and for routine problems there usually exist matrices—various types of prefabricated bridges—which will do the job; though it may require a certain amount of sweat to adjust them to the terrain.[23]

Some discoveries—Koestler called these "original discoveries"—take place without the prefabricated matrix. In such cases intuition leads the scientist or researcher to make certain choices about which characteristics to emphasize in the analogy. This process takes place, Koestler maintained, not in the conscious but in the unconscious mind. Verbal, conscious thinking helps very little in either recognizing analogies or cultivating the circumstances that can produce such "original discoveries." Indeed, conventional, conscious repetition of

dates, numbers, and so forth may lead to habit, which Koestler felt
was the opposite of creative originality.

> Habit and originality, then, point in opposite directions in the
> two-way traffic between conscious and unconscious processes. The
> condensation of learning into habit, and the automatization of skills
> constitute the downward stream; while the upward traffic consists
> in the minor, vitalizing pulses from the underground, and the rare
> major surges of creation.[24]

Koestler further advocated daydreaming and unstructured, un-
constrained environments to make "the rare major surges of creation" more possible.

Although he was writing about the contributions of mature scientists, Koestler's observations on analogy and creativity have major
implications for education at all levels. What he has advocated is in
direct opposition to what goes on in most schools and, ironically, to
what is particularly common in science classes. The suggestion that
we might profitably provide time to daydream or cast about for
analogies to help explain puzzling phenomena may be met with
disbelief or derision by some teachers, but the idea is worthy of
serious consideration since time so spent has occasionally produced
such spectacular results. And, as Jerome Bruner has noted, the same
process of intuition is also of great value in the arts and social
studies.[25]

Koestler also discussed another matter that we, too, have emphasized: the connection of logic and intuition. Koestler recognized
that intuition can often be most effective when it is aided by knowledge and a willingness to use logic to aid in discovery. The story of
Louis Pasteur's pioneering achievements in immunology supports
Koestler's argument for using *both* intuitive and analytical, rational
modes. Pasteur, we read, was the first to extend the idea of vaccina-
tion from smallpox to other diseases. Although such a connection
seems obvious in retrospect, Pasteur was unique among his contemporaries in recognizing the analogous situation. His knowledge of
the field, ability to draw logical conclusions, and intuitive grasp of
relationships led him to the realization that vaccinations could be
used against many illnesses. This realization changed medicine pro-
foundly and ultimately had an influence on the lives of millions of
individuals for decades to come. This combination of logic and intuition, focused in a lightning flash of insight on a particular relationship, had as great an impact on human history as the more celebrated
deeds of generals and statesmen.

Koestler has thus pointed the way toward a wedding of intuitive and rational modes in the classroom or laboratory that could greatly enrich formal education. Without having to discard all of the paraphernalia or procedures of the conventional classroom, teachers can combine intuitive processes with more traditional ones. For science teachers and students, Koestler's accounts of scientific breakthroughs make fascinating and inspiring reading. For those who want to understand more, part one of *The Act of Creation* provides a challenging model of the conscious and unconscious that may change how teachers will want to approach their subjects and students. Taken as a whole, *The Act of Creation* is an important book making a real contribution to the fostering of intuition in scientific research and thus, indirectly, to education.

SUMMARY

The preceding pages have provided only a glimpse of some of the current thought regarding intuition. Varied as the material is, it nevertheless provides a suggestive basis upon which to build some generalizations about contemporary trends in thinking about intuition.

First, intuition is a topic that interests a large segment of the population to a greater extent than at any time in the past several hundred years. Psychologists, social critics, scientists, therapists, anthropologists, popular writers, and others are incorporating notions of nonrational knowledge and wisdom in their explanations of human behavior, creativity, communication, and other phenomena. At the same time, readers are eagerly imbibing the various and often conflicting theories making use of intuition and in many cases taking the speculations of one or several writers to heart. Clearly, the general public and, to a lesser extent, some segments of the intellectual community are ready to listen to an explanation of the human mind that includes a nonlinear, nonrational component. The reasons are complex and, as we mentioned briefly in chapter 2, include an increasing awareness of Eastern mysticism and other intuitive philosophies, such as the one Carlos Castaneda has described, as well as a general dissatisfaction with our traditional scientific, rationalist approach to learning and knowledge.

In sampling the bewildering range of literature devoted to nonrational and intuitive thought, we are struck by the intensity of this rejection of rationalism and all its works. Any schema that reduces the importance of rational thought is quickly seized upon by a growing number of people who are dissatisfied with current culture and its values. This eagerness to accept even an undocumented claim for nonrational knowledge of any sort goes beyond mere open-mindedness and poses a double threat to the serious study of intuition. First, it leaves naive readers vulnerable to deception and exploitation by the incompetent or unscrupulous; and, because of the sensational or uncritical nature of some of the popular literature, this eagerness to accept any literature on the nonrational contributes to the alienation of the scientific and academic communities and discourages them from joining in a serious study of the potential benefits of intuition. Nowhere are these dangers greater than in educational theory, which is under constant criticism for being too susceptible to fads. The solution to these problems lies in educating both educational theorists and laypeople about intuition and in teaching the latter to discriminate between works making responsible and those making reckless claims concerning intuition and the nonrational.

Second, it is clear from the works examined here that there is little agreement among popular writers about what intuition is and that many writers have not even attempted to define it. The problems of definition are not new, as we saw in chapter 1, but for educators they remain urgent, for it is unwise to design any sort of educational program including intuition without a clear sense of what the word means. No doubt some adherents of Zen and other mystical philosophies would object to a verbal definition of a concept that is fundamentally nonverbal and nonlinear. We sympathize with this perspective but still maintain that so long as our educative efforts are mainly verbal, we need a useful definition and elaborated verbal description of intuition to guide our instructional efforts.

Third, the books and organizations discussed here offer a dazzling spectrum of possible uses for intuition. Even when we set aside the most specious and naive presentations, there still remain many possible directions in which research on intuition can be developed: interpersonal relations, social change, studies in creativity, intellectual activity, and other areas. Most of the material written so far constitutes a preliminary investigation of these areas and only hints at the possible developments that may occur in the coming decades. The collection of essays edited by Ornstein by itself gives an idea of the variety of topics related to intuition which are only beginning to be explored. Ultimately, many of these areas may be of great significance to education; some, such as the techniques for enhancing intuitive modes discussed in chapter 5, are already of obvious value.

The current writing on intuition, therefore, suggests a field of study that, despite its ancient and reputable origins, has not yet reached maturity. At present the field is still inchoate and uncertain, sprawling across several disciplines and ranging even further into areas of pseudoscience and mysticism. The long-range prospects for the emergence of an accepted serious view of intuition are good, though. Writers with the talent and intelligence of Hofstadter and Koestler have presented ideas about the mind that include a notion of intuition that is far more than the mere "sloppy thinking" Siegfried and Therese Engelmann, quoted earlier in chapter 1, mistakenly associate with intuition. With serious study of intuition by such writers and by reputable research organizations, we can hope for greater involvement of educational theorists and practitioners in the study of and development of intuition.

Chapter 9

CONCLUSION

> We shall not cease from exploration
> And the end of all our exploring
> Will be to arrive where we started
> And know the place for the first time.
> T. S. Eliot, "Little Gidding"

WE STARTED OUR INVESTIGATION by tracing the development of intuition as a concept from the days of the ancient seers to the present. We saw that intuition, like the humans who possess it, has had its ups and downs. It has been glorified as the only certain form of knowledge and castigated for its unreliability; it has been associated with truth and light and also with the dark and sinister; it has served science and art in all their domains of creativity and yet has been claimed as the special gift of mystics and cultists. Perennially a topic of interest, it has rarely been studied seriously in the field of education.

The question of what intuition is occupied us at length. We found that intuition is an object oriented capacity, one that organizes the material of inner and outer perception into representation for both reason and Will. It is driven by the Will's quest for meaning. It is, in a deep and poetic sense, the eyes, ears, and fingers of the soul. Even after struggling with the initial question for many years and through many pages, we found it most useful—for the purposes of education — to describe intuitive activity in the form of "intuitive modes." The intuitive mode, as we described it, is characterized by the commitment of the Will, receptivity, involvement of the senses, the quest for understanding, and a tension between subjective certainty and objective uncertainty.

Because our main interest is in education, we concentrated on the role of intuition in intellectual activity, but it is clear that educators might profit from a close examination of intuitive activity in other domains: the aesthetic, social, spiritual, practical, and moral. We did, of course, discuss each of these to some degree, but much more needs to be done in these areas. The moral domain, especially, requires the careful attention of educators. When moral situations are approached intuitively, we refuse to "think" the persons we engage; instead, we encounter them directly—we receive them, feel what they feel, and put our motivational energies into their service. The field of moral education is virtually sterile today, completely dominated by approaches that rely almost entirely on reason and logic. This represents a loss not only for moral education but for *all* of education, because the love required to meet others morally also induces a joy and excitement in intellectual activity that sustains both teacher and student. Further, that love, and the intellectual activity it nurtures, protects its recipients from the onslaught of all sorts of unhealthy and unscrupulous attempts to capture their hearts and minds.

In chapter 8, we acknowledged that many popular, inspiring, and useful books that refer to intuition have, in spite of their lack of rigor, made important statements on the larger issues of human social activity. This sort of emphasis needs to be reconsidered in education as well. We did not review the work of educational critics that was so prominent in the sixties but, if we had, we would have noted that much of it suffered from a similar lack of specificity and rigor. Inspiring and essentially "right" in its opposition to the dullness and moral insensitivity of modern education, it did not provide a sufficiently rigorous theoretical base upon which to build a well-articulated structure. Thus, when we educator-critics return to reform efforts, we should launch our attacks from a well-fortified central, theoretical structure. This book represents an effort, however anticipatory, to get started in the right direction.

There are several questions raised by our exploration that remain unanswered and even more intriguing now than at the beginning of our search. One is whether machines can have intuition. To be consistent with our own theoretical base, we have to answer this question in the negative. Any intelligent person hesitates to give such an answer. No one wishes to risk being classified with those who predicted that humans would never fly, walk on the moon, or talk with each other across vast spaces. Still, we cannot brush aside what we have been at such pains to make explicit. Intuition is a capacity directed by and reporting directly to the Will, that dynamic, basic self that cares about its own survival and well-being and, thus, about its physical body. We can well imagine disembodied mind in the restricted form of *reason*, but we cannot imagine disembodied mind in the form of intuition, because intuition is exactly that part of intellect that connects body and mind. Body, with its urge to exist, procreate, and secure meaning for itself, is the receptacle of intuition.

Now, of course, we can (and, wisely, shall) hedge our answer a bit. Certain *manifestations* of intuition may be reproduced in machines. It may be possible for a machine to acquire a limited intuitive-like response to language; to cast up all sorts of possible combinations and select promising ones by certain pre-established criteria; to sense by electrical and chemical means that a human being is lying to it. Magnificent as such accomplishments will surely be, and enormously difficult as they will be to produce, they are yet only a portion of what human intuition accomplishes. To be intuitive, we have implied, requires that the intuiter be part of a thing that lives and wants to live, that fears, hopes, loves, and longs for. We can certainly program machines to "say" things that we would take, said by human beings, to be expressions of fearing, hoping, and loving. But can a machine *feel* the despair a mother feels holding the hand of a dying child, the terror a man feels in the presence of death, the love felt by a lover in the arms of the beloved? Well, one may respond, we must remember "Hal" in *2001*. Yes. But "Hal" is so far a fiction.

We may be wrong on several counts. Perhaps what we are calling intuition is not necessary, as we suppose it is, to a complete intellect. Perhaps, machines can come to "be" in the sense of having Will and, thus, develop intuition. Perhaps, more interestingly, we can rid ourselves eventually of both intuition and body and become eternally conscious things entirely different from human beings. This last is, perhaps, the most intriguing notion of all, but we note that few of us are eager for such a transition just as, in the past, few of us have been eager to pass prematurely to disembodied existence in "heaven."

Another question, considerably less esoteric, that begs to be answered concerns the role of familiarity in intuitive activity. We have insisted, with considerable support, that familiarity is neither necessary nor sufficient for the production of intuitions. But we have taken the more or less standard position that familiarity and intuition are usually positively correlated. Discoveries are made by well-prepared minds. But how "well-prepared" and in what way "well-prepared"? This is a fascinating and important question. Much recent research seems to indicate that successful innovations are created by the "wrong" persons in the "wrong" places.[1] Innovations come not from the persons who are charged with producing new products but from people working alone and on the periphery. If this result is as general as it now seems to be, we need to investigate very carefully the nature of "preparation" possessed by innovators and that of standard workers.

What can we recommend for education based on mere anticipation of the true relation between familiarity and intuition? We discussed at some length the need to induce familiarity prior to the presentation of major concepts and principles. This still seems distinctly right. But the sort of "familiarity" we described in that connection might more properly be termed "facility." One needs facility with the routine skills, symbols, and modes of communication associated with a field of study. But facility-familiarity must not proceed to and be limited to complete routinization. Some things must be routinized so that one can move about a domain freely, but routinization must not *characterize* one's activity. To create, to innovate, one must see things afresh; hence, there must be unexplored territories within or connected to the domain of familiarity, and one must have the courage to enter them.

In education, we believe that strong arguments should be made for branching out—for connecting particular subjects with all sorts of other subjects. Students should acquire facility in basic routines, study important ideas, and then move out temporarily to a wide variety of applications, appreciations, and even loose associations. Then they should re-enter the original domain, extend their familiarity, and move out again. Similarly, teachers should probably not be allowed to teach only algebra, certainly not only "algebra one." Nothing kills intuitive activity so quickly as removing the need to look because everything has already been seen.

So, finally, we present the last question as a challenge: Can education change so that our students can become present-day *seers*? Surely, it is possible to make many of the changes we have suggested. Most of them seem entirely practical financially, structurally, and pedagogically. But the question may, nevertheless, induce negative responses from many persons simply because any sort of change in schools is so difficult to make. Change in the direction we envision requires commitment, a willingness to abandon self-interest and the comfort of well-entrenched methods. Education, obviously, *can* be changed. Will it change? We can only leave the question as challenge and hope that a positive answer is as attractive to other educators as it is to us.

NOTES
BIBLIOGRAPHY
INDEX

NOTES

Chapter 1
INTUITION: HISTORICAL AND TOPICAL
DEVELOPMENT OF THE CONCEPT

1. Jerome S. Bruner, *The Process of Education* (Cambridge, Mass.: Harvard University Press, 1977), p. 59.

2. Ibid., p. 55.

3. Benedetto Croce, *Aesthetic*, trans. Douglas Ainslie (New York: Noonday Press for Farrar, Straus and Giroux, 1972), p. 12.

4. Max Wertheimer, *Productive Thinking* (New York: Harper, 1945), pp. 234–36.

5. Henri Bergson, *Time and Free Will*, trans. F. L. Pogson (London: George Allen & Unwin, 1910), p. 237.

6. Zen Buddhism is perhaps the best known of Asian philosophical and religious systems dealing with intuition. A lucid account of the Zen understanding of intuition is found in Diasetz Teitaro Suzuki, *The Awakening of Zen*, ed. Christmas Humphreys (Boulder, Colo.: Prajna Press, 1980), pp. 24–27.

7. An overview of women's involvement in the mystical and intuitive is found in M. Esther Harding, *Woman's Mysteries, Ancient and Modern: A Psychological Interpretation of the Feminine Principle as Portrayed in Myth, Story, and Dream.* (New York: Putnam, 1971).

8. Siegfried and Therese Engelmann, *Give Your Child a Superior Mind* (New York: Cornerstone Library, 1981), p. 62.

9. A striking example of the importance of oracular or visionary members of a society to a contemporary preliterate culture is cited by Sir James Frazer in "Adonis, Attis, Osiris," Part 4 of *The Golden Bough: A Study in Magic and Religion*, vol. 2 (London: Macmillan, 1963), p. 107. In the Pelew or Palau Islands of the Pacific, some women are considered to be the wives of gods. These women make oracular pronouncements that are very highly regarded. Furthermore, men also may have special powers of insight that enable them to become wealthy and influential. Frazer notes the parallels between the Pelew Island culture and the religious and social systems of

ancient Egypt and western Asia, and suggests that the power of the mother-kin dominated priesthood was strong in both Pacific and Asian cultures. The intriguing link between women and institutionalized uses of intuition is encountered repeatedly in a study of ancient and prehistoric civilizations.

10. See *I Ching*, trans. John Blofeld (New York: Dutton, 1968). Tossing the yarrow sticks was not a chance operation, like throwing dice today, but a form of revelation.

11. A representative work drawing on Hindu intuitions of the nature of reality is Alan Watts, *Beyond Theology: The Art of Godmanship* (Cleveland, Ohio: World Publishing Company, 1967).

12. Plutarch, "Nicias," *The Lives of the Noble Grecians and Romans*, trans. John Dryden (New York: The Modern Library, Random House, reprint of Arthur Hugh Clough's edition, 1864), pp. 645–46.

13. In the *Phaedo* (107d), Plato has Socrates assert that an δαιμων watches over the life of an individual. In the *Apology* (31d) Socrates admits that a voice (φωνη) has been guiding him in his actions since childhood, never urging him on, but dissuading him from many things. This voice did not dissuade Socrates from taking the position he did during his trial, and so he lost his life.

14. Immanuel Kant, *Critique of Pure Reason*, trans. F. Max Müller (Garden City, N.Y.: Doubleday, 1966).

15. Aristotle, *Posterior Analytics*, vol. 2, 100b.

16. Ibid., 99b.

17. Plotinus, *Sixth Ennead* IX, 10. The Neoplatonists, like many other philosophical schools of antiquity, sought knowledge from nonrational spiritual sources so that, although the tradition of the seer eventually faded, the belief in the value of intuition as an inner vision remained strong in many quarters. The word used by some of the Greek philosophers including Plotinus to describe this kind of insight or intuition was γνωσις (*gnosis*), which is linguistically related to the words *Gnostic* and *gnomon*. Although γνωσις is frequently translated as "intuition," the word should not be taken in the sense that Kant and other later philosophers meant it. Γνωσις frequently carries the connotation of spiritual illumination and enlightenment and is closer to Eastern concepts of intuition than to Kant's rigorous philosophical definition. In the New Testament γνωσις acquires the meaning of the deep spiritual understanding of the mysteries of God and His Son and suggests the esoteric theology of the Gnostics.

One must be cautious, moreover, in translating the word as "intuition" whenever it appears in the Gospels. Clearly, the New Testament γνωσις meant an unveiling of both knowledge and truth, but only a very specific category of knowledge and truth. One could not call this type of intuition "problem solving" except in an odd spiritual sense. Yet the meaning of γνωσις to early Christians is closely linked to both Aristotelian and later concepts of intuition.

This use of the word γνωσις in the Gospels began a tradition of investigations into intuition, within the frame of reference of Christianity, which deemphasized its rational aspects. This tradition was nurtured for centuries by the Catholic Church as well as by other denominations in more recent times. Indeed, it is a tradition that persists today. The Christian approach to intuition influenced many philosophers, including Spinoza and Kant. It is also apparently this tradition that ultimately provided the English word *intuition* with all of its implications of γνωσις. At about the same time that the Gospels were being written, Philo, a Hellenized Jew of Alexandria, was, independent of Christian writers, incorporating an idea of intuition into his own religious philosophy. Like the early Christian theologians, Philo had no great confidence in the ability of ordinary human reasoning to bring knowledge of God to man. Instead, Philo suggested that the highest knowledge of God could be attained only through intuition, a divinely inspired, insightful experience. This view puts Philo much closer to medieval mystics than to earlier Greek or Hebrew thought. Philo may even be seen as a bridge between pagan and Christian views of intuition, and as an important link to Eastern notions of the intuitive experience. The spiritual aspects of intuition are important and resurface persistently throughout its history in the West, while at the same time they also form a major part of the concept of intuition in the Hindu tradition.

18. The Cynics received their name, which means "doglike," from their detractors, who claimed that the Cynics' aggressive style of arguing resembled the snarling of dogs. The negative connotation of *cynic* has lasted until the present.

19. Norman W. DeWitt, *Epicurus and His Philosophy* (Minneapolis, Minn.: University of Minnesota Press, 1954), p. 122.

20. See Julian Jaynes, *The Origin of Consciousness in the Breakdown of the Bicameral Mind* (Boston, Mass.: Houghton Mifflin, 1976), for a different perspective on the role of the intuitive "inner voice" in several ancient societies.

21. There are a number of good sources of information about African oracles and seers. Among the best are Geoffrey Parrinder, *West African Religion* (London: Epworth Press, 1901), pp. 136–55; and T. O. Ranger and Isaria Kimambo, *The Historical Study of African Religion* (Berkeley: University of California Press, 1972). For the Islamic world, see R. B. Serjeant, "Islam," in *Oracles and Divination*, ed. Michael Loewe and Carmen Blacker (Boulder, Colo.: Shambhala, 1981), pp. 215–32. A thorough description of the intuitive Sufi philosophy is found in Idries Shah, *The Sufis* (Garden City, N.Y.: Doubleday, 1964).

22. St. Bernard de Clairvaux (1090–1173) typified medieval theologians in his view of intuition, which he saw as a product of contemplation that yielded religious truth. This definition of intuition is far removed from that of twentieth-century aestheticians and psychologists but does show that nonrational paths to illumination remained intellectually respectable during the medieval period. For more information on this important theologian and adversary of Abelard, see Watkin W. Williams, *Saint Bernard of Clairvaux* (Manchester, England: Manchester University Press, 1935).

23. Meister (or Master) Eckhart (ca.1260–1327) was a member of the

Dominican Order and one of the great mystics of the High Middle Ages. He was heavily influenced by both Plotinus and St. Thomas Aquinas and was also familiar with the works of St. Bernard de Clairvaux. Eckhart's position was that the contemplation that led to contact with God was not purely ecstatic but was, in fact, predominantly intellectual. Eckhart also emphasized the union of the soul with God and so foreshadowed the writings of such later theologians as Schleiermacher. Eckhart's understanding of the spiritual intuitive experience shows as much influence from pagan philosophers of antiquity as it does from the New Testament and is especially indebted to the Neoplatonists. Eckhart's influence has increased during the twentieth century and today he is considered an important contributor to the visionary legacy of Christianity. For further discussion see the article on Meister Eckhart in the *New Catholic Encyclopedia* (New York: McGraw-Hill, 1967), vol. V, pp. 38–40.

24. Lettre au Marquis de Newcastle, March or April 1648, quoted in J. H. Randall, *The Career of Philosophy: From the Middle Ages to the Enlightenment* (New York: Columbia University Press, 1962), p. 388.

25. Spinoza distinguished between rational thought and intuition by saying that rational thought uses general principles from which it can deduce its conclusions, while intuition apprehends truth in an immediate fashion without the use of any general principles. Although Spinoza asserted that intuition and reason are both sources of adequate ideas and necessary truths, he believed that in two aspects intuition was superior. First, intuition can arrive at knowledge of individual essences in a concrete way that abstract reason cannot. Second, knowledge reasoned from general principles is, from an epistemological standpoint, insecure and incomplete. Intution, according to Spinoza, provides the complement to this incomplete reason.

What is of particular value to us in our development of the notion of intuition in education is Spinoza's recognition of intuition as immediate apprehension. Moreover, while the notion of intuition as a sure key to truth is no longer tenable, Spinoza's development of the concept remains an important step toward the crucial work of Kant 150 years later, and to an understanding of the later works of Schleiermacher and others.

26. For a discussion of the mechanistic views of the period, see Dudley Shapere, "Isaac Newton," *The Encyclopedia of Philosophy*, vol. 5, ed. Paul Edwards (New York: Macmillan, 1967), pp. 489–96.

27. Kant, *Critique of Pure Reason*, "Transcendental Logic," 1, p. 45.

28. A. S. Neill, *Summerhill: A Radical Approach to Childrearing* (New York: Hart Publishing, 1960). Although Neill makes no direct reference to intuition, he clearly espouses an intuitive approach to learning as he allows his students to discover the world and themselves with a minimal amount of adult guidance.

29. F. H. Jacobi (1743–1819), sometimes called the "faith-philosopher," rose to challenge the Godless, passionless universe of the eighteenth-century rationalists. Metaphysical truth must be reached, asserted this apostle of intuition, not by the "mediate" knowledge of ideas, but by a type of immediate perception which Jacobi called *Glaube* (faith) and what might today be

called intuition. Jacobi thus redefined Kant's conception of intuition to include not only a dispassionate perception that illuminated, but a deeply spiritual experience that led to contact with God. This intuitive approach to metaphysics had much in common with the mysticism of some medieval theologians; but it has not survived well in a rational comparison with Kant's more epistemologically based notions of intuition, since Jacobi did not provide a detailed explanation of how this contact took place. We see in his efforts the continuing attempt to associate intuition with the mystical. But progress in conceptualizing intuition went forward; there was, and obviously still is, an important role for intuition in nonmystical knowing.

30. Friedrich Schleiermacher, *Ethics*, quoted in Richard B. Brandt, *The Philosophy of Schleiermacher* (New York: Harper, 1941), pp. 319–20.

31. Gioberti drew heavily on the teaching of A. Rosmini-Serbati (1797–1855), another Italian theologian. Rosmini-Serbati's conception of intuition included a moral component, and thus both Gioberti and Rosmini-Serbati may be considered precursors of the nineteenth-century revival of intuitionism. Rosmini-Serbati, in particular, continues to exercise a considerable influence on the philosophy of Christian spiritualism and has had some impact on pedagogical practices in European parochial schools.

32. Friedrich Wilhelm Joseph Schelling (1775–1854), Schopenhauer's contemporary, focused on Kant's idea that our aesthetic (i.e., perceiving) sense may contain perceptions of ultimate truth. Schelling's ideas were largely ignored, however, and he was the last major European philosopher until Bergson to write extensively on intuition.

33. See Christopher J. Lucas, *Our Western Educational Heritage* (New York: Macmillan, 1972), pp. 409–11, for a concise discussion of Froebel's pedagogy of symbols. For a sharp criticism of Froebel's attempt to build an intuitively apprehended symbolic universe, see John Dewey, *Democracy and Education* (New York: Free Press, 1966), pp. 58–59.

34. Among the many individuals exploring intuition at this time were Franz Brentano and James Sully.

Franz Brentano (1838–1917), a noted Austrian teacher and philosopher, divided all presentations into two classes: those having "intuitive unity" and those having "attributive unity." Presentations having intuitive unity were divided into intuitions and abstractions, the latter obtained by simplifying and generalizing intuitions. Brentano disagreed with Kant and denied that we have *a priori* knowledge of three-dimensional space. He also made the improbable claim that inner perceptions do not differ from individual to individual. Instead, our interior intuitions have a unity with all other intuitions experienced in the same time and place. Like many others grappling with the problem of intuition, Brentano was hampered by his unclear terminology and unprovable assertions. Yet Brentano's discussion is worth noting because of the influence his teaching had on subsequent writers on intuition, especially Edmund Husserl. See Franz Brentano, *Psychology from an Empirical Standpoint*, ed. Oskar Kraus, trans. A. C. Rancurello, D. B. Terrell, and L. L. McAlister (New York: Humanities Press, 1973).

James Sully (1842–1923) attempted to link Darwinism and Spencerian notions of human and animal development to aesthetics in a series of essays entitled *Sensation and Intuition*. Intuition, for Sully, meant a broad range of aesthetic experiences, all related to the recognition and appreciation of beauty. Sully was also concerned with the development of emotional and moral sensibility, which he referred to as "The Aesthetic Aspects of Character." While presenting a somewhat confusing potpourri of psychology, musicology, and ethics, among other subjects, Sully did reflect the desire of the Victorians to identify, categorize, and integrate all aspects of the human personality.

35. Bergson laid out his concept of intuition in *The Introduction to a New Philosophy*, trans. Sidney Littman (Boston: John W. Luce, 1912), pp. 1–12.

36. A. A. Michaelson, address at the dedication ceremony of the Ryerson Physical Laboratory, University of Chicago. Quoted in *Bartlett's Familiar Quotations* (Boston: Little, Brown, 1968), p. 827.

Chapter 2
THE TWENTIETH CENTURY

1. Carl Gustav Jung, *Psychological Types*, trans. H. Godwin Baynes (London: Kegan Paul, Trench, Trübner; New York: Harcourt Brace, 1946).

2. Ibid., p. 568.

3. Eric Berne, *Intuition and Ego States: The Origins of Transactional Analysis* (San Francisco: TA Press, 1977), pp. 25–26.

4. Ibid., p. 31.

5. Benedetto Croce, *Aesthetic*, trans. Douglas Ainslie (New York: Noonday Press for Farrar, Straus and Giroux, 1972).

6. Croce's view of intuition differs from Kant's, for it can exist without space or time, and includes an expressive component. This notion that "intuition is expressive knowledge" is the most important contribution Croce made to the theory of intuition, since it suggests a close relationship between intuition and the affective domain. Another important contribution of Croce from our point of view is his emphasis on the power of intuition to enlighten the powers of reason. Unfortunately his ideas in this area are not developed sufficiently. Croce maintained, with Kant, that intuition creates nonconceptual representations, but he allowed both emotional and "cosmic" representations to be apprehended by intuition. He maintained that a picture of an object or relationship is essential to the intuitive process. In making such a claim Croce appears to be close to Wertheimer and other Gestalt psychologists who stress the importance of visualization in problem solving. The connection Croce wished to make between artistic creation and intuition is not as clear, however.

7. Edmund Husserl, *Ideas*, trans. W. R. Boyce Gibson (New York: Macmillan, 1962), p. 83.

8. Sartre argues specifically against the transcendental ego in *Being and*

Nothingness, trans. Hazel E. Barnes (New York: Washington Square Press, 1966), pp. 9–24.

9. "Now my reflecting consciousness does not take itself for its object when I effect the *cogito.* What it affirms concerns the reflected consciousness. Insofar as my reflecting consciousness is consciousness of itself, it is non-positional consciousness. It becomes positional only as directed upon the reflected consciousness, which itself, before being thus reflected upon, was not a positional consciousness of itself. Thus the consciousness which states 'I think' is not the consciousness which thinks. Or rather it is not its own thought which it posits by this thetic act. We are accordingly justified in inquiring if the I which thinks is common to the two superimposed consciousnesses, or if it is not rather the I of the reflected consciousness. No reflecting consciousness reflects upon itself; it remains unreflected upon until a third act of consciousness at a higher level posits it. But there is no infinite regress here, since a consciousness does not need a reflecting consciousness to reflect upon it, in order to be conscious of itself. It simply is conscious of itself without positing itself as its object. Is it not the reflective act which brings the Me to birth in the reflected consciousness? This would explain how every thought apprehended by intuition possesses an I without our running into the difficulties previously noted." Jean-Paul Sartre, *The Philosophy of Jean-Paul Sartre,* ed. R. D. Cumming (New York: Random House, 1965), pp. 52–53.

10. Whitehead claimed intuitive judgment arises from the integration of what he called an imaginative feeling with an indicative feeling. In intuitive judgment one experiences the same integration of a physical feeling and a propositional feeling that occurs in conscious perception. In conscious perception, Whitehead maintained, the propositional feeling is derived from the same physical feeling, while with intuitive judgment, the apparent propositional feeling is based on two physical feelings, one being what Whitehead called the indicative feeling and the other direct physical recognition. F. Rasvihary Das describes the distinction between conscious perception and intuitive judgment in a concise fashion: "The difference . . . is based on the difference between the two physical feelings which serve as the indicative feeling and the physical recognition. If one and the same feeling serves both, we have conscious perception; and if the indicative feeling and the physical recognition are two distinct feelings, they give rise to intuitive judgment." Rasvihary Das, *The Philosophy of Whitehead* (New York: Russell and Russell, 1964), p. 123.

The problem with Whitehead's approach is in the term *feelings,* which is so difficult to define, since it has both a physical and emotional connotation. However, Whitehead does give a clue to the educator when he makes the distinction between physical recognition and the indicative feeling. Whitehead defines the latter as "a physical feeling in which the actual entities are given which are the logical subjects of the proposition." The difference between indicative feeling and physical recognition parallels the acts of inspection and insight into deeper structure that Wertheimer and others would develop later.

11. Alfred North Whitehead, *The Aims of Education* (New York: Free Press, 1967), pp. 17–18.

12. Wiener writes: "Russell started as a Platonist but turned to a more empiricistic nominalism under the influence of operationalist developments in the logic of the sciences. Leibniz, on the other hand, started as an atomist, but turned to a more realistic metaphysic in keeping with the seventeenth-century belief that science like art held the mirror of man's mind up to nature. In Russell's theory of knowledge, logical analysis has broken the mirror into so many atomic sense-data that it makes no sense to talk about mind as a mirror at all. The analysis of meaning becomes a matter of logical construction in which sense-data and universals serve as neutral and transparent building blocks, and truth involves a rather obscure relation of logical correspondence. Thus, Russell has effectively criticized the simple mirroring relation that Leibniz's monads have to each other in their divinely preestablished harmony. But a certain sort of Platonism still haunts Russell's theory of truth by logical correspondence in which atomic statements stalk like ghosts of eternal truth." Philip Wiener, "Method in Russell's Work on Leibniz," in *The Philosophy of Bertrand Russell*, ed. P. A. Schilpp (New York: Tudor Publishing Co., 1951), p. 274.

13. See A. E. Dungan Jones, *Butler's Moral Philosophy* (Harmondsworth, Middlesex, England: Penguin, 1952). See also James McCosh, *Intuitions of the Mind, Inductively Investigated* (New York: R. Carter, 1872).

14. See Henry Sidgwick, *The Methods of Ethics* (Indianapolis, Ind.: Hackett Publishing, 1981).

15. Max Wertheimer, *Productive Thinking* (New York: Harper, 1945), pp. 1–12.

16. Jerome S. Bruner, *The Process of Education* (Cambridge, Mass.: Harvard University Press, 1977).

17. Ibid., p. 61.

18. Jerome S. Bruner, *On Knowing: Essays for the Left Hand* (Cambridge, Mass.: Harvard University Press, 1966).

19. Ibid., p. 102.

20. See Friedrich Schleiermacher, *The Christian Faith*, ed. H. R. Mackintosh and J. S. Stewart (New York: Harper & Row, 1965), for a statement of Schleiermacher's theology.

21. R. Buckminster Fuller, *Intuition* (New York: Anchor Press, 1973), p. 50.

22. See M. Esther Harding, *Woman's Mysteries, Ancient and Modern: A Psychological Interpretation of the Feminine Principle as Portrayed in Myth, Story, and Dream* (New York: Putnam, 1971); also Erich Neumann, *The Great Mother: An Analysis of the Archetype*, trans. Ralph Manheim (Princeton, N.J.: Princeton University Press, 1955).

23. See Virginia Woolf on this topic with respect to women and fiction: *A Room of One's Own* (New York: Harcourt, 1929).

24. Marilyn Ferguson, *The Aquarian Conspiracy: Personal and Social Transformation in the 1980s* (Los Angeles: J. P. Tarcher, 1980).

25. Douglas R. Hofstadter, *Gödel, Escher, Bach: An Eternal Golden Braid* (New York: Basic Books, 1979).

26. Richard Rorty, "Intuition," *The Encyclopedia of Philosophy*, vol. 4, ed. Paul Edwards (New York: Macmillan, 1967), pp. 204–12.

Chapter 3
WHAT IS INTUITION?

1. Hans Hahn, "The Crisis in Intuition," in *The World of Mathematics*, ed. James R. Newman (New York: Simon & Schuster, 1956), p. 1976.

2. See Arthur Schopenhauer, *The World as Will and Representation*, trans. E. F. J. Payne (New York: Dover, 1969).

3. D. W. Hamlyn, *The Theory of Knowledge* (Garden City, N.Y.: Doubleday, 1970), p. 275.

4. Immanuel Kant, *Critique of Pure Reason*, trans. F. Max Müller (Garden City, N.Y.: Doubleday, 1966), "Transcendental Aesthetic," 3.

5. Hamlyn, *Theory of Knowledge*, p. 276.

6. Rudy Rucker, *Infinity and the Mind* (Boston: Birkhauser, 1982), p. 208.

7. C. S. Peirce, "The Essence of Mathematics," in Newman, *The World of Mathematics*, pp. 1776–77.

8. Ibid., p. 1773.

9. Philip Davis and Reuben Hersh, *The Mathematical Experience* (Boston: Birkhauser, 1981).

10. See Charles Parsons, "Foundations of Mathematics," *The Encyclopedia of Philosophy*, vol. 5, ed. Paul Edwards (New York: Macmillan, 1972), pp. 188–213.

11. Hermann Weyl, "The Mathematical Way of Thinking," in Newman, *The World of Mathematics*, p. 1836.

12. Ibid., p. 1845.

13. Richard von Mises, "Mathematical Postulates and Human Understanding," in Newman, *The World of Mathematics*, p. 1748.

14. Hahn, "Crisis in Intuition," in Newman, *The World of Mathematics*, p. 1976.

15. G. Spencer Brown, *The Laws of Form* (London: George Allen & Unwin, 1969).

16. In contrast, Jung uses the expression for only abstract intuition. See Carl Jung, *Psychological Types*, trans. H. Godwin Baynes (London: Kegan Paul, Trench, Trübner; New York: Harcourt Brace, 1946), p. 568–69.

17. See Edmund Husserl, *Ideas*, trans. W. R. Boyce Gibson (New York: Macmillan, 1962).

18. Max Wertheimer, *Productive Thinking* (New York: Harper, 1945), pp. 183–84.

19. See Husserl, *Ideas*.

20. Jean-Paul Sartre, "The Emotions: Outline of a Theory," in *Essays in Existentialism*, ed. Wade Baskin (Secaucus, N.J.: Citadel Press, 1965), p. 246.

21. Ulric Neisser, *Cognitive Psychology* (New York: Appleton-Century-Crofts, 1967), p. 3.

22. Jacques Hadamard, *The Psychology of Invention in the Mathematical Field* (New York: Dover, 1954).

23. Schopenhauer, *The World as Will*, p. 112.

24. See Nel Noddings, *Caring: A Feminine Approach to Ethics and Moral Education* (Berkeley: University of California Press, 1984).

25. Martin Buber, *I and Thou*, trans. Ronald Gregor Smith (New York: Scribner's, 1958), p. 8.

26. Linus Pauling, "A Chat with Linus Pauling," California Living, *San Francisco Examiner and Chronicle*, July 17, 1977, p. 13.

27. Henri Poincaré, "Mathematical Creation," in Newman, *The World of Mathematics*, p. 2048.

Chapter 4
INTUITIVE MODES

1. See Martin J. Gardner, *The Annotated Alice* (New York: World Publishing, 1972), p. 191.

2. Ibid., p. 192.

3. e. e. cummings, "what if a much of a which of a wind," *Collected Poems* (New York: Harcourt Brace, 1923).

4. Quoted in Jacques Hadamard, *The Psychology of Invention in the Mathematical Field* (New York: Dover, 1954), p. 16.

5. Martin Buber, *I and Thou*, trans. Ronald Gregor Smith (New York: Scribner's, 1958), p. 8.

6. E. T. Bell, *Men of Mathematics* (New York: Simon & Schuster, 1965), p. 254.

7. Thomas Hardy, "The Impercipient," *Collected Poems* (New York: Macmillan, 1925). Reprinted by permission of the publisher.

8. Thomas Hardy, "Hap," ibid.

9. Robert Frost, *Complete Poems* (New York: Henry Holt, 1949), p. viii.

10. Ibid., p. vi.

11. Ibid., p. vii.

12. See Hadamard, *The Psychology of Invention*; Bell, *Men of Mathematics*; and Stanley Rosner and Lawrence E. Abt, eds., *The Creative Experience* (New York: Grossman, 1970).

13. See the description in Henri Poincaré, "Mathematical Creation," in *The World of Mathematics*, ed. James R. Newman (New York: Simon & Schuster, 1956), pp. 2041–50.

14. Warren S. McCullough, *Embodiments of Mind* (Cambridge, Mass.: MIT Press, 1965).

15. Karl Pribram describes the correlation in "Toward a Neuro-

psychological Theory of Person," in *Mood, States and Mind*, Brain and Behavior, vol. 1, ed. K. H. Pribram. (Harmondsworth, Middlesex, England: Penguin, 1969), pp. 462–75.

16. Frederick C. Bartlett, *Thinking* (New York: Basic Books, 1958).

17. Morris Kline, *Why Johnny Can't Add: The Failure of the New Math* (New York: Vintage, 1974), p. 191.

18. Hadamard, *The Psychology of Invention*, p. 112. But note his attempt to make sense of the distinction, pp. 113–15.

19. John Holt, *How Children Fail* (New York: Dell, 1964), p. 99.

20. Philip Davis and Reuben Hersh, *The Mathematical Experience* (Boston: Birkhauser, 1981), p. 403.

21. Ibid., p. 404.

Chapter 5
ENHANCING INTUITIVE MODES

1. James R. Newman, editorial comment on "The Elusiveness of Invention," in *The World of Mathematics*, ed. James R. Newman (New York: Simon & Schuster, 1956), p. 2039.

2. Henri Poincaré, "Mathematical Creation," in Newman, *The World of Mathematics*, pp. 2041–50.

3. D. T. Suzuki, *An Introduction to Zen Buddhism* (New York: Grove Press, 1964), p. 105.

4. Quoted in a prefatory note to Immanuel Kant, *Critique of Pure Reason*, trans. F. Max Müller (Garden City, N.Y.: Doubleday, 1966).

5. See the account in E. T. Bell, *Men of Mathematics* (New York: Simon & Schuster, 1965), pp. 218–69.

6. Milton Cross and David Ewen, eds., *Milton Cross' Encyclopedia of the Great Composers and Their Music*, vol. 1 (Garden City, N.Y.: Doubleday, 1953), p. 15.

7. Jean-Paul Sartre, quoted in *Existential Encounters for Teachers*, ed. Maxine Greene (New York: Random House, 1967), pp. 85–86.

8. For an account of inquiry training, see Richard Suchman, "A Model for the Analysis of Inquiry," in *Analyses of Concept Learning*, ed. H. J. Klausmeier and Chester W. Harris (New York: Academic Press, 1966).

9. See the essays in *Learning By Discovery*, ed. Lee S. Shulman and Evan R. Keisler (Chicago: Rand McNally, 1966).

10. David Kreps, quoted in *Campus Report*, Stanford University, 27 October 1982, p. 3.

11. Edmund Husserl, *Ideas*, trans. W. R. Boyce Gibson (New York: Macmillan, 1962).

12. Michael Bennett, "Creativity and Knowledge—An Alternative View," *Theoria to Theory*, 1979, 12, p. 334.

13. See Alfred North Whitehead, *The Aims of Education* (New York: Free Press, 1967).

14. Robert Frost, "The Witch of Coös," *Complete Poems* (New York: Henry Holt, 1949), pp. 247–52.

15. Elliot W. Eisner, "Instructional and Expressive Educational Objectives: Their Formulation and Use in Curriculum," *Instructional Objectives*, AERA Monograph Series in Curriculum Evaluation, no. 3 (Chicago: Rand McNally, 1969), pp. 1–31.

16. Frederick C. Bartlett, *Thinking* (New York: Basic Books, 1958).

17. *Celebrated Cases of Judge Dee (Dee Goong An)*, trans. Robert Van Gulick (New York: Dover, 1976), p. 5.

18. Isaac Bashevis Singer, "The Last Demon," in *The Collected Stories* (New York: Farrar, Straus and Giroux, 1982), pp. 179–87.

19. *Biological Science: Molecules to Man*. Boston: Houghton Mifflin, 1973), p. 2.

20. Quoted in Morris Kline, *Why Johnny Can't Add: The Failure of the New Math* (New York: Vintage, 1974), p. 58.

Chapter 6
CURRICULUM AND INSTRUCTION: INTUITIVE
ARRANGEMENTS AND PRESENTATIONS OF SUBJECT MATTER

1. Jerome S. Bruner, *The Process of Education* (Cambridge, Mass. Harvard University Press, 1977), p. 28.

2. Max Beberman, "An Emerging Program of Secondary School Mathematics," in *New Curricula*, ed. Robert W. Heath (New York: Harper & Row, 1964), p. 14.

3. John Dewey, *Experience and Education*. (New York: Macmillan/Collier Books, 1963), p. 67.

4. Martin Buber, "Education," in *Between Man and Man*. (New York: Macmillan, 1965), p. 90.

5. Rick Billstein, Shlomo Libeskind, and Johnny W. Lott, *A Problem-Solving Approach to Mathematics for Elementary School Teachers* (Menlo Park, Calif.: Benjamin/Cummings, 1981), p. 177.

6. R. B. Zajonc, "Feeling and Thinking: Preferences Need No Inferences," *American Psychologist*, 1980, *35*(2), 151–75.

7. Genevieve Lloyd, "The Man of Reason," *Metaphilosophy*, 1979, *10*(1), p. 27.

8. Benedict Spinoza, *The Ethics*, trans. R. H. Elwes (New York: Dover, 1955), Part V, Prop. VII.

9. Douglas R. Hofstadter, *Gödel, Escher, Bach: An Eternal Golden Braid* (New York: Basic Books, 1979), p. 564.

10. Ernest Hemingway, *The Short Stories of Ernest Hemingway* (New York: Scribner's, 1953), p. 207.

11. Nel Noddings, *Caring: A Feminine Approach to Ethics and Moral Education* (Berkeley: University of California Press, 1984).

12. Jean Dieudonné, "L'Abstraction et L'Intuition Mathematique," *Dialectica*, 1975, *29*(1), p. 44.

13. Ibid., p. 43.

14. Everyone is, of course, familiar with *Alice in Wonderland*. The others are Edwin A. Abbott, *Flatland: A Romance of Many Dimensions* (New York: Dover, 1952); and Clifton Fadiman, ed., *Fantasia Mathematica* (New York: Simon & Schuster, 1958).

15. Virginia Woolf, *To The Lighthouse* (New York: Harcourt, 1927), p. 161.

16. See the essays in Frank K. Lester and J. Garofalo, eds., *Mathematical Problem Solving* (Philadelphia: Franklin Institute Press, 1982).

17. Zoltan P. Dienes and E. W. Golding, *Approach to Modern Mathematics* (New York: Herder and Herder, 1971).

18. L. Vygotsky, *Mind in Society* (Cambridge, Mass.: Harvard University Press, 1978).

19. See Nel Noddings, "The Use of Small Group Protocols in Analysis of Children's Arithmetical Problem Solving" (paper presented at annual meeting of the American Educational Research Association, New York, 1982).

20. The following example is suggested by the description in Priscilla Chaffe-Stengel and Nel Noddings, "Facilitating Symbolic Understanding of Fractions," *For The Learning of Mathematics*, 1982, 3(2), pp. 42–48.

21. Michael Polanyi, *Personal Knowledge: Towards a Post-Critical Philosophy.* (New York: Harper & Row, 1964), p. 130.

22. Henri Poincaré, "Mathematical Creation," in *The World of Mathematics*, ed. James R. Newman. (New York: Simon & Schuster, 1956), p. 2041.

23. Ibid., p. 2043.

24. Ibid., p. 2050.

25. Efraim Fischbein, "Intuition and Proof," *For The Learning of Mathematics*, 1982, 3(2), p. 10.

26. Ibid., p. 10.

27. See Morris Kline, *Why Johnny Can't Add: The Failure of the New Math* (New York: Vintage, 1974); Robert B. Davis, "Discovery in the Teaching of Mathematics," in *Learning by Discovery*, ed. Lee S. Shulman and Evan R. Keisler (Chicago: Rand McNally, 1966).

28. Bertrand Russell, "Mathematics and the Metaphysicians," in Newman, *The World of Mathematics*, p. 1578.

29. Fischbein, "Intuition and Proof," p. 11.

Chapter 7
INTUITION, LOVE, AND EDUCATION

1. See Nel Noddings, *Caring: A Feminine Approach to Ethics and Moral Education* (Berkeley: University of California Press, 1984), for a discussion of caring as a central theme of education.

2. Rollo May, *Love and Will* (New York: W. W. Norton, 1969), p. 78.

3. Among the many references in the New Testament to *agape* are: "God is *agape*" (I John 4:8); "Greater *agape* than this has no one, that he lay down his life for his friends" (John 15:13); and "*Agape* covers a multitude of sins" (I Peter 4:8).

4. Isocrates, *Antidosis*, 268. The philosopher Empedocles also subscribed to this view.

5. *Caritas*, which is related to the words *charity, caring,* and *cherish,* is a Latin word meaning regard, affection, esteem, and love, and also has the connotation of preciousness. It is thus an excellent word to express the emotions that help bring about insightful, compassionate teaching.

6. Quoted in Leo Buscaglia, *Living, Loving, and Learning* (New York: Holt, Rinehart & Winston, 1982), pp. 6–7.

7. Quoted in Douglas R. Hofstadter, *Gödel, Escher, Bach: An Eternal Golden Braid* (New York: Basic Books, 1979), p. 254.

8. See D. T. Suzuki, *Zen Buddhism* (Garden City, N.Y.: Doubleday, 1956), p. 160.

9. Ibid., p. 248.

10. Buscaglia, *Living, Loving, and Learning,* p. 64.

11. Suzuki, *Zen Buddhism,* p. 236.

12. *Pestalozzi's Educational Writings,* ed. J. A. Green (New York: Longmans, Green, 1912), p. 161.

13. For a more complete discussion of Pestalozzi's vision of the mother's role in moral education see Kate Silber, *Pestalozzi: The Man and His Work* (London: Routledge and Kegan Paul, 1960), pp. 172–84.

14. Zen writings do make frequent mention of "Buddha-Nature," a quality that may be found in inanimate objects or living things. This, however, does not mean that Zen posits an anthropomorphic Buddha force moving through the physical world.

15. For a short survey of Pestalozzi's practical educational accomplishments, see A. Pinloche, *Pestalozzi and the Foundation of the Modern Elementary School* (New York: Scribner's, 1901).

16. Martin Buber, *I and Thou,* trans. Ronald Gregor Smith (New York: Scribner's, 1958), pp. 15–16.

17. Ibid., p. 39.

18. Ibid., p. 43.

19. Ibid., p. 75.

20. The Greek pedagogue was often a companion for many years, teaching the youth or youths in his charge all the wisdom he knew. Although these pedagogues were frequently slaves, they were held in high regard by their students, who sometimes freed them when the latter reached maturity.

21. George Leonard, *Education and Ecstasy* (New York: Delacorte, 1968), p. 230.

22. See Paul Goodman, *Growing Up Absurd* (New York: Vintage, 1960), p. 80.

23. Quoted in Leonard, *Education and Ecstasy,* p. 231.

24. Jerome S. Bruner, *The Process of Education* (Cambridge, Mass.: Harvard University Press, 1977), p. 64.

25. See Larry Cuban, "Determinants of Curriculum Change and Stability, 1870–1970" in *Value Conflicts and Curriculum Issues,* ed. Jon Schaffarzick and Gary Sykes (Berkeley: McCutchan, 1979), pp. 139–90.

26. Paul Tillich, *The Courage To Be* (New Haven, Conn.: Yale University Press, 1952), pp. 47 and 82.

Chapter 8
RECENT INTEREST IN INTUITION

1. Frances E. Vaughan, *Awakening Intuition* (Garden City, N.Y.: Anchor/Doubleday, 1979).
2. Robert E. Ornstein, ed., *The Nature of Human Consciousness* (San Francisco: W. H. Freeman, 1973).
3. Robert E. Ornstein, *The Psychology of Consciousness* (New York: W. H. Freeman, 1972).
4. Ibid., p. 167.
5. *Institute of Noetic Sciences: Research Projects and Conferences* (San Francisco: Institute for Noetic Sciences, n.d.), p. 1.
6. *Intuitive Consensus: A Novel Approach to the Solution of Difficult Scientific and Technical Problems* (San Francisco: Center for Applied Intuition, n.d.), p. 2.
7. Charles A. Reich, *The Greening of America* (New York: Random House, 1970).
8. Marilyn Ferguson, *The Aquarian Conspiracy: Personal and Social Transformation in the 1980's* (Los Angeles: J. P. Tarcher, 1980).
9. Reich, *The Greening of America*, p. 225.
10. Ferguson, *The Aquarian Conspiracy*, p. 297.
11. Flora Davis, *Inside Intuition* (New York: McGraw-Hill, 1971).
12. Alan Watts, *The Joyous Cosmology: Adventures in the Chemistry of Consciousness* (New York: Pantheon, 1962).
13. Ibid., p. 63.
14. Ibid., p. 64.
15. Jean Shinoda Bolen, *The Tao of Psychology: Synchronicity and the Self* (San Francisco: Harper & Row, 1979).
16. Ibid., p. 89.
17. D. T. Suzuki, *The Awakening of Zen*, ed. Christmas Humphries (Boulder, Colo.: Prajna Press, 1980).
18. Ibid., p. 24.
19. Ibid., p. 68.
20. Carlos Castaneda, *The Teachings of Don Juan: A Yaqui Way of Knowledge* (Berkeley: University of California Press, 1968).
21. Douglas R. Hofstadter, *Gödel, Escher, Bach: An Eternal Golden Braid* (New York: Basic Books, 1979).
22. Arthur Koestler, *The Act of Creation* (New York: Macmillan, 1964).
23. Ibid., p. 201.
24. Ibid., p. 211.
25. Jerome S. Bruner, *The Process of Education* (Cambridge, Mass.: Harvard University Press, 1977), p. 67.

Chapter 9
CONCLUSION

1. See Thomas J. Peters and Robert Waterman, *In Search of Excellence: Lessons from America's Best Run Companies* (New York: Harper & Row, 1982); see also Thomas J. Peters, "The Mythology of Innovation, or A Skunkworks Tale Part I," *The Stanford Magazine*, Summer 1983, pp. 13–21.

BIBLIOGRAPHY

Aristotle. *Nichomachean Ethics.*

Aristotle. *Posterior Analytics.*

Bartlett, Frederick C. *Thinking.* New York: Basic Books, 1958.

Bell, E. T. *Men of Mathematics.* New York: Simon & Schuster, 1965.

Bergson, Henri. *Time and Free Will.* Translated by F. L. Pogson. London: George Allen and Unwin, 1910.

Berkeley, Bishop George. "A Dialogue Concerning the Principles." *Selections from Berkeley: Annotated.* Edited by Alexander Campbell Fraser. Oxford: Clarendon Press, 1899.

Berne, Eric. *Intuition and Ego States: The Origins of Transactional Analysis.* San Francisco: TA Press, 1977.

Bolen, Jean Shinoda. *The Tao of Psychology: Synchronicity and the Self.* San Francisco: Harper & Row, 1979.

Brentano, Franz. *Psychology from an Empirical Standpoint.* Edited by Oskar Kraus. Translated by A. C. Rancurello, D. B. Terrell, and L. L. McAlister. New York: Humanities Press, 1973.

Bruner, Jerome S., et al. *Beyond the Information Given: Studies in the Psychology of Knowing.* Edited by Jeremy M. Anglin. New York: W. W. Norton, 1973.

Bruner, Jerome S. *The Process of Education.* Cambridge Mass.: Harvard University Press, 1977 (1960).

Buber, Martin. *Between Man and Man.* New York: Macmillan, 1965.

Buber, Martin. *I and Thou.* Translated by Ronald Gregor Smith. New York: Scribner's, 1958.

Buscaglia, Leo. *Living, Loving, and Learning.* New York: Holt, Rinehart & Winston, 1982.

Capra, Fritjof. *The Tao of Physics.* Berkeley: Shambhala, 1975.

Carlyle, Thomas. "Characteristics." *Critical and Miscellaneous Essays*, vol. III. London: Chapman and Hall, 1899.

Croce, Benedetto. *Aesthetic.* Translated by Douglas Ainslie. New York: Noonday Press for Farrar, Straus and Giroux, 1972.

Cross, Milton, and Ewen, David, eds. *Milton Cross' Encyclopedia of the Great Composers and Their Music.* Garden City, N.Y.: Doubleday, 1953.

Davis, Philip, and Hersh, Reuben. *The Mathematical Experience.* Boston: Birkhauser, 1981.

Descartes, René. *Discours de la Méthode.*

Dewey, John. *Experience and Education*. New York: Macmillan/Collier Books, 1963.

Dienes, Zoltan P., and Golding, E. W. *Approach to Modern Mathematics*. New York: Herder and Herder, 1971.

Eliot, T. S. "Little Gidding." *Collected Poems and Plays 1909-1950*. New York: Harcourt Brace, 1952.

Encyclopedia of Philosophy, The. Edited by Paul Edwards. New York: Macmillan, 1972.

Epicurus. *On Nature*.

Ferguson, Marilyn. *The Aquarian Conspiracy: Personal and Social Transformation in the 1980's*. Los Angeles: J. P. Tarcher, 1980.

Fromm, Erich. *The Art of Loving*. New York: Harper & Row, 1956.

Fuller, R. Buckminster. *Intuition*. New York: Anchor Press, 1973.

Goodman, Paul. *Growing Up Absurd*. New York: Vintage, 1960.

Green, Maxine, ed. *Existential Encounters for Teachers*. New York: Random House, 1967.

Hadamard, Jacques. *The Psychology of Invention in the Mathematical Field*. New York: Dover, 1954.

Hamlyn, D. W. *The Theory of Knowledge*. Garden City, N.Y.: Doubleday, 1970.

Hocking, William Ernest. *Types of Philosophy*. 3rd ed. New York: Scribner's, 1959.

Hofstadter, Douglas R. *Gödel, Escher, Bach: An Eternal Golden Braid*. New York: Basic Books, 1979.

Husserl, Edmund. *Ideas*. Translated by W. R. Boyce Gibson. New York: Macmillan, 1962.

I Ching. Translated by John Blofeld. New York: Dutton, 1968.

Jaynes, Julian. *The Origin of Consciousness in the Breakdown of the Bicameral Mind*. Boston: Houghton Mifflin, 1976.

Johnson, Samuel. Quoted in James Boswell, *Life of Johnson*. L. F. Powell's revision of George Birbeck Hill's edition. Oxford: Clarendon Press, 1934.

Jung, Carl Gustav. *Man and His Symbols*. Garden City, N.Y.: Doubleday, 1964.

Jung, Carl Gustav. *Psychological Types*. Translated by H. Godwin Baynes. London: Kegan Paul, Trench, Trübner; New York: Harcourt Brace, 1946.

Kant, Immanuel. *Critique of Pure Reason*. Translated by F. Max Müller. Garden City, N.Y.: Doubleday, 1966.

Klausmeier, H. J., and Harris, C. W., eds. *Analyses of Concept Learning*. New York: Academic Press, 1966.

Kline, Morris. *Why Johnny Can't Add: The Failure of the New Math*. New York: Vintage, 1974.

Koestler, Arthur. *The Act of Creation*. New York: Macmillan, 1964.

Leonard, George. *Education and Ecstasy*. New York: Delacorte, 1968.

Lester, Frank K., and Garofalo, J., eds. *Mathematical Problem Solving*. Philadelphia: Franklin Institute Press, 1982.

Loewe, Michael, and Blacker, Carmen, eds. *Oracles and Divination*. Boulder, Colo.: Shambhala, 1981.

May, Rollo. *Love and Will*. New York: W. W. Norton, 1969.

McLuhan, Marshall, and Fiore, Quentin. *The Medium is the Message: An Inventory of Effects*. New York: Bantam, 1967.

Memmert, Wolfgang. *Die Geschichte des Wortes "Anschauung" in Pädagogischer Hinsicht Von Platon Bis Pestalozzi*. Doctoral dissertation, Nürnberg University, 1968.

Neumann, Erich. *The Great Mother: An Analysis of the Archetype*. Translated by Ralph Manheim. Princeton, N.J.: Princeton University Press, 1955.

Newman, James R., ed. *The World of Mathematics*. New York: Simon & Schuster, 1956.

Noddings, Nel. *Caring: A Feminine Approach to Ethics and Moral Education*. Berkeley: University of California Press, 1984.

Nostradamus. *Centuries*.

Ornstein, Robert E. *The Psychology of Consciousness*. San Francisco: W. H. Freeman, 1972.

Ornstein, Robert E., ed. *The Nature of Human Consciousness*. San Francisco: W. H. Freeman, 1973.

Patmore, Coventry. "Seers, Thinkers, and Talkers." *Religio Poetae*. Uniform ed. London: Bell, 1907.

Plato. *Phaedo*.

Plato. *Republic*.

Plotinus. *Enneads*.

Plutarch. *The Lives of the Noble Grecians and Romans*.

Polanyi, Michael. *Personal Knowledge: Towards a Post-Critical Philosophy*. New York: Harper & Row, 1964.

Pribram, K. H., ed. *Mood, States, and Mind*. Brain and Behavior, vol. 1. Harmondsworth, Middlesex, England: Penguin, 1969.

Roszak, Theodore. *The Making of a Counter Culture*. Garden City, N.Y.: Anchor/Doubleday, 1969.

Rucker, Rudy. *Infinity and the Mind*. Boston: Birkhauser, 1982.

Sartre, Jean-Paul. *Being and Nothingness*. Translated by Hazel E. Barnes. New York: Washington Square Press, 1966.

Schleiermacher, Friedrich. *The Christian Faith*. Edited by W. R. Mackintosh and J. S. Stewart. New York: Harper & Row, 1965.

Schopenhauer, Arthur. *The World as Will and Representation*. Translated by E. F. J. Payne. New York: Dover, 1969.

Shah, Idries. *The Sufis*. Garden City, N.Y.: Doubleday, 1964.

Shulman, Lee S., and Keisler, Evan R., eds. *Learning by Discovery*. Chicago: Rand McNally, 1966.

Sidgwick, Henry. *The Methods of Ethics*. Indianapolis, Ind.: Hackett Publishing, 1981.

Spinoza, Benedict. *The Ethics*. Translated by R. H. Elwes. New York: Dover, 1955.

Stephens, James. *The Crock of Gold*. New York: Macmillan, 1926.

Suzuki, D. T. *An Introduction to Zen Buddhism*. New York: Grove Press, 1964.

Suzuki, D. T. *Zen Buddhism*. Garden City, N.Y.: Doubleday, 1956.

Vaughan, Frances E. *Awakening Intuition*. Garden City, N.Y.: Anchor/ Doubleday, 1979.

Vygotsky, L. *Mind in Society*. Cambridge, Mass.: Harvard University Press, 1978.

Weizenbaum, Joseph. *Computer Power and Human Reason: From Judgment to Calculation*. San Francisco: W. H. Freeman, 1976.

Wertheimer, Max. *Productive Thinking*. New York: Harper, 1945.

Weyl, Hermann. *Mind and Nature*. Philadelphia: University of Pennsylvania Press, 1934.

Whitehead, Alfred North. *The Aims of Education*. New York: Free Press, 1967.

Wilder, Raymond L. "The Role of Intuition." *Science*, vol. 156, May 1967, pp. 605-10.

Woolf, Virginia. *A Room of One's Own*. New York: Harcourt Brace, 1929.

INDEX